Military Intervention

Military Intervention

Cases in Context for the Twenty-First Century

WILLIAM J. LAHNEMAN

ROWMAN & LITTLEFIELD PUBLISHERS, INC.
Lanham • Boulder • New York • Toronto • Oxford

ROWMAN & LITTLEFIELD PUBLISHERS, INC.

Published in the United States of America
by Rowman & Littlefield Publishers, Inc.
A wholly owned subsidiary of The Rowman & Littlefield Publishing Group, Inc.
4501 Forbes Boulevard, Suite 200, Lanham, MD 20706
www.rowmanlittlefield.com

P.O. Box 317, Oxford OX2 9RU, UK

British Library Cataloguing in Publication Information Available

Library of Congress Cataloging-in-Publication Data

Lahneman, William J., 1952-
  Military intervention : cases in context for the twenty-first century / William J.
Lahneman.
      p.   cm.
Includes bibliographical references and index.
  ISBN 0-7425-2950-9 (cloth : alk. paper) — ISBN 0-7425-2951-7 (paper :
alk. paper)
  1. Humanitarian intervention—Case studies. 2. Peacekeeping forces—Case
studies. I. Title.
JZ6369.L34 2004
341.5'84—dc22

2003024888

Printed in the United States of America

♾™ The paper used in this publication meets the minimum requirements of American National Standard for Information Sciences—Permanence of Paper for Printed Library Materials, ANSI/NISO Z39.48-1992.

Contents

Contents

Abbreviations and Acronyms

ACBAR	Agency Coordinating Body for Afghan Relief
ACORD	Agency for Cooperation and Research Development
ACSSOM	African Charity Society for Maternity and Childhood
ADRA	Adventist Relief and Development Agency
AFRC	Air Force Reserve Command
AFSC	American Friends Service Committee
AICF	International Action Against Famine
AMA	Africa Muslims Agency
APC	All Peoples Congress
APEC	Asia Pacific Economic Cooperation
ASEAN	Association of Southeast Asian Nations
ATA	Afghan Transitional Administration
AWO	Abu Dhabi Welfare Organization
BBTG	Broad-Based Transitional Government
CARE	CARE International
CARICOM	Caribbean Community
CCOVS	Coordination Committee of Organizations for Voluntary Service
CDP	Cambodian People's Party
CENTCOM	Central Command
CGDK	Coalition Government of Democratic Kampuchea
CISSM	Center for International and Security Studies at Maryland
CMOC	Civilian Military Operations Center
CNEH	National Federation of Haitian Educators

CRS	Catholic Relief Services
CWS	Church World Services
DAWA	Munzamai Islamic Society
DCI	Director of Central Intelligence
DDRR	Disarmament, Demobilization, Resettlement, and Rehabilitation
DGC	Diakonic Care Germany
DK	Democratic Kampuchea
DOD	Department of Defense
DPA	Department of Political Affairs
DPKO	Department of Peace Keeping Operations
DRC	Democratic Republic of the Congo
ECOMOG	Economic Community of West African States Monitoring Group
ECOSOC	Economic and Social Council
ECOWAS	Economic Community of West African States
FAd'H	Haitian Armed Forces
FAO	Food and Agricultural Organization
FAR	Rwandan Armed Forces
FRCS	Federation of the Red Cross Society
FRY	Federal Republic of Yugoslavia
HPZ	Humanitarian Protection Zone
IARA	Islamic African Relief Agency
ICFY	International Conference on the Former Yugoslavia
ICRC	International Committee of the Red Cross
IDP	Internally Displaced Persons
IDRA	International Development and Relief Agency
IGAD	Intergovernmental Authority on Development
IGADD	Inter-Governmental Agency on Drought and Development
IIRO	International Islamic Relief
IMC	International Medical Corps
INARA	National Institute of Agrarian Reform
INTERFET	International Force East Timor
ISAF	International Security Assistance Force
MAUK	Muslim Aid UK
MCF	Muwafaq Charity
MERCY	Mercy International
MICAH	International Civilian Support Mission in Haiti
MICIVIH	International Civilian Mission in Haiti
MNF	Multi-National Force
MOD	Marreexaan, Ogaadeen, and Dhulbahante
MONUC	UN Organization Mission in the Democratic Republic of the Congo
MRND	National Revolutionary Movement for Development
MSF	Doctors Without Borders (Médecins Sans Frontières)
NATO	North Atlantic Treaty Organization
NIC	National Intelligence Council
NIE	National Intelligence Estimates
NMG	Neutral Monitoring Group
NMOG	Neutral Military Observer's Group
NORCROSS	Nordic Red Cross
NPFL	National Patriotic Front of Liberia
NRA	National Resistance Army

NSC	National Security Council
OAU	Organization of African Unity
O.G.I.T.H.	Organization of Haitian Industrial Workers
OPL	Organization of People in Struggle
OSCE	Organization for Security and Co-operation in Europe
OXFAM	Oxford Famine Relief
PRK	People's Republic of Kampuchea
PROP	Assembly of Popular Organization Power
PSF	Pharmacists Without Borders (Pharmaciens Sans Frontières)
Renamo	Mozambican National Resistance
RIHS	Revival Islamic Heritage
ROE	Rules of Engagement
RPA	Rwandan Patriotic Army
RPF	Rwandese Patriotic Front
RTLMC	Radio Télévision Libre des Mille Collines
RUF	Revolutionary United Front
SCF	Save the Children
SCR	Swedish Church Relief
SNM	Somali National Movement
SOS	Children's Emergency Services
SRSG	Special Representative of the Secretary General
SSDF	Somali Salvation Democratic Front
TNA	Transitional National Assembly
ULIMO	United Liberation Movements of Liberia for Democracy
UNAMET	UN Mission in East Timor
UNAMIR	UN Assistance Mission in Rwanda
UNAMSIL	UN Armed Mission in Sierra Leone
UNCTAD	UN Conference on Trade and Development
UNDP	UN Development Program
UNESCO	UN Educational, Scientific, and Cultural Organization
UNHCR	UN High Commission for Refugees
UNICEF	UN International Children's Emergency Fund
UNITAF	United Task Force
UNMIH	UN Mission in Haiti
UNMISET	UN Mission of Support in East Timor
UNOMSIL	UN Observer Mission in Sierra Leone
UNOMUR	UN Observer Mission Uganda-Rwanda
UNOR	UN Office in Rwanda
UNOSOM	UN Operation in Somalia
UNPROFOR	UN Protection Force
UNREO	UN Rwanda Emergency Office
UNTAC	UN Transitional Authority in Cambodia
UNTAET	UN Transitional Administration for East Timor
USAID	U.S. Agency for International Development
USC	United Somali Conference
USFORSOM	U.S. Forces Somalia
USGET	U.S. Group East Timor
WFP	World Food Program
WHO	World Health Organization
WMD	Weapons of Mass Destruction

Acknowledgments

I would first like to thank the authors for their superb contributions to the volume as well as for their active participation in various events of the *Project on Internal Conflict*. Thanks are also due to all of the other scholars and nongovernment experts who participated in project events. These include Deborah Avant, George Washington University; Frances Burwell, University of Maryland; Christian Davenport, University of Maryland; Graham Day, U.S. Institute of Peace; I. M. "Mac" Destler, University of Maryland; Peter Dombrowski, U.S. Naval War College; Joshua Epstein, Brookings Institution; William Flavin, U.S. Army Peacekeeping Institute; Timothy Gulden, University of Maryland; Ted Robert Gurr, University of Maryland; Barbara Harff, U.S. Naval Academy; Len Hawley, independent consultant; Ali Jalali, Voice of America; Tom Johnson, IIT Research Institute; Edward Laurance, Monterey Institute of International Studies; Milton Leitenberg, University of Maryland; Tom Leney, Association of the U.S. Army/Project on the Role of American Military Power; Monty Marshall, University of Maryland; Manus Midlarsky, Rutgers University; Edgar O'Ballance, author; Chantal de Jonge Oudraat, Carnegie Endowment for International Peace; Miles Parker, Brookings Institution; Barry Posen, Massachusetts Institute of Technology; George Quester, University of Maryland; Donald Rothchild, University of California, Davis; MG Robert Scales, U.S. Army (ret.); David R. Segal, University of Maryland; Julie Sirrs, independent consultant; Charles Stevenson, National Defense University; Carola Weil, University of

Maryland; and Ernest W. Wilson III, University of Maryland. Their presentations and the lively discussions that ensued contributed greatly to the project's understanding of internal conflict and intervention. I would also like to thank the many members of the U.S. intelligence community who actively participated in project events. Their expertise and perspective were invaluable.

I would like to specially thank and acknowledge the vital role played by Major General John Landry, U.S. Army (ret.), the national intelligence officer for conventional military issues on the National Intelligence Council. General Landry conceived the idea of commissioning a study to examine internal conflict, military intervention, and the relevance of these phenomena to U.S. foreign policy. He was a leading force in charting the project's course and actively presided and participated in all project events. Special thanks are also due to Clyde Owan, deputy national intelligence officer for conventional military issues. Clyde also guided the project's course and worked with me to determine appropriate combinations of experts to turn general intentions into intellectually stimulating events.

I am indebted to John Steinbruner, director of the Center for International and Security Studies at Maryland (CISSM) and codirector of the National Intelligence Council (NIC) Project. John played a pivotal role in shaping the direction of the project in consultation with General Landry. He also worked closely with me to identify appropriate experts, to structure project events, and to develop event proceedings. Many thanks are also due to Ernest W. Wilson III, director of the Center for Development and Conflict Management at the University of Maryland and the NIC Project's other codirector, for his guidance and participation in project events.

I wish to acknowledge and thank Jim Stokes, Matt Lewis, Gil Peleg, Shirley Hsieh, and Lloyd McCoy, my graduate assistants for the project, for their superb research assistance, excellent compilation of event proceedings, and support during project events. Many thanks also to Sariel Ende, who handled all logistical and administrative aspects of the numerous project events in her customarily outstanding fashion.

Very special thanks to Kristen Jancuk, CISSM's coordinator, whose expert editing and liaison with the publisher were invaluable in transforming a series of individual efforts into a finished manuscript.

On behalf of all the authors, I want to thank the National Intelligence Council and the Center for International and Security Studies at Maryland for providing the financial support that made this volume possible.

The views contained in this volume are those of the respective authors alone. The other persons thanked above are not responsible for its content and should not be blamed for any defects that might be present. The views expressed in this volume do not represent the views, attitudes, or policies of the authors' parent institutions, the National Intelligence Council, or any other agency or component of the U.S. government.

Introduction

William J. Lahneman

Internal or intrastate conflict is a form of organized violence in which factions *within* a country engage in violent conflict with each other. Sometimes this violence can expand to include neighboring countries and entire regions. Internal conflict is the most frequently occurring type of organized armed conflict, eclipsing interstate conflict—war *between* countries—by a considerable margin.[1]

Internal conflicts have tended to occur in a so-called "arc of instability"[2] comprising Africa, the Middle East, Central Asia, and Southeast Asia, although the Western Hemisphere is not exempt, as evidenced by the inclusion of a case study on Haiti in this volume. In the 1990s, it became increasingly common for individual states or coalitions of states to intervene in internal conflicts. Sometimes intervention was limited to diplomatic or economic initiatives to resolve internal conflict, but more often it involved military intervention to monitor a peace accord, implement a cease-fire agreement, or even compel warring parties to cease hostilities.

Military interventions in internal conflict since the end of the Cold War share three major characteristics that appear to warrant categorizing this type of operation as a new phenomenon in international relations. First, the developed countries conducted military intervention largely for "nontraditional" reasons—

to provide humanitarian assistance to starving Somalis, to halt genocide in Rwanda and "ethnic cleansing" in Bosnia, to stop gross abuse of human rights in East Timor, and to restore the democratically elected government of Haiti—in contrast to the "traditional" driving reason of responding to threats to one's own national interests. Second, intervening nations usually conducted military intervention pursuant to a United Nations mandate authorized by a Security Council resolution, which provided these operations with legitimacy in the eyes of the international community. Third, military intervention was generally conducted "reluctantly" with the clear goal of terminating intervention as soon as possible, particularly its military dimension.

As the lone superpower, the United States usually found itself at the center of discussions about intervention. After all, as the world's predominant military power following the collapse of the Soviet Union, the United States was one of the few states for which intervention was more or less always an option and the only power with worldwide military reach. Conventional wisdom held that if the United States failed to participate in a particular case of military intervention, even if it only provided logistical support for intervention by military forces from other countries, the probability of success diminished significantly. However, American elite and public opinion were divided on several issues surrounding military intervention in internal conflict. For example, when should the United States intervene? Should policymakers risk the lives of American military personnel over issues that do not affect U.S. vital national interests? How many U.S. casualties were "acceptable" in such ventures? If the United States did decide to intervene militarily, how should intervention be conducted? What would be the goals of the intervention? To halt mass starvation? To prevent abuse of human rights? To rebuild government, economic, and civil institutions? Were troops adequately trained for such "nation-building" missions? What other groups might be more appropriate? When should troops be withdrawn? Should the United States intervene only under United Nations authorization? If the U.S. military became primarily a peacekeeping force, would it still be able to fight and win the nation's future wars?

In response to this debate, the National Intelligence Council (NIC)[3] commissioned the University of Maryland in the summer of 2000 to study the phenomenon of internal conflict. This study, designated the *Project on Internal Conflict*,[4] sought to answer four principal questions:

1. Is the frequency of internal conflict increasing or decreasing?
2. What factors increase the magnitude or duration of internal conflict?
3. Under what circumstances is third-party intervention in internal conflict necessary?
4. When military intervention is deemed to be necessary, how should it be conducted, both in terms of tactics and strategy?

The project first conducted a series of workshops that tapped the scholarly community's understanding of these issues. Workshops explored the leading research about the causes, frequency, duration, and severity of internal conflict, including forecasts of future trends. The project next turned its attention to issues surrounding third-party intervention in internal conflict, particularly issues surrounding military intervention because this was the aspect of intervention that had proven most contentious in the United States and the rest of the developed world. The project determined that, while much of the knowledge concerning internal conflict was the product of quantitative analyses, information about military intervention was based almost exclusively on expert opinion and was thus predominantly qualitative in nature. The project decided to test the validity of the information concerning military intervention by commissioning seven studies of recent cases of military intervention: Somalia, Bosnia, Cambodia, Rwanda, Haiti, East Timor, and Sierra Leone. The author of each study agreed to be guided by a list of nine questions designed to ensure that each case study directly addressed the project's tentative findings. The questions are:

1. What were the principal circumstances that prompted third-party intervention?
2. What was the nature of the intervention force, for example, military forces, police units, civilian administrators, humanitarian nongovernmental organizations (NGOs), intergovernmental organizations (IGOs)?
3. At what phase of the internal conflict did intervention occur, for example, pre-conflict, during the initial phase of hostilities, during major armed conflict, in the aftermath of major hostilities?
4. What were the goals of the intervention? Authors were asked to include all goals associated with political, military, economic, and social justice aims. To what extent did the various actors involved in the intervention have different goals, and to what degree did goals clash? Authors were asked to include both policy-making bodies (national governments of states performing the intervention and IGOs) and the functional groups involved in policy implementation (military forces, police units, civilian administrators, humanitarian NGO workers).
5. How might intervening forces have improved goal attainment? Would earlier intervention have improved the situation? Would a more powerful military intervention force have improved the situation?
6. To what extent were the military aspects of intervention necessary and sufficient to resolve the internal conflict?
7. To what extent were the nonmilitary aspects of intervention (e.g., rebuilding damaged infrastructure, stabilizing the economy, reconstituting civil society, establishing representative government) necessary and sufficient for producing a lasting peace?
8. Did a clear exit strategy exist at the start of intervention? Did this strategy evolve over the course of the intervention?
9. Was the intervention a "success"? Specifically, which goals were attained and which were not? On balance, did the goals that were attained significantly alleviate death, suffering, and violation of individual and collective

human rights? Did intervention reduce the probability that internal conflict would recur in the future?

As the case studies were nearing completion, the terrorist attacks of 11 September 2001 occurred and, shortly thereafter, the United States and its allies began military action to overthrow the Taliban regime in Afghanistan and attack the al Qaeda terrorist organization's personnel and bases in that country. This operation was both an *invasion* and an *intervention*. On one level the operation was an interstate war: the United States and its allies invaded Afghanistan in response to the terrorist attacks when the ruling Taliban regime refused to surrender the members of al Qaeda responsible for the attacks. However, the U.S. invasion was also a clear case of military intervention in internal conflict. Internal conflict was raging in Afghanistan at the time of the U.S. intervention—the ruling Taliban regime was fighting the Northern Alliance, a loosely knit group of factions, for control of significant areas of Afghanistan—and the country had experienced internal conflict almost without pause since the late 1970s. This military intervention had many similarities to the military interventions studied by the project. For example, since the U.S.-led coalition possessed far more military power than that of the Taliban and al Qaeda combined, the outcome of the intervention was never in doubt as long as the United States and its allies possessed the political will to commit large numbers of forces. However, how to wage the combat phase of the intervention most effectively remained an important question. In addition, American policymakers knew that they would need to reestablish some measure of law and order in postconflict Afghanistan following the defeat of the Taliban, since leaving Afghanistan as a "failed" state would allow terrorist groups to continue using the country as a base of operations. Accordingly, the United States and its allies would need to engage in some measure of reconstruction or "nation building." But what aspects of reconstruction should be accomplished, and how? It became clear that the project's findings could provide answers to many of these important policy questions.

In response to this situation, the final event of the project, which had originally been scheduled for 12 October 2001, was rescheduled for 7 December 2001. This delay provided case study authors with time to consider how their studies could provide specific lessons to help guide U.S. policies in Afghanistan. The delay also provided time to arrange for several Afghanistan area specialists to participate in the day's program. As a result, the project's final event not only allowed case study authors to summarize and discuss their findings, but also allowed a number of regional experts to comment on the putative lessons learned from the case studies. The regional experts also used this forum to offer advice about how Afghan culture, politics, and other factors might affect U.S. policy in post-Taliban Afghanistan.

This volume describes and explains the project's findings. It describes the state of knowledge about internal conflict and focuses on the role of military intervention in such conflicts. Chapter 1 summarizes the current state of knowledge about internal conflict and intervention, including discussion of conflicting findings when appropriate. Chapters 2 through 8 contain individual case studies. Chapter 9 describes several central themes pertinent to military intervention in internal conflict derived from both the case studies and project events. It also briefly summarizes the main lessons from each case study.

The fact that all case study authors used the same set of guidelines to write their studies greatly enhanced the ability to perform comparative analysis and extract conclusions that are potentially applicable to military intervention in current and future cases of internal conflict. Lessons learned fall into two main categories, each of which is equally important as far as the ultimate effectiveness of intervention is concerned. Strategic lessons learned deal with the decision to intervene, the determination of the intervention's initial goals, and the means for achieving them (the "exit" or "engagement" strategy). They address the appropriateness of military intervention, the advisability of obtaining United Nations resolutions authorizing intervention, the importance and nature of consultations with allies, considerations surrounding coalition building, and determination of the broad goals of the intervention (e.g., humanitarian assistance, nation building). Strategic lessons learned occur throughout the volume but are summarized primarily in chapters 1 and 9. In contrast, tactical lessons learned offer advice regarding how to conduct military intervention once the decision to intervene has been made. For example, should a strong military force be employed? Should this force attempt to remain impartial? What kind of organization should perform the nonmilitary aspects of intervention? How will civil-military coordination be achieved? Who should be in charge, and what kind of chain of command should be employed? What about the role of humanitarian NGOs? How should local actors be engaged? Should the former combatants be disarmed? Chapters 2 through 8 contain the bulk of tactical lessons. Chapter 9 includes a brief summary of the most significant tactical lessons from each case.

While the frequency of internal conflict appears to be decreasing, new cases and potential cases of military intervention continue to emerge and demand attention. The joint U.S./British military operations against Iraq that began in March 2003 are similar to those in Afghanistan in that one must view them on two levels to fully appreciate the issues involved. The U.S. invasion of Iraq constituted an interstate war, but it was also a military intervention in Iraq's ongoing internal conflict. As with intervention in Afghanistan, intervening forces possessed overwhelming military superiority over their Iraqi opponents, and the United States has acknowledged the need to conduct substantial postconflict reconstruction to produce a stable, peaceful Iraq.

While intervention in Iraq is still in its opening stages, two other cases of military intervention in internal conflict have already arisen. First, in June 2003, the United Nations authorized a French-led multilateral military force to intervene in the Democratic Republic of the Congo to help stop an internal conflict that has claimed an estimated four million lives. Second, in August 2003, two hundred U.S. marines landed in Liberia to bolster an earlier military intervention by Nigeria and other West African countries. This intervention, also strongly endorsed by the United Nations, hopes to end Liberia's fourteen-year internal conflict that has killed at least 200,000 people.

There is every reason to hope that an understanding and appreciation for the mistakes and successes associated with military interventions in the 1990s will improve the probability of success in both current and future cases of this difficult undertaking.

Notes

1. For example, there were twenty-seven major armed conflicts around the world in 1998. All but two—those between India and Pakistan and between Ethiopia and Eritrea—were internal conflicts. This proportion has remained essentially constant for many years. For more information, see *SIPRI Yearbook, 1999. Armaments, Disarmament and International Security*, Stockholm International Peace Research Institute (Oxford: Oxford University Press, 1999).

2. Policymakers have used this term at least as far back as 1978, when Zbigniew Brzezinski, National Security Advisor in the Carter administration, used it to describe the area running from Angola to Afghanistan where the United States was losing ground to a number of Soviet-sponsored revolutionary movements. See Robert Levgold, "The Super Rivals: Conflict in the Third World," *Foreign Affairs* 57, no. 4 (Spring 1979): 755. Since this time, the term has been used in several contexts. The National Intelligence Council's use of the term expands upon Brzezinski's meaning to include all of Africa, the Middle East, Central Asia, and Southeast Asia.

3. The National Intelligence Council (NIC) is the Intelligence Community's center for mid-term and long-term strategic thinking. Its primary functions are to support the Director of Central Intelligence (DCI) in his role as head of the Intelligence Community; to provide a focal point for policymakers to task the Intelligence Community to answer their questions; to reach out to nongovernment experts in academia and the private sector to broaden the Intelligence Community's perspective; to contribute to the Intelligence Community's effort to allocate its resources in response to policymakers' changing needs; and to lead the Intelligence Community's effort to produce National Intelligence Estimates (NIEs) and other NIC products. See www.cia.gov/nic for more information.

4. The Project on Internal Conflict was a part of the National Intelligence Council (NIC) Project, a program at the Center for International and Security Studies at Maryland (CISSM). CISSM is a research center at the School of Public Affairs of the University of Maryland, College Park. In addition to commissioning the seven case studies contained in this volume, the project conducted several workshops and conferences to explore the phenomenon of military intervention in internal conflict. The names and affiliations of the scholars and other nongovernment experts who participated in the project are listed in the acknowledgments at the beginning of the volume. For more information about the NIC Project, see www.cissm.umd.edu/NIC.htm.

1

Perspectives on Civil Violence: A Review of Current Thinking

John Steinbruner and Jason Forrester

Over the course of the past decade, security policy in the United States has been struggling to contend with a precipitous shift in the perception of threat. The dominant concern of the Cold War period—surprise attack on a continental or intercontinental scale—remains a reference for military planning but is clearly not an imminent possibility. For most of the decade, the American political system as a whole did not recognize any immediate threat to the United States itself, and on those occasions when military forces engaged in combat the justification was prominently questioned. After the terrorist attacks of 11 September 2001 it is now broadly accepted that there is an imminent threat and indeed an active war. There is as yet no detailed consensus, however, regarding the nature of that threat or the appropriate conduct of the war.

The initial military actions against the al Qaeda network in Afghanistan were generally successful and did not generate any major dispute within the United States. The subsequent assault on Iraq was initially more contentious, in part because the connection to terrorism was less convincingly established, but forceful removal of the Saddam Hussein regime was broadly endorsed after the fact. If it turns out that the global network of terrorist organizations has been damaged to the point that they cannot undertake further attacks of major significance, then as far as the American public is concerned the war might prove to be

1

short and decisive. In that case its extended implications would presumably be limited. The current general expectation, however, is that there will be additional episodes of terrorism and that the United States will continue to initiate major military actions designed to eradicate the threat. In an extended sequence of that sort, some inherently difficult and divisive issues are likely to arise. Among the more prominent of these is the connection between acts of terrorism directed against the United States and the various instances of civil conflict that have been encountered in other parts of the world. The question is not only or even primarily whether the same individuals and organizations have been involved, but more fundamentally whether there are common causes of enduring significance.

There certainly are reasons to suspect common causes powerful enough to be a major security concern. The pattern of economic growth associated with the process of globalization has so far been highly inequitable. Concentrations of wealth have increased throughout the world. Standard of living improvements have disproportionately benefited the top 20 percent income bracket. Total population increases have occurred almost exclusively in the lowest 20 percent income bracket whose net standard of living, as best it can be measured, appears to have declined over the past twenty years. An additional two billion people are expected to be added to the total world population by 2030 with 97 percent of the increase occurring at the lowest income levels worldwide. That projected pattern of economic growth among the affluent and population growth among the poor presents obvious issues of social equity. It is prudent to ask whether they might be serious enough to bring basic social coherence into question on a global scale. In many areas of endemic economic austerity that have emerged in the uneven pattern of globalization the ability to preserve social coherence and thereby control violence is already a very serious question. If terrorist activity and localized outbreaks of civil violence are in fact manifestations of a general erosion of legal order, then the containment and reversal of that underlying process will have to become a priority security objective. In any given instance, marauding militia and suicide terrorists can probably be defeated with sufficient determination to do so, but a global contagion of civil violence could be overwhelming.

This latter possibility is hardly a welcome thought, nor is it one that can readily be examined in the exacting manner appropriate for a priority security objective. The extensive data collection efforts so far undertaken in support of national security have been preoccupied with traditional forms of warfare and generally have not attempted to comprehend in comparable detail either the determining conditions or the organizational dynamics of civil conflict. The fact that the al Qaeda organization could be generally known but its capacities misunderstood for many years is a specific indication of that situation. Similarly, large amounts of data are collected to document aggregate economic performance and extensive analysis is done to support efforts to manage economic growth, but the process of income distribution has not been documented or analyzed in comparable detail. Without the supporting investment in data collection that would be necessary, no individual or institution is in position to understand the genesis of civil violence in the penetrating detail that emerging circumstances now appear to require. Those who nonetheless attempt to assess the problem are forced to rely on expedient measures and to indulge in speculation, neither of which provides an adequate foundation for effective policy. The question is now recognized to be urgent, but the capacity to address it remains primitive.

There have been some valiant pioneers, however, and their efforts provide the available point of departure for better comprehension of the situation. If it is not realistic at this point to look for robust conclusions, it is nonetheless important to consider the clues that can be extracted from those who have presented aggregate statistical analysis of civil conflict as well as from those who have attempted to draw lessons from specific instances.

Aggregate Impressions

Published tabulations suggest that the various forms of organized conflict have inflicted casualties at an average rate of more than one million people per year over the past century. For example, a recent compilation of the estimates issued for 156 specified conflicts occurring between 1945 and 2000 cites a figure of 40 million deaths, including civilians as well as direct combatants.[1] That result is derived from point estimates for each of the episodes and is not accompanied by an uncertainty range. In very few if any of the listed circumstances were the cited figures based on a systematic count of individual victims. Comparable figures for the entire twentieth century, including uncertainty bands of some 12 million for the two world wars, indicate that 121 to 133 million deaths occurred that were attributable to armed conflict. Estimates that include deaths deliberately caused by other means, such as extreme repression and systematic starvation, add more than 80 million to the twentieth-century total.

Estimates of deaths caused by acts of terrorism cannot be disentangled from the twentieth-century totals, but it is evident that they represent a very small fraction of the general category of conflict casualties. The United States State Department reports that 24,068 deaths worldwide were caused by terrorist actions during the seven-year period 1995 through 2001, an average of about thirty-five hundred victims per year. The average murder rate for the United States alone during those years was more than seventeen thousand people—a factor of five higher than the global terrorism toll. Terrorist violence is intended, of course, to have greater psychological and political impact than ordinary acts of crime, and that intent certainly succeeded in the case of the September 11 attacks. In terms of physical attrition, however, the significance of terrorism has so far depended largely on its connections to other forms of conflict. That empirical fact is not likely to change unless terrorists start using mass destruction technologies, and even in that very somber case the connections to other forms of conflict would be extremely important.

Since the tabulations of conflict casualties clearly do not emerge from any systematic accounting system, they are best treated as quantified judgments rather than as a literal measure of individual deaths. They offer a crude sense of magnitude but not a credible basis for determining trends over time or statistical correlates that might indicate underlying causes. Most of those who have attempted to detect trends and causes have felt the need to devise a measurable unit that in principle could be considered to be more accurate and more stable over time and circumstance. The typical choice has been an "event" defined as a circumstance in which deaths attributable to conflict exceed some threshold (usually one thousand) in a given country in a given year. Events are recorded by teams of researchers, usually graduate students, using largely mass media sources as their base of information. They use a standard set of instructions as to what to look for and then apply individual judgments as to whether they have seen it in the available documentation. Some efforts are made to harmonize judgments and to check variations by examining the results of overlapping assignments. That creates a somewhat systematic accounting system for codifying publicly reported information.

One of the most prominent recent assessments of trends using coded event data of this sort indicates that the total magnitude of conflict has declined over the past decade from a peak that roughly corresponded to the end of the Cold War.[2] The measure of magnitude is based on a ten-item index for each conflict event since 1946. The index includes the number of combatants, the number of casualties, physical damage, population dislocations, and various other elements of social impact, all of which have been judged by teams of coders. The annual sum of magnitude scores for all events increased with some minor fluctuations from 1945 to 1990, mostly between the years of 1960 and 1990. The total magnitude score nearly tripled during the later thirty-year period and then declined by about 40 percent from its peak during the ensuing decade. Conflicts primarily occurring within a given state, as distinct from those across state boundaries, were the major component both of the thirty-year increase and of the ten-year decline. The number and proportion of states involved in conflict rose and declined by the same amounts as the total magnitude scores and on the same schedule, indicating that the observation is a global phenomenon.

The authors of this survey attribute the recent decline in the magnitude of conflict to the extension of democratic forms of government and to more active forms of international mediation in the wake of the Cold War period. They note, however, that countries engaged in a transition to democracy from more autocratic forms of government are more than twice as susceptible to violence than are the established democracies. To a somewhat lesser extent, societies with transitional governments have also been more susceptible to violence than those that remain autocratic.[3] Those observations lead to the further question as to what determines a successful transition to democracy and whether it is democracy itself or some related set of circumstances that has produced the observed decline.

Basic clues about those questions were provided by a report of the State

Failure Task Force, a consortium of prominent academic specialists organized in 1994 to assess the connection between the outbreak of civil conflict and the decay of governmental institutions in some parts of the world. That exercise identified 113 cases where conflict occurred between 1955 and 1994 in countries other than the United States with populations greater than five hundred thousand people. Those cases were compared with a randomly chosen set of countries and years where no comparable episode occurred, and more than two million items of data were examined to determine the characteristics distinguishing the instances of conflict from the randomly chosen set. The single best statistical model to emerge from that effort used three variables—labeled "openness to international trade, infant mortality, and democracy," respectively—to distinguish 70 percent of the conflict outbreaks from the randomly chosen set two years in advance.[4] The outbreak of conflict was associated with low levels of openness to trade, high infant mortality, and low levels of democracy.

Since infant mortality is considered to be a measure of economic development and trade openness—defined as the ratio of exports and imports to total economic product—to be a measure of participation in the global economy, the suggestion emerging from the State Failure Task Force report is that the incidence of violence is ultimately related primarily to basic economic performance. That suggestion is supported by a separate series of studies undertaken by the World Bank. Their analysis confirms that conflict, as recorded in event data, occurs disproportionately in countries with low per capita income. It also suggests that conflict has the perverse effect of further reducing the income of those countries.[5]

This basic observation has led to an image of conflict emanating from the World Bank that emphasizes the importance of comparative economic opportunity. The highest statistical of risk of conflict in their analysis occurs in countries where primary commodity exports contribute between a quarter and a third of the overall economic product. In an initial report, which examined forty-seven conflict episodes, countries with primary commodity exports accounting for 26 percent of GDP had a 23 percent statistical chance of experiencing conflict, whereas the calculated chance for an otherwise similar country with no primary commodity exports was less than 1 percent.[6] In a subsequent iteration of the analysis, the peak risk of conflict was calculated to be 22 percent at the level of 32 percent primary commodity exports, with the contrasting case of no commodity exports again having a less than 1 percent risk of conflict.[7] The interpretative supposition is that civil conflicts are actually economic battles over the control of resources waged under conditions in which allocation cannot be managed by legal methods or legitimate government domination.

That contention is reinforced by several additional observations drawn from the forty-seven episode data set. The risk of initiating conflict in that body of evidence proved to be:

- higher in countries with dispersed populations—where the extension of legal control is more difficult to achieve,

- higher in countries with faster growing populations,
- higher in countries with lower economic growth,
- higher (for reigniting a previous conflict) when an external diaspora was available to provide support for internal rebels, and
- lower in countries providing greater access to secondary education.[8]

The implication is that conflict is a violent form of business that can be expected to flourish at the expense of normal economic development when there is money to be made by engaging in it and where productive economic opportunities are scarce—the "greed" theory, as it has come to be known. Since that process can in principle be self-reinforcing, there is reason for concern that it might become the dominant pattern in transitional societies. In that case, the reduction in the total magnitude of violence recorded in the past decade would presumably be in jeopardy.

The greed theory was initially presented as an alternative rather than a complement to the more traditional view, which holds that conflict is generated by underlying social grievances based on ethnic or religious distinctions. Such distinctions are prominent in the public perception and historical discussion of most conflicts, and it has long been widely assumed that they are not merely an artifact of civil violence but a causal source. In support of the contention that greed is actually the dominant determinant, statistical analyses of the aggregate event data were presented indicating that the degree of ethnic fractionation in a society does not vary directly and continuously with its risk of conflict, as presumably would be the case if ethnic tensions were the prime cause.[9] Moreover, in at least one study the apparent influence of varying levels of democracy on the incidence of conflict disappeared when differences in economic development and economic growth were taken into account.[10] If ethnic identity were the issue rather than economic opportunity, then presumably the institutions of democracy would be able to control conflict to the extent that they are developed.

A recent elaboration of event data analysis has suggested, however, that the greed and grievance theories refer to fundamentally different types of conflict and that valid statistical analysis must distinguish between conflicts that are generated by identity considerations (ethnic and religious distinctions) and those that are not.[11] To test that argument, annual event data were compiled for 161 countries over a forty-year period specifying whether a conflict of either type did or did not occur in each country in each year. Over that time, seventy-seven wars were initiated that were judged to be ethnic in character as compared to thirty-two initiated wars that did not meet the criteria for that designation.[12] Of the 818 observations of warfare in the data—out of a total of 6,440 possible observations (country/year combinations)—600 fit the definition of ethnic conflict and 218 did not. The difference in the means of the two categories is statistically significant, indicating that they are in fact different phenomena.

When the two categories of conflict are analyzed separately, the level of democracy proves to be a significant determinant of ethnic conflict—countries with higher levels of democracy having fewer outbreaks of conflict.[13] For the other category, apparently representing greed-driven conflicts, the level of democracy was not a statistically significant determinant.[14] Similarly, for ethnic wars only, the degree of social diversity—"ethnic heterogeneity"—has a continuously increasing effect on the probability of conflict, and that effect is separately mitigated by the level of democracy and the level of economic development to about the same extent.[15] Those observations suggest that greed and grievance conflicts both occur but for different reasons. The apparent implication is that efforts to prevent each type of conflict would depend on accurate categorization and would have to be tailored to their different determinants.

The Issue of Data Resolution

Before any practical conclusions are derived from the event data, however, there are important questions to be raised about the outcome measurement—the dependent variable in statistical terms—that is used in virtually all of the studies. As noted, event data are derived largely from news media sources that differ considerably in character and quality across the many conflict episodes being recorded. The media sources do not have equal access to the events they are reporting nor do they have equal attitudes about those events or equal standards of reporting. Each "event" being detected in the stream of reports extends over the course of as much as a year in an area that varies with the size of individual countries, and it involves one thousand or more individual casualties. That definition is a practical choice under the circumstances, but it certainly does not provide the basis for refined observation. It is prudent to ask how understanding might be affected by higher resolution measurement.

Fortunately there is sufficient information from at least one conflict to address that question. The conflict occurred in Guatemala between 1960 and 1996. It involved military, paramilitary, and police units of the Guatemalan government operating against individual or loosely organized civilians whom the government considered to be insurgents. Virtually all of the casualties—some 95 percent of them—were on the civilian side, however, indicating to independent observers that the events in Guatemala had more to do with violent government repression rather than with armed insurgency. That fact attracted the attention of human rights advocates who made three separately organized and somewhat competitive efforts to determine the time and place of individual deaths by the laborious process of interviewing the families of victims. The resulting data record more than forty thousand individual fatalities over the thirty-six-year period, and statistical inferences made from comparisons of the separately generated lists indicate that somewhere between eighty thousand and four hundred thousand total fatalities occurred.[16] The correct number is probably in excess of two hundred thousand. The victims fell largely into two social categories distinguishable in economic, ethnic, and geographic terms—urban middle-class Ladinos and rural Mayan peasants.

The striking feature of the Guatemala data is the pattern that emerges when the measure of conflict used in the event data studies—one thousand deaths or more in a given year—is decomposed into more precise time and place specification. The Guatemala conflict was below the standard threshold for most of the thirty-six-year period, but it exceeded the threshold in the years 1979–1983 in what appears in the annual data to be a single surge of violence rising to a peak of fifteen thousand documented deaths in 1982. Standard event data analysis would record only five years of conflict during the thirty-six-year period and would not notice the extraordinary surge that occurred in 1982. The magnitude of conflict scale would record the 1982 surge but not the numerous surges and declines that appear when the incidence of violence is examined by month and by location (figure 1.1). Although one cannot draw general inferences from the history of a single conflict, there are patterns in the disaggregated Guatemala data that suggest underlying statistical regularities that, if replicated in other instances, would have strong practical implications:[17]

- First, the fact that conflict fatalities in the disaggregated data do not occur continuously in time but in episodic peaks and declines suggests that there are important localized features of the story, not merely the effects of underlying causes. Those localized interactions represent in principle a focus for emergency control. They also may be statistically predictable in some sense or at any rate identifiable, since they appear to follow a power law distribution recognized in other regularly occurring phenomena.[18]

- Second, the more detailed data reveal two distinguishable operational patterns, one in which Guatemalan government units were using violence as a tactic—attempting to suppress the insurgency and consolidate the power of the state—and another involving killing as a strategy to eliminate the rural indigenous population which was seen as a source of support for current and future insurgents. For the first of these patterns—tactical violence designed to support other strategic ends (one might call this "regular warfare")—the size and frequency of incidents closely resembles the Zipf distribution that applies to many natural phenomena. Should that prove to be generally true, it would provide very important analytic leverage. Knowing the size (number of deaths) of the few largest episodes of a conflict would allow roughly accurate estimates of the number of incidents and the total number of people killed. Given any one of these three parameters, one could infer the other two.[19] The other type of operation—which consisted largely of indiscriminate attacks on Mayan villages—did not follow the Zipf distribution, but that distinguishing fact, if generally true, would be an important diagnostic tool. Those attacks were judged by a Guatemalan review commission to fit the criteria of genocide. A statistical technique that is able to isolate genocidal violence from other forms of conflict would be of broad interest.

Figure 1.1: Killing Data for Guatemala

Annual Killings, Guatemala

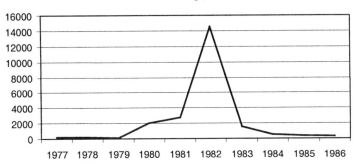

Monthly Killings, Guatemala

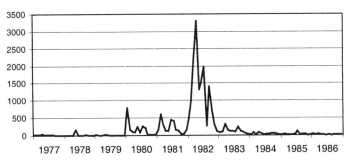

Monthly Killings, Nebaj

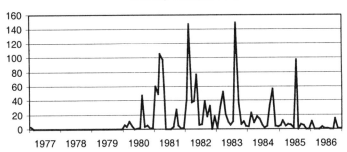

Source: Timothy Gulden "Spatial and Temporal Patterns of Civil Violence: Guatemala, 1977–1986," working paper 26, Center on Social and Economic Dynamics, Brookings Institution, Washington, D.C., 2002, 8.

- Third, the location of incidents in the detailed Guatemala data displays a very striking pattern. Just over half of the deaths recorded in the entire conflict occurred in municipalities in which the Mayan population comprised 80 to 90 percent of the inhabitants. Municipalities with that characteristic are only 8 percent of the total number of municipalities in the country and contain only slightly over 8 percent of the total population. Forty-five percent of the Mayan population in Guatemala live in municipalities in which they represent over 90 percent of the inhabitants, and in those municipalities the incidence of violence was substantially less than it was in the 80 to 90 percent Mayan villages. If that pattern is a recurring one, it would provide quite important guidance to any intervention effort.
- Fourth, the monthly data in Guatemala appear to have provided warning of the mass outbreak in 1982. In early 1980 and again in early 1981 there were significant increases in the number of deaths occurring as a result of attacks on individuals—largely Ladinos—in urban areas. There were several unusually large episodes of that type of violence during the two-year period preceding the campaign against the Mayans. That indicates the twenty-year-old conflict was entering a more violent phase. It also indicates that operations against individuals and against general populations are connected and that a surge in the former anticipates an outbreak of the latter. If a statistical signal of that sort generally occurs, it would provide early warning for emergency control efforts.

When considered together, these evident patterns suggest that if conflict episodes are subjected to more refined scrutiny they may regularly display some of the recognized features of complex adaptive systems.[20] If so, then practical leverage might be achieved by exploring the implications. That contention cannot be confirmed or developed exclusively on the basis of the Guatemalan data, but that single case is suggestive enough to make the examination of comparably refined data from other conflicts a priority matter. Until that is accomplished, it is prudent to be cautious about judging the aggregate trends and underlying determinants of civil conflict.

The practical problem, of course, is organizing the major effort required to gather more refined data. The private organizations that did it in the Guatemala case do not have either the capacity or the mandate to do it more comprehensively. In most instances the traditional intelligence organizations that are most likely to have both the interest and the resources are not likely to be allowed the access to witnesses and relatives of victims that is required. Systematically generating high-resolution data on civil conflict would appear to depend on much more substantial institutional innovation than is usually considered possible. If civil violence in its various forms does come to be recognized as the principal threat of the globalization era, however, such an innovation is likely to be one of the eventual consequences.

Practical Lessons

Practical experience with specific civil conflicts over the past decade has provided a substantially different and generally more prominent source of impression. The various conflicts involving Israel, the Palestinians, and the surrounding Arab states have been so prominent, in fact, and such an enduring preoccupation of international diplomacy that they are treated largely as a unique problem without much reference to other instances. Conflicts in Bosnia, Somalia, Rwanda, and Kosovo, however, have also entangled the international community extensively enough to command general public attention and to generate significant political reactions throughout the world. In those instances and to a lesser extent in numerous others as well, substantial efforts have been made to draw general lessons from specific experience and comparison among the cases has been considered relevant.

Retrospective assessment is not complete for any of the recent conflict episodes, and the general lessons to be derived are still a matter of active debate, but there are some evident themes in the ongoing discussion. Most careful observers contend that the international community as a whole—as distinct from some of its individual members—has reacted belatedly and inadequately to the major instances of civil conflict rather than excessively. The errors of omission are considered to have been greater than the errors of commission. With the advantages of retrospect, it appears that better outcomes could have been achieved in all of the major instances in which international intervention was undertaken if the resources and level of effort that were eventually committed had been made available earlier and had been applied with a clearer conception of purpose.[21]

Beneath that generalization there are some unresolved arguments, the most fundamental of which is the question of interest and the related question of locus of responsibility. Those who believe that the prime cause of civil conflict is usually indigenous to the society in which it occurs are also inclined to believe that the responsibility for settling it properly and practically remains within that society. Both the interest and the effective leverage of the international community are assumed to be limited to an extent that depends generally on geographic proximity and cultural resonance. That basic assessment can be meaningfully altered when a commodity of general importance, such as oil, is at stake, but the principal calculus of interest is considered to be first local, then regional, and only weakly global. That perspective emerges from the traditional realist view of international relations. In contrast, those who take a globalist view of international relations see both the sources of conflict and the interests at stake in broader perspective. Globalist assessments of the specific conflicts emphasize the significance of endemic economic austerity in generating them and trace the determinants to faulty connections to international finance and commodity markets, a view that parallels the World Bank's statistical analysis. Those assessments see greater reason for direct international intervention to control civil conflict—most notably, to counteract market defects that might undermine the emerging global economy and to defend the basic legal provisions that are necessary to sustain it.

This underlying difference in perspective is reflected in a more specific argument about the principles to be used in designing constructive intervention efforts. Adherents of the traditional realist perspective tend to argue for picking an indigenous winner. Those reflecting a globalist perspective suggest, on the contrary, that intervention efforts should preserve an equitable balance between the contending parties. One assessment of the events in Somalia in the 1980s and 1990s, for example, argues that a better outcome could have been achieved in that instance if the international community had unambiguously supported at the outset one of the contending clan leaders (Al Mahdi) with some loose conditions regarding civil rights behavior.[22] That was the basic formula used to control violence in Lebanon in the 1980s, where the Syrian leader, Hafez al-Assad, was the chosen agent with very few awkward questions asked as to how he did it. The general contention of that perspective is that no intervention could ever be truly neutral and should not attempt to be. Other accounts of the Somalia conflict argue, however, that no single figure could alone have commanded sufficient allegiance to establish a viable government but that a power-sharing arrangement among all the major clan leaders had nearly been achieved and could have been consolidated had there been a sustained international effort to do so.[23] The general implication is that any international effort to pick a winner will create dangerously festering internal grievances, and that is the common judgment in the Bosnian case. Most assessments of that episode contend that no single figure or ethnic faction had a superior claim to legitimacy and that as a practical matter none of them had the capacity to end the conflict by decisive use of force.

The major practical issue emerging from these conflicting assessments is whether it should be the principal purpose of international intervention to support the effective exercise of political power or to establish the basis for equitable consensus—the two being related but not equivalent. In most conflict circumstances there is considerable immediate tension between efforts to establish authoritative power and efforts to assure social equity. Basic common sense suggests that both objectives are important and that a successful outcome requires a judicious balance of both considerations. Virtually no objective observer has been willing to argue that a commendable balance has actually been achieved in any of the recent conflict episodes—no result as yet that could be cited as a model of effective practice. Even in Bosnia and in Kosovo, where substantial international interventions conducted primarily through the United States alliance system did succeed in controlling murderous civil conflicts, that was accomplished essentially by forceful segregation of the antagonistic communities and is widely believed to depend on the indefinite presence of international forces to preserve the separation. The general judgment is that those conflicts would reignite if the international presence was removed, and that is not considered to be a reasonable standard of success.

Somalia

In summarizing the evolving process of practical assessment, it is useful to compare experience in Somalia with that in Rwanda. Both are African countries with beleaguered economies relatively disentangled from the various issues associated with international conflict. Neither has strong resonance with the epicenter of conflict in the Middle East, although Somalia is nearby. In both cases the internal divisions of identity that defined the opposing parties required considerable emersion in the culture even to perceive, let alone to comprehend. The international community in general and the United States in particular approached both cases with a detached sense of interest and a presumption that the issues in question were almost entirely local—in genesis and in implication. In Somalia that presumption was overturned with subsequent regret. In Rwanda it was upheld, also with subsequent regret.

The immediate sequence that generated intervention in Somalia began in January 1992, an election year in the United States. In that month, driven by warnings of impending starvation, the UN Security Council invoked Chapter VII of the Charter to declare the internal violence and humanitarian emergency in Somalia a general threat to peace. In April the Security Council formally established a peacekeeping operation (UNOSOM I). Military forces were not authorized to enforce its resolutions until July, however, and did not actually deploy until September when a lightly armed contingent of 500 Pakistani soldiers was sent to Mogadishu under orders to operate only with the consent of the local parties. It quickly became apparent that they could not prevent the plundering of humanitarian relief supplies and were in effect hostages of the militia leaders. In March 1992, a representative of the UN Secretary General, James O. C. Jonah, negotiated a cease-fire agreement between the two principal leaders in the Mogadishu area whose forces were responsible for the most serious violence, Ali Mahdi Mohamed and Mohamed Farah Aideed, but that effort did not include the less belligerent clan leaders in other parts of the country whose participation would clearly be necessary for the reconstruction of a viable government. A subsequent attempt to broaden the mediation effort by UN Special Representative Mohamed Sahnoun was largely absorbed in negotiating the terms of deployment for UNOSOM I with Ali Mahdi and Aideed. It took Sahnoun several months to work out agreement for a September deployment. By October 1992, Sahnoun had resigned, explicitly complaining that difficulties with the Somali clans had been compounded by acerbic relations with the UN bureaucracy.[24]

That pattern was suddenly amended by the United States in late 1992 as it became evident that UNOSOM I could not protect humanitarian relief operations in Somalia and that a catastrophic level of starvation loomed. According to a December 1992 U.S. Centers for Disease Control and Prevention report, the crude mortality rates (CMRs) reported in the Somalia villages of Baidoa and Afgoi were "among the highest ever documented by a population survey among famine-affected civilians."[25] The various NGOs involved in the relief effort were assertively warning of an accelerating disaster and the imminent collapse of their own efforts.[26] The U.S. government was in the midst of a presidential transition at the time—not normally the moment for major initiative. It nonetheless managed a rapid reaction effective enough to overcome the immediate problem. On 25 November, the United States offered to organize and undertake a military operation to ensure the delivery of relief supplies in Somalia if such an action were to be authorized by the Security Council. On 3 December the Security Council passed resolution 794 providing the authorization, and on 9 December the first elements of a UN task force (UNITAF) arrived in Mogadishu under the command of a U.S. Marine Corps general operating through the national command channels of the United States. A total of thirty-seven thousand troops were assigned to UNITAF by over twenty countries, but its primary combat capability was provided by an authorized force of twenty-eight thousand U.S. troops.[27] Reflecting the national character of the operation, the United States also supplied its own coordinating official, Ambassador Robert Oakley, to manage the associated diplomacy. With far more authority and operational capacity at his disposal than Sahnoun had enjoyed, Oakley arranged the uncontested deployment of UNITAF six days after the authorizing resolution, and, by the end of January of 1993, UNITAF had established sufficient control over the southern third of Somalia, where militia violence and exposure to starvation had been concentrated, that effective humanitarian operations could be resumed. The action is authoritatively believed to have saved the lives of hundreds of thousands of people.

As the initiative evolved over the ensuing year, however, it came to be perceived in the United States as a political disaster, primarily because eighteen American soldiers were killed in a battle with Aideed's militia in October 1993. In response to public outrage at that event, inflamed by television images of an American soldier being dragged through the streets of Mogadishu, U.S. military operations associated with the UN force were immediately restricted to prevent any additional casualties, and all American troops were ordered to withdraw from Somalia by the end of March of 1994, a month before the genocide began in Rwanda. The apparent implication, repeatedly articulated in public commentary, was that no casualties could be tolerated in conducting humanitarian operations, and residual UN operations were aligned with that rule.[28] Some thirty thousand troops from twenty-eight countries constituted as UNOSOM II and operating under UN command authority remained in Somalia following UNITAF's withdrawal.[29] With neither the capacity nor the mandate to control the predatory militia, they were compelled to survive by accommodation, and the continuing violence that had to be tolerated overshadowed whatever was prevented. Both UNITAF and UNOSOM were recorded in immediately prevailing political judgment as decisive failures of the sort never again to be attempted. With the benefit of retrospect, however, and with renewed interest in Somalia as a potential haven for international terrorist operations, it is more evident that the original intervention might have been more successful had it been better designed and more resolutely pursued.

In its initial phase, UNITAF clearly demonstrated the international capacity to suppress militia operations and to restore some approximation of normal life at feasible levels of effort and cost. That was particularly apparent in rural areas outside of Mogadishu,[30] but even there, at the major point of contention between the Aideed and Ali Mahdi forces, the situation was not militarily unmanageable up to and including the fateful battle on 3 and 4 October 1993, which U.S. forces initiated. Had the United States chosen to prosecute that engagement rather than withdraw from it, Aideed's forces would have been severely degraded and the UN would have been in commanding position to negotiate political accommodation. Moreover, had UNITAF's operations been more assertive from the start and more systematically coordinated with diplomatic effort to reconstruct a viable government, there is good reason to believe that a direct battle of that intensity could have been avoided. UNITAF's uncontested arrival was negotiated with the militia leaders that might have resisted it, but the speed with which that was accomplished against the immediately preceding background of contempt for UN operations clearly indicates that those leaders were usefully chastened by the large and sudden commitment of the United States. That effect was quickly dissipated, however, by the extremely limited purpose that the United States projected and by the correspondingly cautious behavior of the UNITAF operation. In announcing the action, President George H. W. Bush emphasized that it would be exclusively devoted to the delivery of humanitarian aid and would be completed within a few weeks, a formulation so outlandishly impractical under the circumstances that it signaled fear of excessive entanglement rather than a determination to succeed. No statement of purpose was issued either at the outset of the operation or at any point thereafter that would justify combat casualties, and that fact was reflected in the decisions of American commanders on the scene. UNITAF's actions were forceful enough to compel the militia to move major weapons out of the urban areas where they could be used in effect to tax and otherwise control the delivery of food supplies, but there was no effort to disarm the militia despite insistent pleas from Secretary General Boutros-Ghali to do so.[31] The militia leaders could readily discern from the unfolding pattern of the operation that the U.S. commitment was politically fragile and that it was not likely to be sustained.

That impression was reinforced by the fitful diplomacy associated with the operation. In the immediate aftermath of the UNITAF deployment, UN mediators working in concert with Oakley staged two formal conferences in Addis Ababa involving the clan factions that had been identified as the principal sources of most of the militia operations. On 27 March 1993 the second of these conferences produced a document committing the fifteen signatory organizations to a program of disarmament and political reconciliation, including the creation of transitional institutions intended to produce a national government within a two-year period. That document was not a complete political settlement, but it was a significant enough step in that direction to suggest that an internationally negotiated reconstruction of the central government was feasible in principle and might actually occur. The Somali factions were compelled to take that possibility seriously since none of them were capable of establishing a comprehensive authority on their own terms. The United States refused to accept responsibility for fashioning a political settlement, however. That was construed to be an exercise in nation building, a derisive term in the American political lexicon at the time. Without the military capacity of the United States, the United Nations could not impose the practical discipline required to manage the delicate transition between coercive and consensual methods of acquiring power. Oakley resigned before the Addis Ababa agreement was issued and primary responsibility for security in Somalia was formally shifted from UNITAF to UNOSOM II a few weeks thereafter. With the departure of the cautious but imposing and nationally commanded U.S. combat forces that had formed the core of UNITAF, the Somali militia began to resume their operations, and in June elements of what was assumed to be Aideed's militia ambushed Pakistani troops assigned to UNOSOM II, killing twenty-four of them. On 17 June, in an apparent effort to establish the operational credibility of UNOSOM II, the Special Representative of the Secretary General in Somalia, retired American Admiral Jonathan Howe, issued a warrant for the arrest of General Aideed setting off an extended manhunt that culminated in the battle that commenced on 3 October. Over the course of that sequence, efforts to develop the Addis Ababa agreement were effectively suspended and collapsed thereafter.[32]

Although it cannot be demonstrated what the consequences would have been if UNITAF had been instructed to support the process of political reconstruction over the two-year period mapped out in the Addis Ababa agreement, it is reasonable to believe that a substantially better outcome could have been achieved with less grief on all sides than was actually suffered. A decade after the watershed battle, no permanent government had yet been established in Somalia, and the international community had reinitiated efforts to create one. The government of Kenya, operating through the East African regional organization, the Inter-Governmental Authority on Development (IGAD), had organized what they termed a peace process involving most of the major political movements in Somalia, with "key members of the international community" said to be "closely engaged at every step."[33] The United States and its European allies were interdicting ship traffic into Somalia for fear that terrorist organizations driven out of Afghanistan might relocate there.[34] Meanwhile, the population of approximately six million people continued to teeter on the brink of a humanitarian catastrophe[35] and international food aid deliveries continued to be impeded by endemic violence.[36] In 1996, the last year for which there was sufficient data to make a statistical assessment, Somalia ranked 172 out of 174 countries on the UN Development Program's Human Development Index. With the advantages of retrospect, including in particular experience in Afghanistan, it now seems evident that a judiciously extended and moderately more willful UNITAF could have achieved a better result.

Rwanda

Similarly it seems evident that massive civil violence in Rwanda, which claimed up to eight hundred thousand lives over the course of one hundred days beginning in April of 1994 and has plagued the entire region ever since, could have been largely prevented. The episode was triggered by a fatal attack on an aircraft carrying the presidents of Rwanda and Burundi as it was attempting to land in the capital area. That was the initiating event of a violent assault undertaken by political extremists, the Interahamwe, belonging to the majority Hutu community against moderate politicians of the same community and against all people identified with the minority Tutsi community. (The population of Rwanda at the time was 85 to 90 percent Hutu, 9 to 14 percent Tutsi, and 1 percent Twa, with the Tutsi generally considered to be the historical elite.)[37] The apparent immediate purpose of the assault was to preempt the imminent implementation of a power-sharing arrangement between the communities that had been formally signed in August 1993 in Arusha, Tanzania, but the underlying intent involved a comprehensive attack on all Tutsi individuals that fit the definition of genocide as well as any event in half a century. That intent was well enough understood and the principal protagonists well enough known that close observers were able to warn of the impending calamity in very specific terms in its earliest stages. A United Nations force, officially named UNAMIR, that had been formed in October of 1993 to oversee implementation of the Arusha Accords already had some twenty-five hundred personnel in the country, including 1,660 infantry troops under the operational command of Canadian Major General Romeo Dallaire. That force would have been enough to stop the slaughter of numerous civilians but was considered to be only about half of what would have been required to control fighting between Hutu government and insurgent Tutsi military forces, known as the Rwandan Patriotic Army (RPA), that was also triggered by the plane crash.[38]

Instead of reinforcing UNAMIR and committing it to decisive intervention, as requested by General Dallaire and recommended by the UN Secretary General, the UN Security Council authorized the withdrawal of its combat troops in response to concerns from the contributing countries about their safety. The bedrock reason was that the United States, the only country capable of undertaking the rapid reinforcement required, was not willing to do so. As the crisis played out, Tutsi military units supported from bases in Uganda seized control of the country but not before a significant portion of Rwanda's Tutsi population had been slaughtered. As the RPA was winning the civil war, an estimated two million Hutu refugees, including many of the perpetrators of the original assault, fled into the eastern portion of what was then known as Zaire (today called the Democratic Republic of Congo) with reverberations that were ultimately fatal for its ruling regime.

The succeeding government in Rwanda has been internally repressive and externally aggressive. In 1996, it launched a military operation against the Democratic Republic of the Congo (DRC) aimed at hunting down some of the fighters that were responsible for the 1994 genocide, claiming that the Congolese government was sheltering Interahamwe forces. As a result of this incursion somewhere between 750,000 and one million Hutu refugees that had fled Rwanda in the wake of the genocide returned to their homeland, but militant bands of anti-Rwandan government fighters remained in eastern DRC, enjoying the apparent support of the DRC government.

By 1997, in the wake of actions of Rwandan soldiers and Rwandan-backed rebels, along with help from Uganda and Burundi, Congolese president Mobutu Sese Seko was deposed. With Rwandan support, Laurent Kabila became president of DRC, but by 1998, accusing the new Congolese president of failing to expel extremist Hutu militias, Rwanda turned its troops and the rebels it was supporting against Kabila. Within a short period of time, Angola, Namibia, and Zimbabwe had joined the fight supporting the DRC, and Burundi and Uganda, along with Rwanda, were supporting the antigovernment of DRC rebels. As the war in the DRC grew, the international community urged Rwanda, which was seen as the most capable military force of the interveners, to remove its soldiers from eastern DRC and to stop supporting rebels there. A peace accord signed in Lusaka in 1999 among the warring factions produced some hope, but the terms were not adhered to. It was not until July 2002, with the signing of a peace accord between DRC and Rwanda, that hope of a settlement of the conflict re-emerged. By this time it was estimated that over two million people had died since 1998, most of them civilians who succumbed to starvation or disease.[39]

The DRC-Rwanda peace accord, signed in Pretoria, South Africa, was looked upon as the most likely means of ending what has been called "Africa's First World War." Under the agreement, the government of Rwanda agreed to pull its approximately twenty thousand troops out of eastern DRC if the DRC government would help in the repatriation of the remaining Rwandan Hutu refugees, including the antigovernment of Rwanda fighters numbering approximately twelve thousand,[40] as well as help in the capture of suspected leaders in the genocide. By early 2003 there was general agreement that Rwanda had lived up to the terms of the agreement, but there were periodic indications that Rwanda would consider reinvading the DRC if it believed that forces opposing it were being mobilized.[41] Helping to monitor the Pretoria Accord is the UN Mission in DRC dubbed MONUC. Unfortunately, as of December 2002, the UN had only been able to assemble a force of forty-two hundred out of a planned monitoring force of fifty-five hundred.[42]

In retrospect it seems evident that the initial rampage could have been contained and most of the ensuing turbulence in the region could have been prevented if UNAMIR had been given the authority to do so along with the reinforcing brigade General Dallaire had requested. Moreover, it is also evident that the humanitarian relief efforts that were undertaken without the support of an intervening force ended up contributing to the reverberating violence. Many of the Rwandan refugees who fled into DRC, Tanzania, and Burundi in 1994 were perpetrators of genocide rather than victims of it.[43] A massive influx of poorly coordinated international aid, clearly needed to prevent large-scale starvation and malnutrition, created semipermanent refugee camps that became a base of support for residual Interahamwe elements committed to extending the conflict.[44] That provided a stimulus and justification for Rwandan government military incursions into the DRC. Since long-term recovery and rehabilitation assistance within Rwanda proved to be only about half the amount spent on external refugees, the humanitarian relief efforts also generated a sense of inequity that burdens the prospects for reconciliation throughout the Great Lakes region.[45] As with Somalia, experience in Rwanda indicates that mastery of major conflict episodes requires an integrated and sustained effort not only to suppress violence and provide immediate relief, but also to engage in longer-term reconstruction. It was again demonstrated that none of these elements will work without the others, but that lesson has emerged more from failure than from constructive example.

What then would be a generally accepted standard of success? There are, of course, differing opinions on that question as well, but most of those seriously attempting to draw practical lessons would probably accept restoration of a society's ability to control conflict through its own internal institutions as a basic criterion. And despite the unresolved arguments about interest and purpose, the fundamental conditions for achieving that basic criterion have been identified in each instance and have been generally acknowledged:

- Basic civil administration services must be provided reasonably equitably for all internal communities, including especially police protection; the administration of justice; and the delivery of food, water, and power.
- A process of political reconciliation must be initiated that is eventually able to distribute power and to formulate and implement policies on a consensual basis.
- A process of economic regeneration must be initiated, inevitably requiring substantial international assistance in its initial phases.

In all of the interventions recently undertaken, these components have been minimally improvised and clearly inadequate—a natural result of the fact that no systematic preparations were made in advance. As long as the United States participates, the international community has ample military capability to suppress the major forms of fighting in any civil conflict. It also has substantial capacity for delivering humanitarian assistance and economic aid, but the institutions that do that have not designed their activities for active conflict situations and have not been integrated into military operations. The international community has virtually no systematically prepared capacity to perform police functions or provide interim civil administration in support of conflict interventions. Not surprisingly, the imbalance in capacity has produced an imbalance in performance. No full scope effort has yet been undertaken that might set a standard of good practice, and most of the retrospective observers would agree that nothing has yet come close to plausible requirements. Without a practical reference of that sort it is very difficult to judge how costly and effective a credible intervention effort might be.

The Implications of Afghanistan

The intervention in Afghanistan initiated by the United States in response to the attacks of 11 September 2001 is clearly a work in progress, and it is especially hazardous at this point to try to visualize the extended implications. There are nonetheless some strong presumptions.

First, it appears that the commitment of United States forces to ground operations in Afghanistan has consolidated acceptance of enduring global engagement within the American political system. Prior to September 11 the use of American military forces in Central Asia would have been so assertively contested as to be infeasible. In the aftermath, the necessity in that instance was accepted as a matter of nearly universal consensus, and the expectation has been established that comparable military action against terrorism would be considered in any part of the world. Moreover, the scope of engagement was expanded to include activities previously denigrated as "nation building."

That progression was especially notable for leading figures of the Bush administration. As the Republican Party candidate during the 2000 U.S. presidential campaign, then-Governor George W. Bush explicitly declared that his administration would be loath to involve itself in any nation-building effort. When asked in the second of three presidential debates with Democratic nominee Al Gore if U.S. soldiers would be used in nation-building operations, Bush stated: "Absolutely not. Our military is meant to fight and win war." Shortly after the September 11 attacks, White House Chief of Staff Andrew Card reiterated this sentiment when he stated: "The president won't want to use troops to rebuild Afghanistan."[46] By 20 August 2002, however, Secretary of Defense Donald Rumsfeld displayed at a regular press briefing a series of "before" and "after" photographs of schools, hospitals, wells, canals, bridges, and roads that the United States and coalition military forces had helped to rebuild or refurbish in Afghanistan.[47] In touting those accomplishments, Rumsfeld explicitly stated:

> Our goal in Afghanistan, clearly, is to create conditions so the country does not again become a terrorist training camp. Terrorists are like parasites; they seek out weak and struggling countries to serve as hosts for their attacks on innocent men, women and children. If we are to ensure that terrorist networks do not return to take over Afghanistan once again, then we have to help the Afghan people build the infrastructure that will allow them to achieve true self-government and self-reliance. . . . And that's why the U.S. Army Civil Affairs teams are working in some ten regions of the country, digging wells, rebuilding schools, bridges and hospitals.[48]

Although it did not include the term "nation building," Rumsfeld's statement was an unambiguous commitment to its basic purposes. That commitment was reiterated on 16 January 2003 by Deputy Secretary of Defense Paul Wolfowitz. "We're clearly moving into a different phase, where our priority in Afghanistan is increasingly going to be stability and reconstruction," Wolfowitz asserted, adding: "There is no way to go too fast. Faster is better."[49] He made the statement outside Kabul's main maternity hospital, which was being renovated with Pentagon funds.

Second, if that expansion of policy is to be enduring and effective it would have to be accompanied by development of the institutional capabilities that have been defective in previous instances; most notably the ability to provide interim police and civil administration services and to undertake a general process of reconstruction. That aspiration has begun to appear in U.S. military operations that were said, as of early 2003, to be evolving from "combat-oriented to reconstruction operations, the fourth and final phase of the Pentagon's overall strategy in Afghanistan."[50] It was specifically exemplified in an initiative to form what was originally termed Provisional Reconstruction Teams (PRTs) designed to provide dedicated security for humanitarian relief efforts operating outside of the Kabul area.[51] By late February 2003, units so designated had commenced operations in Gardez, Bamyan, and Konduz.[52] They included Special Operations soldiers, Army Civil Affair soldiers trained in reconstruction work, and conventional ground troops. Although small in size (forty to sixty soldiers), their mere presence and their ability to call in reinforcement, including air strikes, was considered to be a substantial commitment to the security of relief efforts.[53] The PRTs are at least meant to include representatives of the United States Agency for International Development (USAID) and the State Department, along with others involved in Afghan reconstruction.

The PRTs were not unequivocally endorsed by the humanitarian organizations operating in Afghanistan, suggesting that the concept would have to evolve appreciably if it is to be institutionalized. In a policy brief released in mid-January 2003, a coordinating body for those organizations—the Agency Coordinating Body for Afghan Relief (ACBAR)—questioned both the fundamental purposes and the legal authority of the proposed PRTs. ACBAR expressed concern about the operational autonomy of relief organizations, indicating a reluctance to become directly involved in the hunt for al Qaeda operatives and an assertive interest in addressing human rights abuses wherever they might originate.[54] The humanitarian organizations also questioned the limited scope of the PRT concept as they questioned the limited mandate of the International Security Assistance Force (ISAF)—the five-thousand-soldier peacekeeping force that had been restricted to the Kabul area. Since an expansion of PRT or ISAF to cover all of Afghanistan would require more military personnel—as many as ten thousand according to some estimates[55]—the entire discussion was suspended as a practical matter by the invasion of Iraq in March 2003, and it became evident at that point that policy on reconstruction would be yet more consequentially shaped by the outcome in Iraq. Meanwhile, the United States did continue to provide assistance for military infrastructure, training, and equipment for the Afghan National Army, utilizing $150 million from the Afghan Freedom Support Act.[56] As of the middle of January 2003, four battalions of the rebuilt Afghan National Army had completed training, another two were in the process, and a seventh unit was being formed.

Although those developments remained well short of what a comprehensive reconstruction effort would require, they did provide some indication that one of the main practical lessons from previous experience had been absorbed; namely, that the effective performance of police and civil administration functions were vital to the restoration of a viable society and that interim international involvement in those functions would be required. That principle was repeatedly emphasized by Hamid Karzai after he became president of the Afghan Transitional Administration (ATA) in June 2002. It was acknowledged by James Dobbins who served as U.S. special envoy to Afghanistan—"small-scale violence remains prevalent enough to inhibit the resumption of normal economic activity, and such activity is central to Afghanistan's future"[57]—by Ambassador Lakhdar Brahimi, Special Representative of the Secretary-General (SRSG) for Afghanistan— "There will be no long term solution to the security problems of Afghanistan unless and until a well trained, well equipped and regularly paid National Police and National Army are in place"[58]—and by UN Secretary General Kofi Annan—"the Government and the people of Afghanistan need and ask for international support to provide security while the National Police and National Army are being trained."[59] Annan's statement reflected the fact that during the twenty-three years of Afghan civil war, there was no functioning civilian police force in Afghanistan[60] and that the one being created in the aftermath of U.S. occupation did not yet meet international standards. A report issued by Amnesty International in March 2003 found a "widespread pattern of human rights violations committed by members of the police, including torture and arbitrary arrest."[61] SRSG Brahimi concurred in the Amnesty International findings.[62]

Similarly, a third presumption that reconstruction will have to include serious international investment in economic regeneration has been acknowledged in principle but not implemented in fact either in the amount that would be required or in the design. In January 2002 the United Nations Development Program, Asian Development Bank, and World Bank jointly estimated that between $11.4 billion and $18.1 billion would be required over ten years to rebuild the Afghan economy,[63] but at the donor conference in Tokyo the same month only $4.5 billion was pledged for Afghan relief, recovery, and reconstruction—in per capita terms, about a quarter of the amount pledged for Bosnia.[64] Nine months later U.S. Secretary of State Colin Powell complained that more than a third of the pledges for 2002 had not yet been delivered.[65] Both the amounts pledged and the actual deliveries, moreover, were initially allocated more to relief than to recovery and reconstruction.[66]

The deficiencies have been acknowledged in principle and addressed in limited instances. The United States pledged $80 million to help rehabilitate the main road connecting Kabul, Kandahar, and Herat,[67] for example, and has also committed funds to repair and reconstruct thirty-one bridges, roads, canals, dams, and water systems.[68] Overall U.S. assistance to Afghanistan in fiscal year 2003 was scheduled to be 44 percent more than the $569 million provided in fiscal year 2002.[69] As with support for police and civil administration functions, however, programs for economic reconstruction in Afghanistan as of 2003 documented general awareness of their significance for the effective control of violence but not yet the level of commitment required to assure social stabilization and political regeneration.

In general one can be plausibly hopeful at this point that intervention in Afghanistan has established the basic requirements of reconstruction and that implementing policies are in the initial stages of development. A dedicated optimist might also be hopeful that the yet more consequential intervention in Iraq, undertaken for reasons that extend beyond concern for civil conflict, will accelerate the pace and expand the scale of reconstruction efforts. If necessity is indeed the mother of invention, as the familiar aphorism claims, then enhanced reconstruction should be one of the major implications of the combined ventures. Certainly they have created a compelling necessity. A realist is obliged to note, however, that political rhetoric and practical accomplishment are hardly the same thing. The problem of civil violence has been acknowledged and its fundamental requirements are apparent, but mastery has yet to be constructively demonstrated.

Notes

This chapter was prepared with partial support from the Center for Social and Economic Dynamics at the Brookings Institution, Washington, D.C.

1. Milton Leitenberg, "Deaths in Wars and Conflicts between 1945 and 2000," (occasional paper #29, Cornell University Peace Studies Program, July 2003).

2. Ted Robert Gurr and Monty G. Marshall, *Peace and Conflict, 2003,* Center for International Development and Conflict Management, University of Maryland, College Park, 11 February 2003.

3. Ted Robert Gurr, Deepa Khosla, and Monty G. Marshall, *Peace and Conflict, 2001,* Center for International Development and Conflict Management, University of Maryland, College Park, 1 January 2001, 20.

4. Daniel C. Esty, Jack A. Goldstone, Ted Robert Gurr, Pamela T. Surko, and Alan N. Unger, "State Failure Task Force Report," (working paper, Center for International Development and Conflict Management, University of Maryland, November 1995).

5. Paul Collier and Nicholas Sambanis, "Understanding Civil War: A New Agenda," *Journal of Conflict Resolution* 46, no. 1 (February 2002): 3.

6. Paul Collier, "Economic Causes of Civil Conflict and Their Implications for Policy," World Bank, 15 June 2000, 6. See also Paul Collier et al., "Breaking the Conflict Trap: Civil War and Development Policy," World Bank, 2003.

7. Paul Collier and Anke Hoeffler, "Greed and Grievance in Civil War," World Bank, 21 October 2001, 12.

8. Collier, Hoeffler, "Greed and Grievance," 6–7.

9. Collier, Hoeffler, "Greed and Grievance," 10.

10. James Fearon and David Laitin, "Ethnicity, Insurgency and War," Stanford University, 2000, cited in Nicholas Sambanis, "Do Ethnic and Nonethnic Wars Have the Same Causes?" *Journal of Conflict Resolution* 45, no. 3 (June 2001): 264.

11. Sambanis, "Ethnic, Nonethnic Causes," 259–281.

12. Sambanis, "Ethnic, Nonethnic Causes," 269.

13. Sambanis, "Ethnic, Nonethnic Causes," 273.

14. Sambanis, "Ethnic, Nonethnic Causes," 272.

15. Sambanis, "Ethnic, Nonethnic Causes," 277.

16. Patrick Ball, Paul Kobrak, and Herbert F. Spirer, *State Violence in Guatemala, 1960–1996: A Quantitative Reflection,* 1999, hrdata.aaas.org/ciidh/data.html (July 2000).

17. Timothy Gulden, "Spatial and Temporal Patterns of Civil Violence: Guatemala, 1977–1986," working paper no. 26, Center on Social and Economic Dynamics, Brookings Institution, Washington, D.C., 2002.

18. Gulden, "Guatemala," 10.

19. Gulden, "Guatemala," 15.

20. Joshua M. Epstein, Miles T. Parker, and John D. Steinbruner, "Modeling Civil Violence: An Agent-Based Computational Approach," working paper no. 20, Center on Social and Economic Dynamics, Brookings Institution, Washington, D.C., 2001.

21. John D. Steinbruner, *Principles of Global Security* (Washington, D.C.: Brookings Institution, 2000), chapter 4.

22. David D. Laitin, "Somalia: Intervention in Internal Conflict," Stanford University, 12 October 2001, 14.

23. Terrence Lyons and Ahmed I. Samatar, *Somalia: State Collapse, Multilateral Intervention, and Strategies for Political Reconstruction,* Brookings Occasional Papers, Brookings Institution, Washington, D.C., 1995, chapter 3.

24. Mohamed Sahnoun, *Somalia: The Missed Opportunities* (Washington, D.C.: U.S. Institute for Peace Press, 1994).

25. "Population-Based Mortality Assessment—Baidoa and Afgoi, Somalia, 1992," *Morbidity and Mortality Weekly Report* 41, no. 49 (11 December 1992): 913–917.

26. "Population-Based Mortality Assessment," 33.

27. Telephone conversation with Public Affairs Office of the Fifteenth Marine Expeditionary Unit.

28. As discussed later in this chapter, the application of this lesson would have disastrous consequences for Rwanda.

29. The initial intervention led by the United States and organized as UNITAF was formally terminated in May 1993, and the U.S. forces that had conducted it were withdrawn. UNITAF was replaced by UNOSOM II on 4 May. Fifteen hundred U.S. combat forces remained in the area under national command, however, as available reinforcement for UNOSOM II should that be necessary. The hunt for Aideed and the October battle that resulted were conducted by U.S. Army Ranger units assigned to the U.S. national force.

30. United Nations, *The United Nations and Somalia, 1992–1996* (New York: United Nations Press, 1996), 55.

31. *United Nations and Somalia,* 225.

32. John L. Hirsh and Robert B. Oakley, *Somalia and Operation Restore Hope: Reflections on Peacemaking and Peacekeeping* (Washington, D.C.: United States Institute for Peace Press, 1995).

33. International Crisis Group, *Salvaging Somalia's Chance for Peace*, Africa Briefing, 9 December 2002.

34. International Crisis Group, *Somalia: Countering Terrorism in a Failed State*, Africa Report no. 45, 23 May 2002.

35. Kofi Annan, *Report of the Secretary-General on the Situation in Somalia*, United Nations, S/2002/709, 27 June 2002.

36. Food and Agriculture Organization, "FAO Global Information and Early Warning System on Food and Agriculture," Special alert no. 319, 13 November 2001.

37. This distinction between the Hutu and the Tutsi is based primarily on cultural history and is not reliably evident from language, appearance, or personal name. The Tutsi were warriors and cattle herders, were favored by the German and Belgian colonial administrators, and became over the course of the colonial period the cultural elite. The Belgians systematically reinforced the distinction through a system of identity cards. The Hutu were farmers and were able to come to power when the country acquired independence in 1962 by virtue of their electoral majorities. See Gérard Prunier, *The Rwanda Crisis: History of a Genocide* (New York: Columbia University Press, 1995) and Scott R. Feil, *Preventing Genocide: How the Early Use of Force Might Have Succeeded in Rwanda* (Washington, D.C.: Carnegie Commission on Preventing Deadly Conflict, April 1998), appendix B.

38. In retrospect it seems apparent that the timely arrest of less than one hundred known individuals would have prevented most of the civilian casualties since these were largely inflicted by irregular militia gangs organized explicitly for the purpose. Professional assessments also suggest that a single U.S. infantry brigade—the basic unit capable of undertaking all the aspects of the required operation—could have provided sufficient reinforcement for UNAMIR to control the situation. See Scott Feil, *Preventing Genocide.* As with any argument about how a historical event might have been altered, there is a range of opinion about how decisive a timely intervention in Rwanda would have been. Skeptics argue that controlling the violence would have been difficult and would have required more than a single brigade. Most of the skeptics appear to concede, however, that a meaningfully effective operation could have been undertaken with the level of resources that were reasonably available. See Alan J. Kuperman, *The Limits of Humanitarian Intervention: Genocide in Rwanda* (Washington, D.C.: Brookings Institution Press, 2001) and Alan J. Kuperman, "Rwanda in Retrospect," *Foreign Affairs* 79, no. 1 (January–February 2000): 94–118.

39. John Murphy, "Hopes High as Rwanda, Congo Sign Peace Pact," *Baltimore Sun*, 31 July 2002, 1A.

40. Laurie Goering, "Africans Pin Hope on Dawn of Peace; Congo, Rwanda Reach Agreement," *Chicago Tribune*, 31 July 2002, 1.

41. Leonard Doyle, "Rwanda Warns of Congo Reinvasion If Militias Advance," *The Independent* (London), 18 October 2002, 10.

42. Declan Walsh, "Congolese Hope a Ragged Army of Thousands Will Go Home to Rwanda," *The Irish Times*, 16 December 2002, 10.

43. One analyst has even described this movement of refugees as an "organized political withdrawal." See Norah Nylund, "Rwanda: What Lessons Have Humanitarians Learned?" *Hunger Notes* 22, no. 1 (1996), accessed at: web.archive.org/web/20010420055436/www.brown.edu/Departments/World_Hunger_Program/hungerweb/HN/Articles/RWANDA/NYLUND.html.

44. Steering Committee of the Joint Evaluation of Emergency Assistance to Rwanda, "Recommendations and Lessons Learned—Chapter 12," *The International Re-

sponse to Conflict and Genocide: Lessons from the Rwanda Experience, vol. 4, *Rebuilding Post-War Rwanda* (Copenhagen, Denmark: Steering Committee of the Joint Evaluation of Emergency Assistance to Rwanda, March 1996).

45. Krishna Kumar, "Rebuilding Post-War Rwanda," *Hunger Notes* 22, no. 1 (1996), accessed at: web.archive.org/web/20010420060147/www.brown.edu/Departments/World_Hunger_Program/hungerweb/HN/Articles/RWANDA/KUMAR.html.

46. Bob Woodward, *Bush at War* (New York: Simon and Schuster, 2002), 193.

47. "Department of Defense News Briefing—Secretary [Donald] Rumsfeld and General [Peter] Pace," 20 August 2002, accessed at www.defenselink.mil/news/Aug2002/t08202002_t0820sd.html. See also, Gerry J. Gilmore, "Rumsfeld Praises Civil Affairs' Work in Afghanistan," *Armed Forces Information Service*, 20 August 2002, accessed at www.defenselink.mil/news/Aug2002/n08202002_200208202.html.

48. "DoD News Briefing."

49. Bradley Graham, "Wolfowitz Pushes Faster Afghan Reconstruction," *Washington Post*, 16 January 2003, A20.

50. Jim Wagner, "Civil Affairs Soldiers Adapt to a New Mission," www.defendamerica.mil/articles/feb2003/a010303a.html.

51. James Dao, "Pentagon Official Wants to Speed Rebuilding of Afghanistan," *New York Times*, 15 January 2003.

52. U.S. Department of Defense, "Afghanistan Relief and Reconstruction," briefing, 27 February 2003.

53. Dao, "Speed Rebuilding of Afghanistan."

54. CAREUSA, "NGO Position Paper Concerning the Provisional Reconstruction Teams," *ACBAR Policy Brief*, accessed at www.careusa.org/newsroom/specialreports/afghanistan/01152003_ngorec.pdf.

55. Dao, "Speed Rebuilding of Afghanistan."

56. White House Office of Global Communication, "Rebuilding Afghanistan," *Fact Sheet*, 27 February 2003.

57. James Dobbins, "Afghanistan's Faltering Reconstruction," *New York Times*, 12 September 2002, A27.

58. Briefing by SRSG Lakhdar Brahimi, "Open Meeting of the Security Council: Afghanistan," 30 October 2002.

59. Brahimi, "Open Meeting of the Security Council: Afghanistan."

60. Amnesty International, "Afghanistan—Police Reconstruction Essential for the Protection of Human Rights," ASA 11/003/2003, March 2003, 6.

61. Amnesty International, "Afghanistan—Police Reconstruction Essential," 1.

62. "Transcript of the Press Conference by Lakhdar Brahimi," SRSG for Afghanistan, 20 March 2003.

63. The United Nations Development Program, Asian Development Bank, and World Bank, *Afghanistan: Preliminary Needs Assessment for Recovery and Reconstruction*, January 2002.

64. Rory McCarthy, "The Bombing of Afghanistan," *The Guardian* (London), 7 October 2002, 4.

65. Dao, "Speed Rebuilding of Afghanistan."

66. Dana Milbank, "Bush Bids to End Impasse at U.N., Outlines Iraq Plan," *Washington Post*, 12 October 2002, A1.

67. As of January 2003 the United States had agreed to help rebuild 120 miles of the 600-mile project.

68. White House Office of Global Communication, "Rebuilding Afghanistan."

69. Richard Boucher, spokesman, U.S. Department of State, "U.S. Delegation in Brussels to Reaffirm Its Commitment to Afghanistan," press statement, 17 March 2003.

2

Somalia: Intervention in Internal Conflict

David D. Laitin

Massive international efforts beginning in 1992 to ameliorate the devastating effects of the Somali civil war and to reconstitute a functioning government in that country brought some notable achievements, but they were overshadowed by grievous failures. Section I of this chapter provides background information on the Somali conflict that precipitated the international intervention. Section II delineates the special problems for military intervention in the current era in civil wars like Somalia's. Sections III–V develop three points, listed here, that have implications for future international interventions in civil wars:

- Early decisive diplomatic attention to the Somali crisis, backed by fiscal and military threats, probably could have nipped the civil war in its bud, averting the catastrophe that followed.
- The goals of the humanitarian relief mission, while impressively fulfilled, undermined the chances for a political settlement, and therefore set the stage for an ignominious exit by the international gendarmerie.
- The strategic situation in the United Nations Security Council, between the leading permanent missions (the P-5) and the Secretary General (SG), creates a bias toward ambitious goals combined with paltry resources. The UN's Somali operations reflected that unfortunate bias.

Section VI evaluates the international effort in Somalia.

I. Background Information

In the late 1980s, President Maxamad Siyaad Barre's inner coalition of three clans (Marreexaan, Ogaadeen, and Dhulbahante, called "MOD") were in full-scale war against the Isxaaqs of the former British colony in the northwest (organized into the Somali National Movement, the SNM), the Majeerteens in the northeast (organized as the Somali Salvation Democratic Front, the SSDF), and the Hawiyas to Mogadishu's immediate west and south (organized as the United Somali Congress, the USC). The USC army drove Siyaad out of the country in 1991 and a Hawiya (Abgal subclan) businessman, Cali Mahdi, was installed as president, with the encouragement of the Italian ambassador. The Isxaaq and the Majeerteen armies refused to accept Hawiya rule (proximity to the capital and old colonial ties to the Italians were not sufficient justification for non-Hawiyas) and continued to fight. The issue was especially complex for the SNM. The Isxaaqs fought Siyaad Barre with the greatest loss in personnel (and their major metropolis, Hargeisa, leveled) and were angry that their army did not get to Mogadishu (where Isxaaqs had major land holdings) before the armies of the USC. They were thus reluctant to return to their homeland in the north but eventually did, creating a rump state. Meanwhile, a military leader of the USC army from a different subclan than Mahdi's, Maxamad Faarax Aideed (from the Habar Gidir subclan), challenged Mahdi's right to the presidency. By late 1991 not only was there an interclan war for control over Somalia, but also an intraclan war for control over Mogadishu. Throughout the south, and in Mogadishu especially, warlords (*waraanle*) claimed control over bands of well-armed youths who, with their armed Land Rovers (called "technicals"), roamed the cities and roadways plundering, extorting, and killing. By late 1992, due to the civil war, the entire infrastructure of the country was ruined, mass killing, starvation, and disease afflicted much of the population, there was no central government that could negotiate on behalf of the state, and international relief workers were nearly as vulnerable to attack as was the Somali population.

The UN, more than a year after Siyaad fell from power, brokered a cease-fire in February 1992 between Mahdi and Aideed. Six weeks later, the Security Council established the United Nations Operation in Somalia (UNOSOM I) to monitor the cease-fire and to provide emergency humanitarian assistance. The Secretary General appointed Mohamed Sahnoun, a well-respected Egyptian diplomat, as his special representative (SRSG) and he was provided with a staff of fifty unarmed monitors. In Resolution 751 (April 1992), the UN promised to send a 500-man security force as well, but it was not until September that lightly armed Pakistani troops arrived. The cease-fire did not last. Continued fighting in this impoverished country created massive numbers of starving and diseased victims. The unspeakable horrors of the war, broadcast through international media, gained international attention. Reports on this situation led U.S. President

Map 2.1 Somalia

Bush to commit U.S. forces to airlift relief supplies to the civil war's victims. In this U.S.-support operation of UNOSOM I, called "Provide Relief," more than twenty-eight thousand metric tons of relief supplies were delivered to Somalia.

By November, President Bush agreed to up the ante and to offer U.S. troops to lead a UN military action to avert an even greater human tragedy. On 3 December, the Security Council, combining language of Chapters VI (on peacekeeping) and VII (on peace enforcement) of the UN Charter, passed Resolution 794 creating the United Task Force (UNITAF) with a mandate to create a permanent UN peacekeeping operation to provide humanitarian assistance and to restore order to southern Somalia once the UNITAF ameliorated the human tragedy. From December 1992 through May 1993, UNITAF had about thirty-eight thousand troops from twenty-one nations, including twenty-eight thousand Americans, whose parallel operation during the UNITAF period was called "Restore Hope." President Bush insisted that "Restore Hope" be seen merely as a humanitarian mission to save civilian lives and promised that the mission would be over in a few months' time

The UN was reluctant to manage the transition in which UNITAF would be replaced. But in March 1993, with Security Council Resolution 814, crafted by President Clinton's foreign policy team, UNOSOM II was mandated to replace UNITAF. This was an ambitious resolution calling for the rebuilding of state institutions. Moreover, it was the first ever Chapter VII resolution that was explicit about enforcement, including the disarming of Somali clans. Aideed took advantage of weak administration of the mission in June 1993 when some of his supporters ambushed and killed twenty-four Pakistani soldiers. In response, the UN authorized (through Security Council Resolution 837) U.S. Rangers to apprehend those responsible. This led to a disaster for UNOSOM II. In an operation conducted on 3 October 1993, eighteen Americans were killed and seventy-five wounded in their manhunt for Aideed. President Clinton forthwith announced the phased withdrawal of American troops that would be completed by March 1994, thus ending the role of the international gendarmerie in the Somali civil war.

II. A New Kind of Mission

The collapse of weak states in the post–Cold War world and the concomitant humanitarian tragedies bring new challenges for diplomatic and military operations. For one, many actors involve themselves in these operations, each with its own program, leading to considerable coordination issues. Second, the goals of any operation are ambiguous from the beginning and tend to change in the course of its implementation. Third, rarely do these wars affect the interests of the intervening powers in a direct way. Humanitarian horrors rather than national threat drive the intervention. Therefore, goals are often more ambitious than resolve.

The most evident operational problem for this new type of intervention (clearest in UNOSOM II) comes from the divided command structure, with each part of the command having somewhat different goals. UNOSOM II was under nominal UN control. However, the United States had its own parallel command structure. U.S. Major General Montgomery was both Commander of U.S. Forces Somalia (USFORSOM) and a deputy to the UN Force Commander in Somalia, Lieutenant General Cevik Bir. Furthermore, the U.S. command was itself divided, with a complex command structure that, for example, separated the land forces inside Somalia from the Navy and Marine Corps forces that remained under the U.S. Central Command (CENTCOM). When the Task Force Ranger was deployed to capture Aideed, it had its own chain of command that did not go through either the U.S. or the UN channels in Somalia.

Then there was a problem of command over a diverse multinational army. Several countries besides the United States provided troops to these UN operations. In UNOSOM I, a brigade of uniformed but unarmed Pakistani troops was stationed at the airport, unable to carry out its mission. With U.S. troops leading UNITAF, support contingents from France, Canada, Belgium, Italy, Australia, Pakistan, Botswana, Nigeria, Zimbabwe, Saudi Arabia, Kuwait, the UAE, and six other countries were sent to Somalia. UNOSOM II included troops from Italy, France, Belgium, and Pakistan. In UNOSOM II, different national armies interpreted the Rules of Engagement differently, as to whether technicals should be engaged without provocation or whether they should first be asked to surrender weapons voluntarily. However, the bigger problem was the tendency of national contingents to seek guidance from their governments before carrying out orders. This reached levels of near treachery when the commander of the Italian contingent opened negotiations with Aideed when the Security Council had instructed UNOSOM II to hunt him down. There was no way the Italians could be policed or punished. Nearly all of the problems in plan implementation can be traced at least in part to this ambiguous command structure.

The coordination issues that stymied military command were equally problematical in relations between the military command and the humanitarian operations. Foreign NGO personnel were ubiquitous. Throughout the period thirty NGOs were active in providing humanitarian relief. These included Catholic Relief Services (CRS), International Medical Corps (IMC), Abu Dhabi Welfare Organization (AWO), Diakonic Care Germany (DGC), CARE International (CARE), Adventist Relief and Development Agency (ADRA), Africa Muslims Agency (AMA), Coordination Committee of Organizations for Voluntary Service (CCOVS), International Action Against Famine (AICF), Children's Emergency Services (SOS), Mercy International (MERCY), Doctors Without Borders (MSF), Muwafaq Charity (MCF), Pharmacists Without Borders (PSF), Revival Islamic Heritage (RIHS), Swedish Church Relief (SCR), Nordic Red Cross (NORCROSS), International Committee of the Red Cross (ICRC), Federation of the Red Cross Society (FRCS), Oxford Famine Relief (OXFAM), Church World Services (CWS), Agency for Cooperation and Research Development (ACORD), American Friends Service Committee (AFSC), Islamic African Relief Agency (IARA), International Islamic Relief (IIRO), International Development and Relief Agency (IDRA), Munzamai Islamic Society (DAWA), Muslim Aid UK (MAUK), Save the Children (SCF), and African Charity Society for Maternity and Childhood (ACSSOM). In October 1992, Philip Johnston, president of CARE, helped to create a security coordination mechanism for all NGOs, and this became the U.S.-led Civilian-Military Operations Center (CMOC). Besides the NGOs, several UN humanitarian agencies were also active during the civil war, including the UNHCR, UNICEF, UNESCO, UNDP, UNCTAD, and ECOSOC.

The goals of the NGOs have rarely been examined in a systematic way. Based on the stinging exposé of these goals written by Michael Maren, we can say that oftentimes their publicly stated humanitarian goals are overshadowed by their organizational desires to raise private money and to procure international contracts for their activities.[1] For several of these organizations Somalia was a perfect site for advertising to potential donors the need for greater financial support. Their personnel were there despite an inability to provide the aid that would have justified their presence. In reality, personnel from these humanitarian contingents were constantly in danger from their own (Somali) personnel as well as from militias. There was no clear way that the military command could provide security services to the NGOs. Giving IDs to registered NGO personnel only created a market for such IDs and these IDs were considered a license to bear arms. The CMOC was established in December 1992 to ameliorate some of these problems, but the larger problem was that military commands had to expand goals or be faced with the blood of humanitarian relief workers on their hands. The multiplicity of humanitarian agents without a clear structure of command is a constant in military/humanitarian interventions, and participating organizations need to adjust to this new reality. The CMOC is evidence that the U.S. armed forces are cognizant of the problems and able to adjust to this new reality.

III. Missed Opportunities for Early Decisive Action

In retrospect it seems clearer than it did at the moment that decisive diplomatic action backed by fiscal and military promises and threats could have cauterized the Somali civil war. There were several propitious points for significant diplomatic intervention, but they were squandered.[2]

In 1988, when only small insurgencies were evident, the international community had an opportunity to stem the civil war in its bud. In that year, Somalia made a formal agreement with its archenemy Ethiopia forming the Inter-Governmental Agency on Drought and Development (IGADD). Ethiopia was then housing insurgents from Somalia's north (the Isxaaq-led SNM). In light of this "conflict management agreement" between Ethiopian head of state Mengistu Haile Mariam and Siyaad, Ethiopia forced the repatriation of the SNM into Somalia. The SNM was thereby pressured into military action for survival. Meanwhile, Siyaad brutally bombed Hargeisa, the commercial capital of the Isxaaqs. At this point the United States could have condemned the massacre in Hargeisa and withheld financial support for Somalia, including arms shipments, to compel a cease-fire and an internal dialogue for reconciliation. In part because the United States remained interested in the Berbera base for CENTCOM, it ignored the signs of disaster.

In 1990 an Abgal-led "Manifesto Group" wrote an open letter to Siyaad calling for national reconciliation and democratization. The writers were arrested, but when their trial began riots broke out, and they were released. Italy quietly tried to negotiate on behalf of the Manifesto Group. The United States, had it understood the severity of the crisis, might have pushed the opposition groups to accept mediation and not wait for military victory. Instead, the United States maintained its support for the Siyaad regime.

In January 1991 Siyaad and his entourage escaped from the presidential compound, and the forces of the USC took control over what was left of the administrative apparatus. In the chaos of governmental collapse the United States airlifted its personnel to Kenya. Italy maintained a shadow mission, and its ambassador urged Ali Mahdi to declare himself president (Italy was a long-time ally of the Abgal subclan, going back to the days of the Colony and the Trusteeship). If the Cold War were still being fought, Mahdi would have then declared himself an ally of either the West or East and received consequential military backing from either the United States or the Soviets. The other superpower (having learned the lesson in Congo-Kinshasa in 1960 that African states are not worth fighting over) would have acquiesced. All parties in Somalia would then have had to reconcile themselves to procuring positions in an Abgal-led government. No democracy would have resulted, but there would have been order. That Mahdi received no more external support than his opponents meant that there was no preferred leader who could decisively defeat opposition. This opened the possibility for a war of attrition in which all parties, to prove their resolve, would refuse to negotiate a solution, since showing interest in a cease-fire would be an unwanted sign of the lack of resolve. The Cold War tactic of backing the first leader to occupy the presidential palace and then mollifying opposition was not taken, and this created the conditions for a war of attrition.

In June 1992 (and reconvened in July with wider participation) there was a reconciliation conference in Djibouti with Saudi financial support. Despite widespread Somali public opinion that the time was ripe for a negotiated settlement, the Djibouti conferences failed. The UN did not participate. The organizers (a group of mediators from inter alia Italy, Egypt, and Djibouti) were all interested parties one way or another. The conference reaffirmed the 1960 constitution and the unity of Somalia (thus alienating the SNM) and sought to build a fair transitional government around Mahdi (and thus the Habar Gidirs refused to join in). There was no sufficiently skilled negotiator to capitalize on the de facto cease-fire and to overcome the presumption of Mahdi's presidency so that Aideed could attend. There was also no backing of any sort of military force to enforce any agreement. This was an opportune moment squandered due to lack of leadership.

The Secretary General's special representative, Sahnoun, was entrusted with the administration of Security Council Resolution 751, creating UNOSOM I. While working in Somalia, he learned that his superiors had allowed a Russian plane with UN markings to deliver shipments to Mahdi, thus undermining the UN's impartiality. Later, the UN announced a deployment of three thousand troops to Somalia while he was in delicate negotiations concerning the first five hundred. Exasperated with the UN's inability to articulate and sustain any policy, Sahnoun quit in October 1992.

Sahnoun has argued that more decisive international involvement in mediating the political crisis after the fall of Siyaad would have enabled the installation of a regime capable of legitimate domination, thereby forestalling a civil war. There is clear merit to Sahnoun's argument. If decisive support were given to one of the faction leaders or to a coalition group shortly after the collapse of the Siyaad government, it is likely that other factions would have bargained for positions in the cabinet rather than fight a war of attrition.[3]

In retrospect, the Somali faction leaders were weak and desperate for a compelled solution. They would have yielded early on to a deal brokered by the United States or the UN, if it had substantial fiscal and military backing. But once the war of attrition got under way, none of the parties could accept a negotiated settlement without appearing to have lost resolve, thus making them more vulnerable to attack by rival clans.

IV. Humanitarian Relief and a Political Solution

From an operations point of view, UNITAF was a success. In this operation, 986 airlift missions moved over thirty-three thousand passengers and more than thirty-two thousand short tons of cargo to Somalia. Eleven ships moved 365,000 tons of cargo as well as 1,192 containers of sustainment supplies. To be sure, there were logistical problems. The Mogadishu airport had limited capacities and there was no central airlift control coordinating U.S. government and NGO charters. Additional problems were incurred with the supply of hazardous cargoes on chartered planes and the issue of diplomatic clearance. Furthermore, documentation of sustainable supplies was subject to different accounting systems and failure to have consistent documentation wasted airlift assets. Equally complex problems occurred with the sea lift, and a lack of clear priorities when only one ship could be unloaded at a time led to confusion. Overall, what Allard calls extensive "work-arounds" enabled the UNITAF command to pursue its mission with impressive skill.[4]

However, humanitarian success required compromises that undermined political reconciliation. The biggest problem for the relationship of military to nonmilitary aspects of the intervention is that the military goal of providing rapid distribution of food and medical supplies required accommodation with war-lords. The civilian goal of establishing legitimate government in Somalia required challenging those warlords. This dilemma, often posed as one of an "exit strategy," was never successfully resolved in UNITAF (which emphasized the need to cooperate with the warlords and therefore empowered them) and in UNOSOM II (which sought to diminish the power of those warlords).

There was never a clear exit strategy for the UN operation. Amid the early discussions within the U.S. State Department, John Bolton wrote a memo called "Somalia: Easier to Get into than to Get Out Of." He was correct, and for two reasons. First, the goal of providing immediate relief tended to undermine the later goal of building legitimate authority. Ambassador Robert Oakley, named by President Bush as Special Envoy to Somalia, faced a difficult decision in his attempt to "restore hope." The warlords had the capacity to terrorize anyone who ventured into the countryside. Although the anarchy in the bush made the success of humanitarian efforts precarious even with the warlords' acquiescence, they were the principal threats to the security of the refugee centers that the humanitarian agencies sought to reach. Eliminating the warlords would be a major military and political undertaking, and if that were the first step in a U.S. plan, nearly the entire population of the south would have been put in jeopardy. Such a strategy would have been counter to the presidential admonition that all U.S. troops be gone from Somalia within three months. Although Oakley made several efforts to trim the warlords' sails, for example, in the appointment of governors in the localities and in the appointment of women in all local councils, he necessarily became hostage to the order that the warlords could provide, as this order was the key to the success of the humanitarian effort. The long-term consequence of such a strategy was to make legitimate governance of Somalia (or even illegitimate governance by a hegemonic warlord) virtually impossible. Thus, the best strategy for restoring hope undermined a reasonable strategy of exit under peaceful conditions.

Second, the need for a peaceful effort led to mission creep (even by the Oakley team), and expanded goals made exit ever more distant. By the end of January 1993 Oakley's mission had already expanded beyond relief. He encouraged the formation of local councils and mediated interclan conflicts. Brigadier General Anthony Zinni (UNITAF Deputy for Operations) said, "We did creep outside our mission a lot. . . . I think we went as far as we could go given what we were." General Johnston said, "To the extent that the hand-off was becoming more difficult to execute, the prospect of mission creep became greater. . . . I resisted it strongly, but I also knew that the standup of a police force . . . were stabilizing actions by themselves." Bush resisted for a while, but after the first U.S. casualty, a marine shot in an alleyway, Oakley wrote a stinging message saying that a Somali police force would be crucial for U.S. troop security. Bush relented. UN officials were against this, as it was too minimal, but they went along. By late February, interim police forces were operating not only in Mogadishu but in dozens of towns, and courts began to take shape. Oakley later tried to extend the cantonment program to the outlying areas, but the U.S. Department of Defense (DOD) objected and only wanted cantonment near U.S. troops. Oakley lost this battle. The greatest controversy was on the issue of disarmament, and UNITAF refused a proactive disarmament program. One relief official said, "The fact that weapons were cantoned and then not destroyed probably sent quite a message of comfort to the warlords that, well, yeah, we're just temporarily on hold while these guys are here."[5]

UNITAF believed that its mission had succeeded by January 1993 as the deaths in the camps had stopped. With hostility toward Americans beginning to be felt, many in UNITAF believed this was the opportune time to go. But UN Secretary General Boutros-Ghali refused to allow his people to engage in many of the police and civic programs until UNITAF left the scene, so there was no transition for these efforts. Neither the United States nor the UN was thinking about a viable exit strategy at this time.

The U.S. mission under the UNOSOM II rubric (which, if it succeeded, would have enabled exit) was led by Admiral Jonathan Howe. Given pressure from the Secretary General, from the international lobby of humanitarian agencies, and from the realization that the Oakley strategy provided no easy exit, Howe became further implicated in "mission creep"—the move from humanitarian intervention to nation building. But with entrenched warlords surviving on predation, UNOSOM II did not have civilian leaders with sufficient authority to negotiate a political solution. Those with authority—earned by force and recognized by UNITAF—had little interest in legitimate governance.

V. The Fundamental Strategic Dilemma in International Peacekeeping Operations

The fundamental strategic dilemma for international peacekeeping operations is that the permanent members of the Security Council (the P-5) have an interest in mandating operations that they do not want to fulfill. This leads to systematic underfunding of ambitious mandates. To see how this operates, it is first crucial to analyze the goals of the major actors.

In regard to Somalia, the U.S. goals must be broken down into two periods. From the viewpoint of President Bush, the original U.S. intervention into UNOSOM I and UNITAF was principally for humanitarian purposes, to address the massive starvation and illness that resulted from the Somali civil war. The U.S. ambassador to Kenya, Smith Hempstone, Jr., had sent a cable to Bush called "A Day in Hell" on a visit to a Kenya refugee camp. Bush was moved and told Acting Secretary of State Lawrence Eagleburger to be "forward leaning" on Somalia, with an eye to airlifting supplies. At the U.S. Department of State, there developed a consensus (as opposed to the DOD, which was largely against such a mission) that the United States could help save several hundred thousand people's lives, and no one else could, so the United States should do it. Eagleburger later said, "There was no one in the Bush administration who thought of this as anything other than fundamentally a humanitarian mission. . . . we were prepared to concede that once we fed people and left, it could turn into a mess again. But we consciously were unprepared to try to solve the political mess." Although there was some initial ambiguity about the goals of the mission, eventually Bush wrote to Secretary General Boutros-Ghali, "I want to emphasize that the mission of the coalition is limited and specific: to create security conditions which will permit the feeding of the starving Somali people and allow the transfer of these security functions to the UN peacekeeping force."[6] The expectation of the Bush administration was that after UNITAF finished its mission, UNOSOM II would deal with the issue of disarmament of the factions and a transition to civilian administration.

From the point of view of the U.S. armed services, led by General Powell as chairman of the Joint Chiefs of Staff, there was a grudging acceptance of the mission. Powell was reluctant to have the United States intervene in Bosnia, a much more dangerous operation, and he may have felt that the operation in Somalia would take political pressure off of quick entry into the Bosnian war. He therefore was much more positive to the UNITAF operation than was the DOD. It might be said, then, that a secondary goal of the United States in its entry into Somalia, replacing UNOSOM I with UNITAF, was to deflect public pressure for a military intervention into Bosnia.

In the second period, the Clinton administration was handed the extraordinarily delicate task of exit. This required a rethinking of goals. It decided that the best way to exit would be through a reconstitution of a legitimate government in Somalia under conditions of peace. This was the goal as set in UNOSOM II, a document largely drafted by members of the Clinton administration. Some commentators associated with the Bush administration (e.g., John Bolton) exaggerated the differences in philosophy of the Clinton administration, calling it "assertive multilateralism." While there is some truth to this charge, the change was also due to an inexorable logic of mission creep and to the extraordinary difficulty of developing an exit strategy. When the Aideed forces took advantage of poor surveillance by UN forces, killing twenty-four ill-equipped Pakistani soldiers, the goal of the Clinton administration changed, in support of revenge. When revenge turned into disaster for American Rangers, the goal changed again to immediate exit without any concern for the implications of that exit for Somalia.

The UN had its own perspective. Despite the Charter that mandated that the UN act to end the scourge of war, the UN initially was against any operational involvement in Somalia. The Organization of African Unity (OAU) advised against such an operation because there was no sovereign government requesting help, and thus it could not be justified within the context of the UN Charter. Article 2(7) of the UN Charter, OAU representatives further argued, prohibits intervention in the internal affairs of member states. Secretary General Pérez de Cuéllar showed little interest in a proactive policy.

De Cuéllar's successor as Secretary General, Boutros Boutros-Ghali, had a keener interest in Somali affairs. Furthermore, the new Secretary General was adamant that the international community react to crises in Africa with the same concern as in Europe and shamed the Security Council into active consideration of the crisis in Somalia. In February 1992, the two faction leaders went to UN Headquarters and agreed to a cease-fire. In April, through UN Resolution 751, the Security Council established UNOSOM I to monitor the cease-fire. Sahnoun was deputized as the SRSG, but the Secretary General several times undermined the authority of his Special Representative, who eventually resigned. (The resignation illustrated some internal differences in goals within the UN. The Secretary General, who had, as foreign minister in Egypt, worked closely with Siyaad Barre, was despised by faction leader Aideed, and the feeling became mutual; meanwhile Sahnoun was negotiating closely with Aideed, and this created friction between the SG and the SRSG.)

With the chaos in Somalia when the cease-fire broke down, the Bush plan (as demanded by Powell) called for a massive military operation. Boutros-Ghali had reservations, but given the catastrophe, he had no choice but to accept the U.S. plan. On 3 December 1992 the Security Council unanimously passed Resolution 794, under Chapter VII, allowing for "all necessary means" to get relief food to the refugee camps. This set the basis for the U.S.-led UNITAF. Once in the field, the SG sought to enlarge UN goals to include the disarmament of all factions.

Some consideration should be given to the goals of the P-5, the permanent representatives in the UN Security Council. UNOSOM I was created by Security Council Resolution 751 on 24 April 1992. It was a compromise. It established a peacekeeping operation, but it was modest. It called for fifty unarmed UN observers to overlook the cease-fire, a longer term commitment to five hundred armed peacekeepers to protect relief supplies, and a ninety-day plan to be created to coordinate humanitarian aid. Ambitious resolutions but low funding have been endemic for UN Peacekeeping Operations (PKOs). In part this was caused by the failures in the Somali intervention, but even UNOSOM I was ambitious in words and quite modest in support.

We can infer P-5 goals from their consistent actions. At least in the past decade, and with the horrible failure of the Somali operation in their minds, the rich states have been mindful of four goals in mandating UN peacekeeping policies. First, they (and this is especially true of the European states) don't want refugees. Civil wars produce refugees in large numbers who can become threats to the efficient provision of social services and the national self-images of the developed states. Second, the leading powers in the West will not countenance "private" rule in foreign countries by mercenary armies such as "Executive Outcomes." Therefore, it is desirable that countries suffering from civil wars be "on track" to some form of self-rule. Third, leaders of liberal societies increasingly empathize with civilian victims of civil wars, massacres, and genocides, and cannot callously sit and watch these horrors (e.g., on CNN) without taking ameliorative action. Finally, in light of the psychological effects of media coverage of civil wars, leaders of rich states at least want to be "seen" by their populations as "doing something" about the human tragedy in whatever country is facing massive civilian starvation and death. These goals need to be pursued under a remarkable constraint, especially when military operations are called for. Leaders of rich states do not want body bags of their own citizens as a consequence of their playing the role of international gendarme. If peace is to be bought through combat, the troops whose lives would be on the line should not be from the rich states. The death of U.S. Rangers in Somalia was sufficient cause for President Clinton to end U.S. military engagement. The result of these goals along with the no-deaths constraint is to push for missions under the auspices the DPKO but to underfund them, as showing interest and stemming refugee flows is more important than sustaining peace. Furthermore, if combat troops are needed, it is best to recruit battalions from the Group of 77 (Third World) armies rather than from the countries that are mandating the mission. While the Somali PKOs were in part the cause of the goals now pursued by the P-5, even in 1992, there was a clear reluctance by the permanent representatives to the SC to fund and to man fully what they mandated.

In light of the unconscionable mismatch between mandates and resources, the UN showed itself unable to assume leadership of an international military engagement. It could not take the lead when member states entrusted it with leadership. This was not merely a failure at the top. The UN's staffing was at that time an international embarrassment. During the negotiations between the United States and the UN over the establishment of UNITAF, for example, the Secretary General did not develop a serious plan (as Resolution 794 called for) for transferring power to UNOSOM II after UNITAF's withdrawal. When a U.S. interagency team went to New York to connect with the UNOSOM team, the Americans were shocked that the Secretary General had virtually no staff working on the problem. The best the UN team could do was to drag its feet, in the expectation that if it did nothing, the Americans would continue keeping guard. There was no command center in the UN committed to getting the operation done correctly. Under UNOSOM II, no UN planners were sent on site before the arrival of the commander (Admiral Jonathan Howe) and his deputy commander. With the UN Command operating with twelve thousand fewer troops than authorized, and many of the troops under strong restrictions as to what kinds of activities they could legally engage in, there was no way Admiral Howe could develop a coherent tactical plan. Furthermore, Howe was authorized to have a staff of 800, but it took months to reach one hundred, and he described the applicant pool as "people that nobody else wants." Stories of UN incompetence in the field are legion. Major-General Lewis Mackenzie, a Canadian and former head of UN forces in Sarajevo, made this comment about UN managerial capacity: "A UN commander in the field should not get into trouble after 5 p.m. in New York, or Saturday and Sunday. There is no one to answer the phone."[7]

A far more powerful intervention force was needed for UNOSOM II success. UNOSOM II was asked to carry out, with about eighteen thousand troops, a much more complex mission than UNITAF, which had about twice that number of troops. Furthermore, the UNITAF troops were better trained and equipped and under a more coherent command structure. The basic point here is that a disarmament mission is far different from arms control. In the words of Allard:

> Removing or limiting the major weapons of an inferior or defeated military force can be thought of as a form of arms control, *but to commit military forces to the mission of forcibly disarming a populace is to commit those forces to a combat situation that may thereafter involve them as an active belligerent. . . . If the disarmament of the population becomes an objective, then there should be no mistaking the fact that the troops given this mission have been committed to combat.*[8]

It should be asked if the failures in Somalia are inherent in UN operations, or if they are just examples of poor management that can be fixed. Under the leadership of Secretary General Kofi Annan, the UN DPKO has been strengthened, and the Brahimi Report issued in August 2000 went a long way to identifying the problems that were evident in Somalia but repeated in Sierra Leone. Suggestions for improvement were both feasible and useful. While the UN seems to be on the road to improvement, I have serious doubts as to whether it should have command and control power in Chapter VII type operations.[9]

Despite the Brahimi Report's acute analysis, bold recommendations, considerable Security Council (and less so, the General Assembly) support, and renewed optimism at the DPKO, several problems lie ahead. First, there is a P-5/Secretary General commitment problem that remains unsolved. In humanitarian crises, the Secretary General will face enormous pressures to seek some form of provisional settlement (as in the Mahdi/Aideed cease-fire of February 1992). If he achieves one, no matter how papered over it is, the Security Council cannot say no or else its members look callous. So instead they say yes but underfund a mission with little concern for its success. Once the Security Council agrees, even with underfunding, the Secretary General can hardly turn his back. After all, he had only a thin strand of a peace agreement originally. In the words of Stephen Stedman, "The Secretary General reasons that once we get a PKO on the ground, 'I can shame [the great powers] to give me the resources to save the day.'"[10] This is mission creep. At best, the Secretary General will hope for "mission creep" to get more resources.

The logic of "mission creep" weakens Brahimi recommendations. Suppose there is a rebel group that signs a peace accord but sees itself being squeezed by the UN PKO forces (as was the case with Aideed). The rebels can then renounce the agreement and become "spoilers." By the terms of the original mission, one that requires agreement on both sides, the UN should leave once there is a spoiler. But when the rebels have caused real damage to the UN troops, the option of just pulling out looks like an ignominious defeat for the UN that would undermine its reputation and credibility in other PKOs. So there is a strong temptation to expand, even without the necessary resolve, to ensure success. This logic explains the call for the U.S. Rangers after Aideed's men ambushed UN troops.

This critical analysis of the logic of mission creep needs to be modified a bit. As one DPKO staff person analyzed the strategic situation of Mr. Annan:

> The Secretary General does *not* have an incentive to misrepresent the costs, as doing so plays directly back into his office. So the idea that he would be motivated by an ideology of "give peace a chance" is not correct. He has discouraged any mission to Congo-B, and has been cautious with MONUC, and pulled out of Angola when the mission was going nowhere. He catches the flak when things go really wrong.[11]

This response is not wholly convincing. The logic of mission creep is more immediate and short-term and thus more decisive than the long-term worries about the integrity of the Secretariat.

The UN DPKO's answer to the spoiler issue is a doctrine of deterrence that reads like the Powell Doctrine in the United States. The UN force should be strong enough so that no group has an incentive to be a spoiler. Furthermore, no original party to the agreement should have the resources to compel the UN mission to leave. Thus, even though an agreement between warring parties still serves as a near necessary condition for a new UN DPKO, if one of the parties pulls out from the agreement the new doctrine of deterrence requires the PKO to hold its course. With sufficient force and presence, the doctrine goes, spoilers disappear into the proverbial woodwork.

The international gendarmerie is demonstrating this more aggressive approach to peacekeeping in Kosovo and even Sierra Leone. In Kosovo, with the UN, NATO, and OSCE involved in operations there, it has become clear that the international presence will not disappear even if the Provincial Government demands that all international organizations leave the country. Under these conditions radicals cannot successfully play spoiler, and they have increasingly agreed to accept the electoral game. After its May 2000 debacle, the United States Mission in Sierra Leone (UNAMSIL) faced a similar situation in Sierra Leone. The UN effectively ignored the Revolutionary United Front (RUF) when it played the role of spoiler and would not leave even if RUF demanded it. Meanwhile, the UN has enlisted the help of Guinea in fighting the RUF. The UN has also helped to corner Charles Taylor, such that even he is reducing Liberia's intervention in favor of the RUF.

However successful UN deterrent effects, these strategies take resources and long-term commitments that the P-5 states are reluctant to provide. Since failures of the UN due to mission creep won't be consequential for the P-5, the great powers will appear to have "done something." Furthermore, the UN will take the heat from a gaggle of critics that will sustain its image as an inefficient organization. Under these conditions, the UN does not provide a credible deterrent.

In light of this analysis, the best role for the UN is to vote for interventions, whether of Chapter VI or VII (or some hybrid), and then to subcontract the operation out to a state or regional organization capable of carrying it out. This is how UNITAF was organized as opposed to the two UNOSOMs. An equitable share-the-burdens taxation scheme for member states would of course be necessary, and this might be facilitated by the Secretariat, but the UN should not be directly involved in the command and control over combat operations.

VI. Conclusion

The initial humanitarian goals of UNITAF achieved some success but at enormous cost. A ballpark figure is hard to come by. Hansch et al., provide reasonable statistical evidence that UNITAF input saved between 10,000 and 25,000 lives, with total lives saved by international efforts during the course of the civil war amounting to 110,000. Supporters of American efforts have given wildly inflated figures. Crocker gives a figure (without any empirical support) of 250,000. Mandelbaum gives the figure of 500,000, again without any empirical justification. Meanwhile, detractors of the policy err in the other direction. De Waal asserts without statistical evidence that the rains of 1991 were the principal cause of the miracle that saved thousands. The overall cost of the operation for the United States from 1992 to 1994 was $2.3 billion, as estimated by Sommer.[12] We should not be embarrassed or defensive about the costs paid. UN- and U.S.-led efforts showed a profound respect for human life.

However, in part the result of a mismatch between goals and resources, the goals of bringing peace to Somalia and nation building were failures. Somalia remains without a state. Two regions (Somaliland in the north and Punt in the northeast) have seceded from Somalia and have attained a degree of peace and prosperity without any UN attention. In the south, where most of the international action took place, the two factions remain entrenched in different parts of Mogadishu. There is a modicum of peace, a transitional government installed in August 2000, but as yet no stable rule. While the goals of UNITAF were partly, albeit expensively, met, the goals of UNOSOM II were not attained.

The analysis herein of the international intervention into the Somali civil war yielded three insights that can be applied in future episodes of state breakdown. First, decisive diplomatic action in constituting state authority can help avert a costly and gruesome civil war. In the Somali case, the international community put insufficient diplomatic pressure, and none backed with fiscal and military threats, to reconstitute state authority in the late Siyaad and the early post-Siyaad periods. Second, humanitarian missions should not be planned in absence of a strategy of reconstituting political authority once the humanitarian crisis is solved. In the Somali case, reliance on warlords to implement the humanitarian program certainly eased the crisis in an efficient way, but the cost was the ceding of authority in Somalia to military units whose leadership had little interest in legitimate rule. Third, the P-5 powers have an interest in creating mandates for the UN that P-5 countries have little interest in implementing. This means that missions are underfunded and weakly staffed. In the Somali case, the mandate for UNOSOM II was far more ambitious than the resources provided to fulfill it. This wasn't a mistake, but is built into the structure of the relationship between the P-5 and the SG. Addressing this issue is crucial for the success of future peacekeeping missions.

Notes

This chapter is based on research that went into my chapter "Somalia—Civil War and International Intervention," in Barbara Walter and Jack Snyder, eds., *Civil War, Insecurity, and Intervention* (New York, Columbia University Press, 1999.)

1. Michael Maren, *The Road to Hell: The Ravaging Effects of Foreign Aid and International Charity* (New York: Free Press, 1997).
2. I. William Zartman, in a chapter in press, develops some of these themes more fully. Terrence Lyons and Ahmed I. Samatar, *Somalia: State Collapse, Multilateral Intervention and Strategies for Political Reconstruction* (Washington, D.C.: Brookings Institution Press, 1995) also emphasize missed diplomatic opportunities that could have forestalled the civil war.
3. Mohamed Sahnoun, *Somalia: The Missed Opportunities* (Washington, D.C.: United States Institute of Peace Press, 1994).
4. Kenneth Allard, *Somalia Operations: Lessons Learned* (Washington, D.C.: National Defense University Press, 1995), 51.
5. Quotes from Susan Rosegrant, "A 'Seamless' Transition: United States and United Nations Operations in Somalia—1992–1993," case program (part A), John F. Kennedy School of Government, Harvard University, Cambridge, Mass., CO9-96-1324.0, 1996, 26–28.
6. Quotes from Rosegrant, "A 'Seamless' Transition," 13–15.
7. Ramesh Thakur, "From Peacekeeping to Peace Enforcement: The U.N. Operation in Somalia," *Journal of Modern African Studies* 32, no. 3 (1994): 393. This changed a bit in 1993 with a 24-hour Situation Room phone in New York.
8. Allard, *Somalia: The Missed Opportunities*, 64, 90.
9. Lakhdar Brahimi, chair, "Report of the Panel on United Nations Peace Operations," A/55/305, S/2000/809, 21 August 2000.
10. In remarks delivered at the annual meeting of the Association for the Study of Nationalities, New York, 5 April 2001.
11. Confidential interview, with a member of the staff of the Secretary General, 3 April 2001.
12. See: Steven Hansch et al., *Excess Mortality and the Impact of Health Interventions in the Somalia Humanitarian Emergency* (Washington, D.C.: Refugee Policy Group and Centers for Disease Control and Prevention, 12 August 1994); Chester Crocker, "Lessons of Somalia," *Foreign Affairs* 74, no. 3 (1995); Michael Mandelbaum, "Foreign Policy as Social World," *Foreign Affairs* 75, no. 1 (1996): 30; Alex de Waal, *Times Literary Supplement* (December 1995), 29; and John G. Sommer, *Hope Restored? Humanitarian Aid in Somalia 1990–1994* (Washington, D.C.: Refugee Policy Group, Center for Policy Analysis and Research on Refugee Issues, 1994). Milton Leitenberg of the Center for International and Security Studies Maryland at the University of Maryland, College Park, points out, in a private communication to me, that UNITAF made possible the fol-

low-on UN mission, and therefore its work saved lives post-1993. This is a reasonable interpretation and would substantially raise the estimates provided by the Hansch team.

3

Intervention in Internal Conflict:
The Case of Bosnia

Steven L. Burg

The case of Bosnia presents analysts with a complex set of circumstances and factors surrounding multiple instances of intervention, carried out by a diverse set of external actors. Indeed, even the distinction between "internal" and "external" might be considered problematic in this case. For the purposes of this analysis, the conflict among Bosnian Serbs, Bosnian Croats, and Bosnian Muslims (who have since adopted the "Bosniac" label) is defined as an internal conflict over the status of the territory and its internal political organization. This conflict erupted as part of the larger set of conflicts surrounding the disintegration of the former Yugoslav federal state, of which Bosnia and Herzegovina was a federal "republic." However, the larger conflict will be treated only as context and not subjected to detailed analysis here. The direct and indirect involvement of the neighboring states of Serbia and Croatia in the internal Bosnian conflict, which could be defined as "external" interventions by local powers, are instead treated here as dimensions of the internal conflict. The involvement of these local powers, and their very real interests in the outcome of the conflict, were important factors affecting the series of decisions by U.S. and other Western policymakers, as well as UN actors, concerning intervention. Recent changes that have moved both Croatia and Serbia in the direction of democratization, disavowal of support for the ethnic dismemberment of Bosnia, and even affirmation of the principle of territorial integrity, have improved the prospect that international intervention will ultimately succeed in establishing some form of multinational state in Bosnia, although the institutional character of such a state remains in doubt. This chapter focuses on the decisions and actions of external policymakers, and U.S. policymakers in particular, as "third parties" to the conflict and the outcomes of their interventions in it.

Interventions in the Bosnian conflict fall into several distinct categories: diplomatic/political *peacemaking* intended to find a solution to the conflict; military/diplomatic *peacekeeping* intended at first to facilitate the delivery of humanitarian relief, then used to secure and maintain the limited agreements reached by the parties during the course of the conflict and, finally, to carry out UN decisions taken without the support of the warring parties; *humanitarian relief* operations carried out with the support of peacekeeping forces and intended to redress the suffering of the civilian population; the imposition of economic and other *sanctions* under the authority of the UN Security Council; acts of *deterrence* carried out through a combination of military threats and the demonstrative use of force; implementation of a comprehensive strategy of *coercive diplomacy* including the use of limited but effective force; and finally, military occupation and *state building* intended to implement the settlement imposed on the warring parties. The humanitarian relief effort in Bosnia was an extension of the UNHCR operations initiated in October 1991 in response to the outbreak of fighting associated with the disintegration of Yugoslavia. It was carried out, with some gaps, for the entire duration of the war in Bosnia and continued on thereafter. Military occupation and state building represent essentially post-conflict involvement, designed to secure the results of intervention. This chapter focuses on the forms of intervention (peacemaking, peacekeeping, deterrence, and coercive diplomacy) that reflected the gradual escalation of direct involvement in the conflict on the part of the United States, the European powers, the United Nations and, in the end, Russia.

Peacemaking

The initial involvement of the European powers in the Yugoslav conflict(s) was motivated by a clearly articulated desire to prevent escalation of the political conflicts surrounding disintegration of the country into armed conflict. Several interests and motivations lay behind this desire. These included the straightforward security interest of the European states in preventing armed conflict in a neighboring state; the political interest of some states in advancing the role of common European (EC and, later, EU) foreign policymaking institutions in international security affairs; the concern that armed conflict would likely generate an influx of significant numbers of refugees into Western Europe, with potentially costly and socially destabilizing consequences; and the pressure of domestic constituencies calling for action. Relatively early in the conflict the

Map 3.1 Bosnia and Herzegovina

European states deliberated and rejected military intervention in favor of a diplomatic effort to facilitate negotiation of a formula for a peaceful settlement among the Yugoslavs. Thus, the initial intervention by outside actors took the form of diplomatic and political peacemaking activities, without the backing of a credible threat of force.[1]

Actual peacemaking efforts by the European powers were preceded by rhetorical efforts to encourage the parties themselves to resolve their differences peacefully. The Europeans expressed their support for existing internal and external borders while the United States discouraged secession. Although the United States left the door open to border changes by "peaceful consensual means," it offered no support for such changes.[2] The European and American positions reflected a mechanistic application of existing Helsinki principles of interstate relations. But these were designed for a period of relative stability, made possible by détente between the superpowers.[3] Their application to intrastate or intergroup relations under conditions of enormous uncertainty and instability was ineffective. The ineffectiveness of Western, and particularly U.S., responses in this early period appear to have been compounded by a failure on the part of state policymaking establishments to mobilize outside expertise in these efforts. It was already clear to many academic and other experts, after a January 1991 meeting of the Serbian and Slovenian leaders, that a negotiated agreement among the regional leaders of Yugoslavia over internal borders would be essential to maintaining peace in that country, that such an agreement was likely to involve changes, perhaps substantial changes, to the status quo, and that such an agreement would be difficult to achieve by consensual means without external assistance in the form of incentives for the Yugoslavs (in the initial stages of dissolution, primarily the Serbs) to avoid the use of force.[4] Little of this thinking appears to have been incorporated into official responses to the emerging crisis.

Convocation of the EC's Conference on Yugoslavia in September 1991 came against the background of escalating conflict in Croatia and a clear European decision, debated in August and September, not to intervene militarily. The fighting in Croatia was not seen by Western policymakers as threatening their national security interests. In the absence of any prospect of external military intervention, the Serbian and Yugoslav army leaderships were free to pursue a strategy of seizing Serb-populated regions of Croatia. As Paul Shoup and I have pointed out,

> at the outset the Serbian leadership used the EC efforts to mediate a settlement among the former Yugoslav republics to nullify more forceful diplomacy by the international community, and in the process encouraged the JNA and Serbian nationalists to pursue their policy of creating a Greater Serbia based on military conquest. But, when the EC took more forceful action, by imposing sanctions on Yugoslavia and calling on the UN Security Council to use its coercive powers to bring peace to the region, the Serbian effort was redirected toward greater cooperation with the international community. Yet, Western policymakers failed to respond to changes in the Serbian position as they de-

veloped, and the opportunities to exploit the nuances evident in Serb positions by early November 1991.[5]

Western pressure in the form of negative sanctions, including the Security Council's adoption of Resolution 713 (25 September 1991) imposing an arms embargo against all of (former) Yugoslavia, was insufficient to reverse Serbian military actions. Cooperation by the Serbs extended only as far as accepting a UN-sponsored cease-fire in November 1991 and establishment of UN-protected areas in those regions of Croatia seized by the Yugoslav army, thus "freezing" Serbian gains and ending Serbian interest in further negotiations. Other provisions of the UN-sponsored Vance plan for Croatia were ignored. Once Croatia achieved international recognition in January 1992, it also had no further interest in negotiations, as these might have compromised its now internationally recognized claim to sovereignty over the protected areas.

In Bosnia, too, international recognition of the state came in the absence of a negotiated agreement among the conflicting parties. As in Croatia, recognition offered the single most powerful positive inducement to cooperation, and granting it (denying it, with respect to the Bosnian Serbs) without first seeking to extract cooperation had the effect of ending any incentives for the parties to negotiate. The timing of recognition was a matter of intense diplomatic maneuvering by the United States and its European allies, the Bosnian government, and Serbia, as well as intense political maneuvering among the Bosnian Muslims, Croats, and Serbs in the period between December 1991 and March 1992. However, much of this effort unfolded after the referendum of 29 February and the Bosnian government's declaration of independence on 3 March. By the time the EC and the United States recognized Bosnia, on 6 and 7 April, respectively, ethnic cleansing and localized fighting were already under way.[6]

International recognition of Croatia in January and of Bosnia-Herzegovina in April came in the midst of unresolved conflicts over the status of these territories. Fighting over the fate of the UN-protected areas of Croatia was delayed until August 1995. In the absence of *either* a constitutional agreement on status among the conflicting Bosnian parties (and their neighbors) *or* an international commitment to defend the newly recognized government of Bosnia, or better yet *both*, recognition contributed to a rapid escalation of the conflict. Eleventh-hour negotiations to achieve such an agreement conducted for the EC by Jose Cutiliero in February and March ended in failure, in part because the lack of U.S. interest in or support for the process signaled to the Bosnian Muslim leadership that they had only to withhold their agreement in order to win eventual U.S. support. In effect, the United States had provided the Muslim-dominated Bosnian government, wittingly or not, with a positive inducement to intransigence. However, it is by no means certain that these negotiations would have succeeded even if recognition had been linked to an agreement. The negotiations began after the Muslim political leadership in control of the government declared Bosnian independence, Serbian and Bosnian Serb preparations for war may already have gone too far to be reversed, and countervailing military action by the

United States or the European powers to avert Serbian (and Croatian) aggression against the newly recognized state appeared already to have been ruled out. Successful negotiations, even if supported by delayed recognition, would almost certainly have had to have begun much earlier, before the onset of dissolution.[7]

The approach taken in these early Western peacemaking efforts was based on the fundamentally flawed principle that the existing internal borders of the constituent units of the Yugoslav federation should become internationally recognized borders. This represented a mechanistic transfer of Cold War era concepts to new circumstances, rather than a nuanced response to the specific characteristics of the conflict. It ignored the lack of correspondence between borders and identities in much of the Yugoslav federation and the dynamic of political conflict that this produced. Even this flawed approach was not implemented consistently, however. The demand for recognition by the Kosovar Albanians, for example, who constituted 90 percent of the population of an autonomous province that had dual status as a constituent unit of the federation and an integral part of the Serbian republic, and thus could arguably have received the same treatment as the republics, was rejected. As Shoup and I have argued, this initial effort at peacemaking might have succeeded had the European strategy been formulated differently; in essence, holding the nationalist ambitions of dominant nations in each Yugoslav republic for international recognition hostage to prior agreement on borders and internal political order, including the effective protection of minority rights. By doing so the Europeans, with support from the United States, would have defined a peaceful path by which each of the Yugoslav nations might have pursued its nationalist goals, a path that not only would have required each to negotiate, but would have enabled them to do so rather than resort to force. Nonetheless, for this strategy of peacemaking to succeed, the intervening powers would have had to have mounted an effective threat to use countervailing force against any party that violated the peace. Neither the Europeans nor the Americans were prepared to make such a threat in the early stages of the Yugoslav conflicts. Indeed, the military option was explicitly dismissed on both sides of the Atlantic. With respect to the United States, at least, this can be attributed to the perception on the part of senior policymakers that no strategic U.S. national interests were at risk.[8]

Despite the Security Council's adoption of Resolution 757 (30 May 1992) imposing economic sanctions against Yugoslavia (Serbia and Montenegro), and the takeover of Sarajevo airport by UN peacekeepers in June 1992, it remained clear that the Western powers were not ready to impose a settlement by force when fighting broke out in Bosnia. Indeed, the agreement opening Sarajevo airport for the delivery of humanitarian relief specifically disavowed any precedent with respect to settlement of the larger conflict.[9] U.S. policymakers did not perceive any vital national interests to be at stake in the fighting. As a result, the United States not only resisted the use of force but remained at the margins of diplomatic efforts to end the conflict in Bosnia for almost two years. The International Conference on the Former Yugoslavia (ICFY) was established in August 1992 under the cosponsorship of the United Nations and the European

Community and cochaired by former U.S. Secretary of State Cyrus Vance (acting in his capacity as special representative of the UN Secretary General) and former British Foreign Minister Lord David Owen (acting as representative of the EC). Vance and Owen attempted to address the competing interests and claims of the warring parties by adopting a strategy of extensive territorial devolution,[10] but each of the parties sought to use the negotiations as means to pursue their own goals, rather than to pursue a genuine solution. The absence of any capacity to compel the parties to compromise led negotiators to offer last-minute concessions to the Serbs in April 1993 that moved the proposal toward a strategy of partition. However, not even a partition plan could work as long as parties on the ground remained wedded to force and major outside powers remained uninterested in compelling them to agree. Despite reports at the time that the United States was ready to commit troops to enforcement of the plan, and that NATO had prepared plans for deployment, the United States and its allies could not agree on exactly how or under what conditions force might be used. The absence of any Western threat of force—either to implement an agreed settlement or to impose a solution in the absence of agreement—led one member of the Vance-Owen team to liken the negotiations to playing "baseball without a bat."[11] These problems—the lack of engagement on the part of the United States and a concomitant absence of a credible threat of force—continued to plague later negotiators even as they moved toward an explicit plan for partition in 1993 and 1994.

Paul Shoup and I have documented the process by which the United States finally became seriously engaged in a strategy of coercive diplomacy in Bosnia in late 1994, when policymakers finally came to perceive the fighting as threatening U.S. national interests.[12] From that point forward the United States became increasingly determined to bring the fighting to an end. The result was the U.S. adoption of a strategy of coercive diplomacy, described below, and what might be described as a successful case of intervention. Thus, it seems clear that the degree to which policymakers perceived the conflict as threatening vital U.S. national interests was the critical factor in explaining the extent of U.S. engagement and "willingness" to intervene in the conflict.

Humanitarian Relief and Peacekeeping

Humanitarian intervention began in Croatia in February 1992 with the establishment of the United Nations Protection Force (UNPROFOR) for those areas of Croatia from which Yugoslav (Serbian) forces were to withdraw under the Vance plan. The mandate of UNPROFOR in Croatia was gradually expanded both territorially and functionally. Similarly, the deployment of UN troops to Bosnia began with the June 1992 action to reopen Sarajevo airport for humanitarian supply efforts and expanded both territorially and functionally over time.

The deployment of a humanitarian relief mission to Bosnia in the midst of continuing fighting reflected both the understanding of Western policymakers that the conflict was not going to end quickly and their reluctance to intervene in it militarily. However, the deployment of a humanitarian mission protected by UNPROFOR gradually took on the characteristics of a limited military intervention. In an effort to secure delivery of humanitarian relief to Bosnian civilians, the Western allies secured adoption of Security Council Resolution 757 (30 May 1992) under Chapter VII authority, imposing sanctions on Yugoslavia and calling for the opening of Sarajevo airport. This was followed by an agreement negotiated locally between UNPROFOR and the Bosnian Serbs and Muslims on 5 June, allowing UNPROFOR to take control of the airport, and a decision by the Security Council on 8 June to expand the UNPROFOR mandate in Bosnia in order to allow it to implement that agreement.[13] The agreement was not implemented, however, until after UN Secretary General Boutros-Ghali issued a vague ultimatum to the Serbs and after French President Mitterand made a dramatic trip to Sarajevo airport that challenged Serb willingness to use force to keep the airport closed. Neither the ultimatum nor the visit offered much of a threat to the Serbs, but the agreement did offer an important positive inducement to the Serbs: control of the airport by a neutral force (UNPROFOR) that would prevent it from falling into the hands of Bosnian government, or Muslim, forces. There is also some evidence to suggest that Milosevic pressured the Bosnian Serb leadership to accept the agreement in an effort to avert implementation of the sanctions called for in Resolution 757.[14] Indeed, the compelling effect of sanctions on Serbian (Milosevic's) behavior would grow stronger over time. It would come to play an important, if not critical, role in the success of coercive diplomacy in 1995.

Continued Bosnian Serb resistance to the delivery of humanitarian relief to Bosnian Muslim populations under siege resulted in further expansion of Western intervention through UNPROFOR. Acting under the coercive authority of Chapter VII of the UN Charter, as it had when it imposed sanctions in May, the Security Council adopted Resolution 770 (13 August 1992) authorizing the use of "all measures necessary" to deliver humanitarian assistance and in Resolution 776 (14 September 1992) once again expanded the UNPROFOR mandate and authorized an increase in its strength. These steps toward a widening intervention in the conflict were contradicted, however, by highly restrictive rules of engagement that reflected the original Chapter VI authorization of the UNPROFOR mission, which made it dependent on the cooperation of local forces.[15] In April 1993 Security Council Resolution 819 (16 April 1993) established Srebrenica as a "safe area." Resolution 824 (7 May 1993) extended this status to five additional areas. In Resolution 836 (4 June 1993) the Security Council again invoked Chapter VII authority to assign UNPROFOR the task of deterring attacks on the safe areas and defending them in the event of attack. As events in Srebrenica in July 1995 would make painfully obvious,[16] these deployments did little to protect threatened populations but did expose UNPROFOR troops to heightened risks and thus inevitably drew them more directly into the military conflict. As the mandate of UNPROFOR expanded, the distinction between "humanitarian" and "peacekeeping" activities, and even military intervention, became blurred. As most of the UNPROFOR troops were drawn from European NATO-member states, the distinction between UN involvement and Western intervention also became blurred.

Ultimately, escalating risks to UNPROFOR troops from NATO-member states on the ground in Bosnia created the impetus for direct U.S. and NATO military intervention to end the fighting. The threat to NATO cohesion posed by the prospect that these troops might be overwhelmed in the absence of support from the United States, and the daunting military and political challenges of waiting to assist them until they were already under attack, created a compelling U.S. national interest in bringing the fighting in Bosnia to a rapid conclusion. While policymakers' initial assessments that no strategic national interest was at stake limited initial engagement in the conflict, over time that engagement tended to expand incrementally in response to events on the ground and, in part, media coverage that created pressure on policymakers to "do something" in response to egregious developments.[17] The gradual expansion of resources committed to the conflict, in turn, created a real national interest in ending it where none had existed before. Thus, the decision to intervene directly in the conflict with military force in support of a strategy of coercive diplomacy reflected a change in national decision makers' calculations of the interests put at risk by the conflict.

Deterrence

Over the course of the war, the United States participated in five attempts to use the threat of force to persuade or compel the Bosnian Serbs either to cease or to refrain from certain actions. Although these were limited in scope and intent,[18] together they had the effect of expanding the Western commitment of material and other resources to the conflict. First, in response to the Serb "strangulation" of Sarajevo in the summer of 1993 that resulted from increased shelling of the city and ground action that suggested an imminent frontal assault on the city, NATO issued a vague threat of future action against those who attacked UN forces or obstructed humanitarian aid. Despite signs of differences among the allies, the Bosnian Serbs ended their immediate threat to the city. Second, in February 1994 the United States and its NATO allies responded to a shelling of the Markala marketplace in Sarajevo attributed to the Bosnian Serbs by issuing an ultimatum to the Serbs to withdraw their heavy weapons from around the city. A threat of NATO air attack led the Bosnian Serbs to withdraw and to the establishment of a heavy weapons exclusion zone around Sarajevo.

The U.S. and NATO threat to use force in connection with the 1993 crisis over the "strangulation" of Sarajevo and in response to the Markala marketplace massacre in February 1994 can be considered successful but limited acts of intervention that displayed some of the characteristics of coercive diplomacy identified by Alexander George. In each case, a threat of air attack was employed to

compel the Bosnian Serbs to pull back from Sarajevo and reduce, at least temporarily, their attacks on the city. Issuance of an ultimatum was accompanied by
crisis negotiations, but in each case special circumstances secured Serb compliance. Shoup and I have pointed out that Bosnian Serb agreement was secured in
no small part by the fact that in 1993 the Serbs were not required to withdraw so
far as to prevent them from renewing artillery fire on the city, were able to secure UN occupation of strategic territory, thereby denying it to the Muslims, and
appeared to have pushed resolution of the conflict in the direction of a UN-
patrolled partition based on the status quo.[19] Similarly, in 1994 negotiators
agreed to prevent the Muslims (Bosnian government) from gaining control over
territory relinquished by the Serbs by deploying Russian peacekeepers to the
territory. In each case the demand advanced by the NATO allies was one to
which the Serbs could agree. The agreements served Serb interests by keeping
alive negotiations for a comprehensive cease-fire that would freeze existing Serb
territorial gains. Thus, the Serbs did comply, at least in the shortrun.

That neither of these episodes led to concessions that advanced the conflict
toward resolution may be attributed to the fact that in both instances negotiations
with the Serbs were not carried out by the coercing party (NATO and the United
States), but by a third party—the UN commander—not under the control of, and
with quite different interests from, those of the coercing party. The goals to
which coercion was applied were in each case limited in scope. The threat of
force used to secure the pullback of the Serbs from around Sarajevo was not
accompanied in either 1993 or 1994 by more comprehensive efforts—at least
not on the part of the principal coercer, the United States—to settle the larger
conflict. Nonetheless, the 1994 action did result in a cease-fire and a significant
easing of the conflict. The use of force in these cases can be attributed to a desire on the part of Western policymakers to contain the conflict and to respond
to media pressure to "do something," rather than a commitment on their part to
end it. There is no evidence that policymakers had changed their view that the
conflict did not threaten strategic interests and therefore did not warrant a significant commitment of national resources to its resolution.

In some respects, however, these attempts to use force made matters in
Bosnia worse. The apparent increase in U.S. and NATO involvement and the
threat of force against the Serbs contributed in each case to a hardening of Bosnian Muslim positions in the negotiations over a political settlement taking place
in Geneva under the auspices of the ICFY. This contradictory outcome suggests
one of the difficulties of intervening against only one party to a conflict involving multiple actors. Because the interests of the Bosnian actors were most often
in opposition, threats or coercion applied against one in order to encourage that
party to negotiate or comply would make one or more of the others less willing
to negotiate or comply. The fact that the threat of force was not actually carried
out in connection with either the "strangulation" crisis or the Markala marketplace massacre, and that the Serbs were able both to keep their immediate concessions modest and to reverse them later, weakened the credibility of subsequent U.S. and NATO threats in the eyes of both the Serbs and the Muslims. In

effect, both these "successful" cases of limited intervention actually "upped the ante" for the later, more comprehensive intervention intended to bring the conflict to an end.

The third use of force for deterrence, in April 1994, consisted of three limited air attacks—derisively characterized in the Western media as "pinpricks"—which were carried out against Serb forces threatening to overrun the Muslim-held enclave of Gorazde in eastern Bosnia. The air attacks were followed by another NATO ultimatum to the Serbs to withdraw and at least some consideration of the use of more extensive force against them. However, any effort to use further force was blocked by Yasushi Akashi, special representative of the UN Secretary General, who exercised "dual key" control over the use of force by the West, which was operating in Bosnia under a UN mandate. This unwieldy command structure reflected the concern among contributing states that UN-PROFOR troops (the majority of which came from NATO-member states) should not be put at risk by the use of air power. It was this concern that had led the Europeans to reject an earlier U.S. proposal to "lift and strike," that is, to lift the arms embargo against the Bosnian government and use air power against the Serbs. An exclusion zone was established around Gorazde in 1994, but the confrontation was allowed to wind down without a definitive conclusion. However, events in Gorazde alerted Western policymakers to another possible constraint on the use of air power in Bosnia: in response to the air strikes, the Serbs had taken some two hundred UN and civilian personnel hostage. Concern for their fate may have contributed to the reluctance of Akashi to authorize further use of force in Gorazde. This standoff over the use of air power between the UN and troop-contributing countries on the one hand and the United States on the other continued until 1995 when the credibility of UN operations was finally expended, their collapse appeared imminent, and the United States had committed itself to deploying troops to secure the safe withdrawal of allied and other UN-PROFOR forces. Only then was the United States able to secure the support of its allies for a strategy of coercive diplomacy. Thus, divisions between the United States and its allies over the proper course of action in Bosnia may have represented as important an impediment to decisive intervention before 1995 as the risks of intervention itself.

The fourth example of deterrence through use of force, in November 1994, consisted of NATO air attacks against a Serb air base and three Serb SAM missile sites in the Bihac area in response to Serb attacks that threatened to overrun the Muslim-held enclave in western Bosnia. The events in Bihac seemed to raise the stakes of the Bosnian conflict for the United States and European policymakers. UNPROFOR forces were caught in the fighting and suffered several casualties. The involvement of Serb ground and air forces operating from the Serb-held territories of Croatia just across the nearby border threatened to escalate the fighting and draw the Croatian regular army into the battle, with the potential to reignite fighting in Croatia. After the Serbs had launched a missile attack using converted SAM missiles and air strikes from their air base in Croatia, NATO planes struck that air base and then, two days later, three Serb SAM sites in the Bihac area. Once again, the Serbs seized UN personnel as hostages to deter further NATO attacks. NATO leaders convened to consider both proposals to demilitarize and secure the Bihac safe area, and proposals to carry out wide-ranging air strikes against the Bosnian Serbs. They could not agree on a course of action. At the same time, however, the Serbs began allowing UN aid convoys into the pocket, and Bosnian Muslim troops began slipping out of the pocket, thereby lessening tensions. Thus, while the allies remained deeply divided over further action, this crisis, too, ended inconclusively with little net change in the status quo.

The fifth and final attempt to use force consisted of the use of airpower against Bosnian Serbs in May 1995. An escalation of fighting on the ground and increased Serb shelling of Sarajevo had raised serious doubts among UN officials about continuation of the UNPROFOR deployment and led to both threats of withdrawal and demands for the use of airpower against the Serbs from the United States and European states. The UNPROFOR commander warned both the Muslims and the Serbs to halt the use of heavy weapons and issued an ultimatum to the Serbs to withdraw from the exclusion zone around Sarajevo. When they failed to comply, NATO carried out air strikes against Serb ammunition bunkers in Pale, east of Sarajevo. These attacks failed to compel the Serbs. Rather, they produced what Alexander George might characterize as an escalatory response. The Bosnian Serbs shelled Tuzla then seized UN personnel as hostages, using them as human shields against further attack—a response that should have been anticipated by NATO policymakers on the basis of earlier Bosnian Serb reactions to the use of airpower against them at Bihac and Gorazde. The Serb reaction not only compelled NATO to cease its use of force, but also forced UNPROFOR to renounce the future use of force by reaffirming its adherence to strict peacekeeping principles as a condition for release of the UN hostages. Thus, while the earlier instances of the use of force did have at least a short-term deterrent effect on the Serbs, the May 1995 events had no such effect. On the contrary, they had the effect of deterring UNPROFOR from further use of force and thereby contributed to both the collapse of the UN mission in Bosnia and the emergence of a comprehensive, U.S.-led strategy of coercive diplomacy.

None of these episodes of more direct military-political intervention in reaction to specific local developments in Bosnia was undertaken on the basis of a clear plan or even concept for ending the larger conflict in which they were embedded. The May air strikes were openly criticized in the West for the lack of preparation behind them. One unnamed U.S. official suggested that the May events amounted to little more than "drop a few bombs and see what happens."[20] More comprehensive strategies of intervention, such as the U.S. proposal to lift the arms embargo and use air strikes to protect the Bosnian Muslims while they armed and prepared themselves for war against the Serbs ("lift and strike"), were considered at various times during 1993 and 1994 but rejected, either by European actors concerned they might subject their troops in UNPROFOR to increased risk or by U.S. policymakers concerned that direct intervention represented a "slippery slope" of involvement in a potential quagmire. In August 1992, then-Deputy Secretary of State Lawrence Eagleburger had publicly drawn direct parallels between intervention in Bosnia and earlier U.S. involvements in Lebanon and Vietnam. In August 1993, an unnamed "top policymaker" in the Clinton administration told Washington reporter Elizabeth Drew that "this thing is a no-winner; it's going to be a quagmire."[21] In the cases of Sarajevo and Gorazde, more expansive or decisive action was precluded by UN resistance to widening the conflict or, especially, putting UN personnel at even greater risk. In the case of Bihac, it was precluded by continuing differences between the United States and at least some of its NATO allies arising out of their differing commitments and attendant risks. However, the threat to alliance cohesion evident in these differences, and particularly the conclusion drawn by some in the media that these events suggested that NATO lacked resolve, led to reconsideration of Bosnia policy by senior U.S. officials and, therefore, the NATO allies. Repeated use of force for deterrence underscored the cumulative impact of limited engagement on the perception of national interests. It was the perception that strategic interests, both U.S. and common U.S./European, had been put at risk that led to adoption of a strategy of coercive diplomacy in 1995.

Coercive Diplomacy

The above examples reinforce the view that limited interventions motivated by humanitarian concerns or policymakers' perceived need to "do something" in the face of mounting public and/or media pressure, rather than by clearly defined national interests, result in poorly conceived and inadequately implemented actions. The uses of force in Gorazde and Bihac represented responses to what were perceived as Serb attempts to alter the military balance decisively in their favor. The threat and use of force in Gorazde and Bihac were only of limited military value and were not accompanied by a serious effort to extract any larger political concessions from the Serbs. Their net effect, if any, appears to have been to deepen divisions within NATO over the use of force and erode the effectiveness of any future threat to do so. Paradoxically, however, the prospect of irreparable damage to the internal cohesion and external credibility of the NATO alliance created a powerful U.S. national interest in bringing the war to an end on terms more favorable to the Muslims and Croats with whom NATO had been cooperating.

The divisions within the alliance that followed the limited use of force against the Serbs at Bihac in November 1994 led U.S. policymakers to adopt a more comprehensive approach to ending the conflict in Bosnia and to begin to intervene more directly in the conflict to implement that approach. U.S. policymakers concluded that the use of force alone was futile, the Serbs had to be given incentives to accept a settlement, and if force were to be used it had to be used to support a political settlement. U.S. diplomats entered into direct negotiations with both Milosevic and the Bosnian Serbs and prepared to back up their negotiating positions with a more credible threat of force. The establishment of a credible threat required intensive diplomatic efforts with NATO allies and Russia, primarily in the context of the Contact Group, so as to establish a set of shared perceptions, commitments, and goals. It also required the continuation of efforts to shift the military balance on the ground in Bosnia against the Serbs. In order to exercise control over negotiations with the target(s) of coercion, the United States had to shift negotiations over a political settlement away from the ICFY and to the Contact Group, and to alter the very nature of those negotiations. Rather than ICFY-mediated exchanges among the warring parties in search of a mutually acceptable solution, the Contact Group powers now negotiated among themselves in search of a solution they all could accept and then impose on the warring parties. The United States can thus be said to have laid the basis for a strategy of coercive diplomacy in Bosnia in late 1994. It was not until July 1995 that policymakers appear self-consciously to have committed themselves to such a strategy. Direct, decisive U.S. intervention in the conflict can thus be dated to either late 1994 or mid-1995.

The decision by U.S. policymakers to intervene more directly in Bosnia was driven for the most part by concern that U.S. troops would be drawn into a potentially costly operation to evacuate UN forces, including those of the NATO allies. UNPROFOR had become the target of increasing attacks in the wake of events at Bihac. According to Richard Holbrooke, following the fall of Srebrenica and Zepa in July 1995 and the realization that the UN operation was heading for failure, "the President saw the degree to which involvement was now inevitable, and how much better it would be to have involvement built on success rather than failure."[22] The resort to coercive diplomacy in 1995 was thus driven by a clear sense of national interest in avoiding a potential military catastrophe that might threaten the survival of the NATO alliance. Policymakers in the Clinton administration, including the president, also turned to coercive diplomacy out of a narrower sense of political self-interest: an interest in resolving the Bosnian issue in time to prevent the presumed Republican candidate for president from using it against the administration in the 1996 election. A journalistic account of the policy debates within the administration in June and July makes clear the intensity with which policymakers felt these concerns.[23]

Unlike the earlier uses of force for deterrence in Bosnia, outlined above, the U.S. intervention that unfolded in late 1994 and 1995 was directed toward a specific, comprehensive goal: achieving an agreement that would put an end to the fighting. This was a goal shared by the United States and its allies, who were also concerned about the consequences of a collapse of the UN mission for their troops on the ground. This convergence of allied goals around a clear shared interest in avoiding catastrophe made the management of alliance politics over Bosnia more tractable in the period July–October 1995 than it had been at any point in the three previous years.

The success of coercive diplomacy in Bosnia in 1995 was built on changes in the military situation on the ground in the direction of a stalemate or standoff between the parties. In the literature on conflict resolution, the emergence of such a stalemate is seen as "ripening" and is characterized as "hurting" when each party is assumed to be neither willing or capable of enduring it, nor able to overcome it. In Bosnia, however, Shoup and I have demonstrated that, contrary to the spontaneous process posited in the literature,[24] the "ripening" process was manufactured or engineered by the coercing power. U.S. support for the development of the regular Croatian army and its war-fighting capacity began more than a year earlier, before coercive diplomacy was adopted as a strategy. Moreover, the stalemate in Bosnia was clearly not "hurting"; it was a stalemate enforced by the United States, which was determined not to allow the strategic balance between Croatia and Serbia essential to regional stability to be tipped in favor of Croatia. It should be noted that the tragedies in Srebrenica and Zepa played a major role in establishing the conditions for this stalemate, which involved genocidal killing of Muslims by Serbs but which were greeted by some U.S. officials as events that eliminated heretofore thorny map problems.[25]

The success of coercive diplomacy in Bosnia also involved a change in the U.S. political position. Alexander George suggests that for a strategy of coercive diplomacy to succeed, the demands imposed on the object of coercion must in the end be ones that can be accepted. In the case of Bosnia, this required the United States to alter its demands from those based on one-sided support for the Bosnian Muslims (and Bosnian Croats, to the extent that these two parties could be kept in agreement) to those based on recognition of the need to address the real and often conflicting interests of all sides, including the outside actors, Serbia (Milosevic), and Croatia (Tudjman). A December 1994 NATO declaration calling for "equitable and balanced arrangements" signaled the onset of this transformation.[26] It was completed by the de facto recognition of "Republika Srpska" and partition of Bosnia incorporated in a 1 September agreement negotiated by Holbrooke with Milosevic and the Bosnian Serbs, which provided the general framework for the later Dayton settlement.

The key to securing Milosevic's cooperation from this point on, including his dramatic role at Dayton,[27] appears to have been the combination of a credible threat that the Bosnian Serbs would be defeated on the battlefield, thereby tipping the larger balance of power in the region against Serbia, and the positive inducements of recognition for the Bosnian Serb republic and a promise to lift sanctions against Serbia (formally the Federal Republic of Yugoslavia or FRY). The threat was made credible by the successes of the Croatian army and by the application of limited but significant U.S. and NATO airpower. As noted earlier, Milosevic's interest in lifting sanctions had been clear since 1993. He had been pursuing that interest in intensive negotiations in May and June 1995 with the U.S. diplomat then responsible for Bosnia, Robert Frasure. Milosevic's cooperation at Dayton appears to have been secured in an apparent deal with Holbrooke in exchange for sanctions lifting.

The final factor in the successful application of coercive diplomacy to end the war in Bosnia was, of course, the use of airpower. These words are often followed by the phrase "against the Serbs," but airpower was used not only to pressure the Serbs into specific action on the ground—primarily a withdrawal from around Sarajevo—but also to pressure the Muslims into accepting the emerging partition of Bosnia. It was the end of bombing that opened the door to a cease-fire agreement and negotiations, not its onset. The agreement on "basic constitutional principles" for Bosnia, signed by the foreign ministers of Croatia, Serbia, and Bosnia on 8 September in Geneva, was reached while the bombing was still in progress, but the bombing did not, in fact, "bring the Serbs to the negotiating table." Milosevic was already moving in early August toward establishing control over the Bosnian Serbs so as to bring them to the negotiating table and had completed his moves before the bombing began. It appears that it was the Bosnian Muslims who were brought to the negotiating table by the bombing or, more accurately, by the threat that it would be ended if they did not agree to the U.S. settlement. The initial decision to "suspend" the bombing on 14 September came in exchange for Bosnian Serb agreement to withdraw their heavy weapons from the exclusion zone around Sarajevo and end the siege of that city.

At the same time, the United States did not allow the combined Croatian-Muslim offensive in western Bosnia that followed the ouster of the Krajina Serbs to inflict too great a defeat on the Bosnian Serbs. To have done so might have drawn Serbia into the conflict directly and threatened the strategic balance in the region. The bombing in Bosnia constituted the "exemplary use of quite limited force to persuade the opponent to back down" consistent with Alexander George's model of coercive diplomacy. George defines "exemplary" as "the use of just enough force of an appropriate kind to demonstrate resolution to protect one's interests and to establish the credibility of one's determination to use more force if necessary."[28] A military analyst points out that the total effort "equated to just about a busy day's sorties count for coalition air forces during the Gulf War" and characterizes it as "a strategically limited, tactically intense, high-technology, coalition air campaign, conducted under tight restraints of time and permissible collateral damage . . . aimed at coercing political and military compliance from a regional opponent who had no airpower." [29] The United States and its NATO allies were careful not to use so much force as to lead either side to believe that all was won or lost, thereby creating real incentives to accept the U.S. settlement.

To a certain extent, the "balancing act" carried out by U.S. diplomats—led by Richard Holbrooke—in their relations with the Serbs, Croats, and Muslims during the bombing was necessitated by the pressures exerted by the British, French, and Russians. The British and French refused to "wage war on behalf of the Muslim-led government,"[30] while the Russians continued to oppose the bombing. However, "balancing" reflected to a far greater extent the difficulties of applying the techniques of coercive diplomacy to the behaviors of multiple parties with conflicting interests. This is a far more difficult task than attempting to affect the behavior of a single opponent. By facilitating the emergence of a Croatian ground army and using airpower against the Bosnian Serb army, the United States encouraged the political and territorial ambitions of the Croats and the Muslims. The United States, therefore, did not prevent the Bosnian Serbs from using artillery withdrawn from Sarajevo and Serbian airpower to stop the Croatian and Muslim advance in western Bosnia. Whereas Holbrooke had blamed the Serbs for the difficulties of negotiations in August and September, for example, by October he was blaming the Muslims for blocking the conclusion of a cease-fire agreement. The cooperation of Milosevic was the direct result of the coercive diplomacy—the combination of threats, inducements, and actual use of force—exercised by the United States. On 4 October, Holbrooke cautioned Bosnian President Izetbegovic that he was "playing craps with the destiny of his country" by refusing to agree to a cease-fire and warned him that "If you want to let the fighting go on, that is your right, but do not expect the United States to be your air force."[31] Despite this threat, the Bosnian Muslims refused to agree to a cease-fire until they had extracted a commitment from the United States to provide them with military assistance. The United States was therefore compelled to supply both positive and negative incentives to cooperation to all the parties directly involved in the Bosnian conflict (the Bosnian Muslims, Serbs, and Croats, and both Tudjman and Milosevic) to ensure success. Thus, even the most successful case of direct intervention in the Bosnian conflict suggests caution: the difficulties of balancing relations among allies—coalition management—magnifies the already difficult task of balancing actions directed against each of the warring parties in a multisided internal conflict.

Military Occupation and State Building

The military-political intervention characterized above as "coercive diplomacy" ended the fighting in Bosnia but did not end the conflict among the Bosnian Muslims, Croats, and Serbs. In an attempt to do so, the United States also engaged in a direct political intervention, imposing its own solution at Dayton, enforcing it through the deployment of NATO and other forces to Bosnia, and establishing a de facto international protectorate over the country. These actions have redirected the conflict to more, but not entirely, peaceful means, but they have been insufficient to resolve the fundamental conflict in any meaningful time frame. The Dayton arrangements have left power divided among the three major ethnic groups and between the central state and its constituent entities (the Federation and the Serb Republic) and lower units (cantons and local governments). Even after more than six years, there are no authoritative institutions capable of formulating and implementing policies for the whole state. As a result, the local representative of international authority in Bosnia, the Office of the High Representative, has had to intervene repeatedly to impose policy decisions where local actors proved unable or unwilling to do so on their own. Paradoxically, to the extent that international institutions continue to perform such a role, Bosnian institutions will remain internally divided and incapable. Yet, there is no clear exit option for international forces in Bosnia that does not increase the risk of renewed violent conflict among the three Bosnian ethnic communities to unacceptably high levels. Intervention in Bosnia has thus taken on the characteristics of an open-ended commitment to administer the territory.

Conclusion: Assessing the Bosnian Interventions

Intervention in Bosnia began relatively early in the conflict, but was limited in scope and objective. It represented the continuation of Western efforts to contain the destabilizing consequences of the dissolution of former Yugoslavia, rather than an effort to facilitate meaningful settlement of the issues driving the conflict to violence. Such an effort appeared to be closed off by the commitment of the West to existing borders and, therefore, recognition of the former republics of the Yugoslav federation as states prior to negotiation among the conflicting parties of an agreement on either new borders or a new political order within the existing borders. The Bosnian case offers a clear example of how even a limited commitment to containment and humanitarian relief may lead, incrementally, to a major commitment to direct intervention. Each commitment of diplomatic energy ("prestige") and military and material resources to peacemaking, peacekeeping, and successive attempts at deterrence created the basis for arguments for further expansion of Western commitments until the level of prestige and resources committed to the conflict created a compelling national interest in securing a favorable outcome. The interests that in the end compelled armed intervention as part of the strategy of coercive diplomacy were not, therefore, the product of the conflict itself; at no point did Western policymakers appear to view the conflict in Bosnia itself as threatening to national interests.

This view of the conflict was at the time and remains today highly controversial. Some in the United States argued then and continue to argue today that the Serbs were committing genocide against the Muslims and that the United States was not only obligated to intervene, but had a moral interest in doing so. The debate over the place of moral values in the definition of American national interest remained unresolved, however. The threats to national interests that in the end motivated U.S. intervention in the Bosnian conflict derived from the consequences of the conflict for NATO cohesion and the potential consequences of the conflict for electoral politics in the United States, not the nature of the war itself. In short, limited intervention itself created the impetus for further intervention by raising the political cost of inaction.

The coordinated military-political intervention or strategy of coercive diplomacy carried out in 1995 can be considered successful because it achieved the primary goals of Western policymakers: it put an end to the fighting, averted a catastrophic withdrawal of allied forces under fire, and established a Bosnian state within existing borders. It also put a halt, however belatedly, to the genocidal killing in Bosnia and stemmed the flow of refugees to the West. But intervention did not settle the conflict; it transformed the struggle among Bosnian Muslims, Bosnian Croats, and Bosnian Serbs from a military to a political conflict. The Dayton agreement left power divided among the three groups and between the central state and its constituent entities (the Bosnian Federation and the Serb Republic), as well as the lower-level cantons and local governments. The difficulties of establishing central Bosnian government authority over the entire country, achieving interethnic reconciliation, resettling refugees in the towns and villages from which they had fled or been "cleansed," and reviving the economy during the more than five years of effective international occupation all reflect the continuation of intergroup conflict in Bosnia. Although there are some limited signs of hope in the emergence of a multiethnic political party that is gaining some power and authority in the country, the international community, through the Office of the High Representative, continues to play a critical role in resolving political deadlocks, imposing public policies on the Bosnian state, and negating political processes that produce unsatisfactory outcomes. This leaves it unclear whether the Bosnian state could survive in the absence of an international civil, police, and military presence. Thus, the postconflict tasks of occupation and state building have turned into an open-ended commitment for the West. At best, it amounts to an effort to "buy time" for the establishment of a stable state within existing borders, the only basis for "exit" of international forces and the conclusion of the Bosnian intervention.

Notes

1. Steven L. Burg and Paul S. Shoup, *The War in Bosnia-Herzegovina: Ethnic Conflict and International Intervention* (Armonk, N.Y.: M. E. Sharpe, 1999), 80–81, 84–88.

2. *U.S. Department of State Dispatch* 2, no. 22 (3 June 1991): 395–396.

3. For discussion of the uncertainties surrounding these principles at the moment of Yugoslavia's dissolution, see Steven L. Burg, *War or Peace? Nationalism, Democracy, and American Foreign Policy in Post-Communist Europe* (New York: New York University Press, 1996), 45–55.

4. Steven L. Burg, "Nationalism and Democratization in Yugoslavia," *Washington Quarterly* 14, no. 4 (Autumn 1991): 5–19.

5. Burg, Shoup, *The War in Bosnia-Herzegovina*, 90.

6. Burg, Shoup, *The War in Bosnia-Herzegovina*, 92–102.

7. For a detailed account of these negotiations, see Burg and Shoup, *The War in Bosnia-Hezcegovina*, 108–117.

8. Burg, Shoup, *The War in Bosnia-Herzegovina*, 120–127, 200–203.

9. Kofi Annan, "Agreement of 5 June 1992 on the Reopening of Sarajevo Airport for Humanitarian Purposes," *Report of the Secretary General Pursuant to Security Council Resolution 757*, S/24075 (6 June 1992).

10. These negotiations are examined in detail in Burg and Shoup, *The War in Bosnia-Herzegovina*, 189–262.

11. Herbert S. Okun, as cited in *New York Times*, 11 July 1993, IV: 7.

12. Burg, Shoup, *The War in Bosnia-Herzegovina*, 307–360.

13. Text of the agreement is cited in note 9. The UNPROFOR mandate is enlarged in UN Security Council Resolution 758 (8 June 1992).

14. Burg, Shoup, *The War in Bosnia-Herzegovina*, 207–208.

15. Andrew Winner points out this source of the contradiction between UNPROFOR mission/mandate and rules of engagement in his recent doctoral dissertation, "You and What Army? Coalitions and Coercive Diplomacy" (Ph.D. diss., University of Maryland, College Park, 2002).

16. See Norbert Both and Jan Willem Honig, *Srebrenica: Record of a War Crime* (New York: Penguin Books, 1997).

17. For a careful examination of the impact of media coverage of these events on Western policymakers, see Nik Gowing, "Real-Time Television Coverage of Armed Conflicts and Diplomatic Crises: Does It Pressure or Distort Foreign Policy Decisions?" working paper 94-1, Joan Shorenstein Barone Center on the Press, Politics, and Public Policy, John F. Kennedy School of Government, Harvard University, Cambridge, Mass., 1994, which offers analysis based on extensive interviews with Western policymakers.

18. These events are examined in greater detail in Burg and Shoup, *The War in Bosnia-Herzegovina*, 140–159, 329, 340–341. These events, as well as those addressed in the following section on coercive diplomacy, are also examined, from the perspective of coalition theory and the politics of coercive diplomacy, in Winner, *You and What Army?* (see note 15).

19. Peter Viggo Jakobsen makes the same point in *Western Use of Coercive Diplomacy after the Cold War: A Challenge for Theory and Practice* (New York: St. Martin's Press, 1998), 92.

20. Cited in Burg, Shoup, *The War in Bosnia-Herzegovina*, 341.

21. Cited in Burg, Shoup, *The War in Bosnia-Herzegovina*, 210 (Eagleburger) and 252 ("quagmire").

22. Burg, Shoup, *The War in Bosnia-Herzegovina*, 325.

23. Bob Woodward, *The Choice* (New York: Simon and Schuster, 1996), 253–270.

24. See I. William Zartman, *Ripe for Resolution: Conflict and Intervention in Africa*, 2nd ed. (New York: Oxford, 1989); "The Unfinished Agenda: Negotiating Internal Conflicts," in *Stopping the Killing: How Civil Wars End*, Roy Licklider, ed. (New York: New York University Press, 1993), 20–34.

25. Burg, Shoup, *The War in Bosnia-Herzegovina*, 326.

26. Cited in Burg and Shoup, *The War in Bosnia-Herzegovina*, 321.

27. Burg, Shoup, *The War in Bosnia-Herzegovina*, 363–364.

28. Alexander L. George, *Forceful Persuasion: Coercive Diplomacy as an Alternative to War* (Washington, D.C.: United States Institute of Peace Press, 1991), 5.

29. Col. Robert C. Owen, USAF, "The Balkans Air Campaign Study," part II, *Airpower Journal* 11, no. 3 (Fall 1997): 8, 20. Part I of the analysis is to be found in *Airpower Journal* 11, no. 2 (Summer 1997): 5–24.

30. Woodward, *The Choice*, 357.

31. Woodward, *The Choice*, 359.

4

Intervention in Internal Conflict: The Case of Rwanda

Gilbert M. Khadiagala

Postcolonial Rwanda was born out of a decisive reversal of power from the minority Tutsi to the majority Hutu occasioned by the 1959 revolution. The revolution inaugurated an era of massive movement of refugees in the region, endemic communal violence, and political frailty. In the early 1980s, the government of Juvenal Habyarimana and the one-party state he had erected since 1973, the National Revolutionary Movement for Development (Mouvement Révolutionnaire National pour le Développement, MRND), were under siege from three fronts. First, as the Habyarimana government grew more authoritarian, the intra-Hutu common political front frayed, shifting military and economic power to the president's narrow northern ruling elites.

Second, inequitable access to resources heightened intra-Hutu cleavages amidst a worsening economy. With the highest population density in mainland Africa (256 persons per square kilometer), Rwanda typifies the dilemma of overpopulation and resource scarcity compounded by severe dependence on coffee production. By the second half of the 1980s, with economic growth rates falling behind a burgeoning population, the government admitted that it could only feed five million people. Internal and external economic shocks were to worsen the class and regional polarization, contributing to the general weakening of the Habyarimana state. Economic decline and external pressure for democratization galvanized domestic opposition groups to demand political reforms. In response, Habyarimana appointed a commission in September 1990 to work out a National Political Charter that would allow the establishment of different political parties.[1]

Third, against the backdrop of economic and political weakness, Tutsi exiles in Uganda organized in the Rwandese Patriotic Front (RPF) invaded in October 1990. Caught in an uncertain exile, RPF units that had been part of Uganda's National Resistance Army (NRA) took the initiative at the opportune instance of regime weakness to force the issue of return, restoration of citizenship rights, national unity, and an end to a dictatorial system that generates refugees.

The Internationalization of the Conflict

Between the RPF's invasion in October 1990 and the signing of the Arusha Agreement in August 1993, the conflict went through two significant stages that form the background to UN intervention: external military intervention to support the belligerents and regional mediation efforts to end the conflict. Regional mediation had two primary phases: November 1990–May 1992 and June 1992– August 1993. These phases are important to analyses of the dynamics of the conflict and international efforts to address it.

Foreign Military Intervention

The fledgling Habyarimana government invited foreign military support in the fall of 1990 from its allies, Belgium, France, and Zaire, to meet the RPF's threat. Responding to this appeal, Belgium sent 535 troops and France sent 300 troops, ostensibly to protect their nationals in Rwanda. Zaire's Mobutu Sese Seko dispatched about 1,000 troops that were deployed in direct combat against the RPF. External support enabled the Rwandese army to inflict heavy casualties on the RPF. As the war raged on, however, Zaire and Belgium withdrew their troops, the latter citing a legal obligation to remain neutral in war situations, while Mobutu's undisciplined troops left in ignominy. After the withdrawal of Zairian and Belgian troops, France was left as the principal supporter of the government. French military commitment to the government included the provision of troops and military advisers, the supply of heavy weaponry such as armored personnel carriers, reconnaissance vehicles, communications equipment, and helicopters. France also provided financial guarantees for purchases of small arms, mortars, and grenade launchers from Egypt and South Africa. Military assistance and training enabled Habyarimana to boost the government army, Forces Armees Rwandaises (FAR), which grew from fifty-two hundred in Octo-

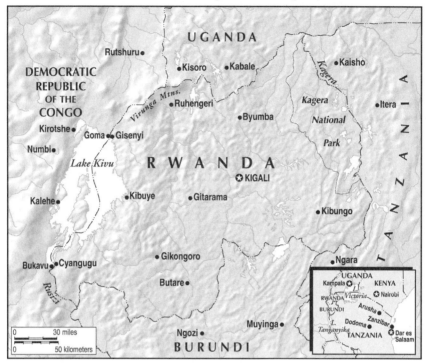

Map 4.1 Rwanda

ber 1990 to fifteen thousand by mid-1991 and thirty thousand by the time the Arusha negotiations began in June 1992.[2]

Uganda's military and political support for the RPF was indispensable to its initial survival. Stemming from the RPF's long-term alliance with Ugandan President Yoweri Museveni's NRA, Uganda provided arms, food, and gasoline and willingly opened its southern border as a military launching pad and place of refuge. In the face of widespread condemnation for the invasion, Museveni remained a dependable RPF ally in regional and international diplomatic circles.

Regional Mediation

Phase One, 1990–1992

The first phase of regional mediation efforts stemmed from Habyarimana's desire to isolate the RPF and Uganda. In a predictable spate of self-denial, this strategy entailed mobilizing the support of Belgium and its European allies to use their economic muscle on regional actors, and enlisting Tanzania and Zaire as mediators between Rwanda and Uganda. Three weeks after the invasion, Belgium sent its prime minister, Wilfried Martens, to East Africa to persuade regional leaders to prevail on Museveni. Martens proposed the creation of a regional intervention force to supervise a cease-fire, with Europe furnishing logistical and financial support. Belgian diplomatic intervention led to regional consultations in November 1990 focusing on a cease-fire and possible establishment of a peacekeeping force.

Efforts to use Tanzania's influence over Museveni to curtail Uganda's logistical and military support to the RPF culminated in various summit meetings in Tanzania in late October 1990. Habyarimana promised to initiate a dialogue with both the internal and external opposition under the auspices of the Organization of African Unity (OAU) to end the conflict and resolve the problem of Tutsi refugees. But this dialogue stalled, predicated, as it were, on Tanzania and Uganda persuading the RPF to essentially return to Uganda. Tanzania's diplomatic intervention failed to stop the war because of Habyarimana's unwillingness to concede the legitimacy of the RPF.

Subsequently, Habyarimana prevailed on Mobutu to embark on a series of diplomatic initiatives to break the impasse. Mobutu's mediation, starting on 26 October 1990 in Gbadolite, Zaire, proposed a cease-fire agreement to be supervised by a fifteen-man OAU Neutral Military Observer's Group (NMOG) drawn from Zaire, Burundi, Tanzania, and Uganda. Mobutu's mediation created a negotiating process without fundamentally altering the government's view of a cease-fire as a prelude to RPF's withdrawal back to Uganda. Even though Mobutu made overtures to the RPF during these talks, the government either refused to participate or sent representatives who had no negotiating mandate. The government's unyielding stance was demonstrated when it scuttled the deployment of OAU military observers, insisting on stationing a military team on the Rwanda-Uganda border to prevent further incursions by the RPF.

With futile regional mediation efforts to stop the war, the focus shifted to finding a regional solution to the problem of Rwandese refugees. The conference on Rwandese refugees in Dar es Salaam, Tanzania, in February 1991 brought together Rwanda's neighbors, the OAU, and the United Nations High Commission for Refugees (UNHCR). Habyarimana promised to remove all obstacles impeding the voluntary return and reintegration of refugees. In return, Uganda, Burundi, Tanzania, and Zaire agreed to naturalize and integrate refugees who opted to settle outside Rwanda. With no end in sight for the war, Mobutu reinvigorated his efforts to find a durable cease-fire culminating in an agreement at N'sele, Zaire, on 29 March 1991, which proposed the immediate cessation of hostilities as a prelude to negotiations on power sharing. At N'sele, the Habyarimana government agreed, for the first time, on direct negotiations with the RPF.

Further favoring the negotiations were fundamental changes in the domestic balance of power engendered by Habyarimana's internal reforms. These reforms created a new multiparty constitution and led to the formation of political parties sympathetic to the RPF's position. In a major breakthrough in April 1992, the major political parties signed a protocol that established a coalition transitional government. As part of this agreement, Habyarimana conceded to the start of negotiations with the RPF.[3]

Phase Two, June 1992–August 1993: The Arusha Peace Process

Tanzania, under the broad mandate of the OAU, mediated the Arusha peace talks from their inception in June 1992 to their conclusion in August 1993. To provide additional sources of leverage, representatives from France, Germany, Belgium, the UN, and the United States attended the talks as observers. Similarly, Burundi, Uganda, Zaire, and the OAU sent observers to give the talks an African imprimatur and demonstrate regional anxiety about a settlement. The multilateral nature of the Arusha talks provided a wider international context of power, but in reality the essentially token participation of major Western countries and the UN from the outset helped shape expectations about the extent of international commitment to Rwanda's peace process. During the negotiations these expectations weighed heavily on decisions about the resources for implementation, postwar economic reconstruction, and refugee resettlement.

From the start of the negotiations, the Tanzanian mediators focused on reaching agreement on a durable cease-fire as a means to build confidence. Previous attempts to establish cease-fire mechanisms in the N'sele agreement of March 1991 provided a blueprint for the negotiations, facilitating a quick agreement that established a fifty-five-man OAU Neutral Military Organization Group (NMOG) composed of troops from Mali, Nigeria, Senegal, and Zimbabwe. As the first multilateral military intervention in the conflict, the NMOG, led by Nigeria's General Ekundayo Opaleye, had the limited task to create and supervise a buffer zone in the north between RPF and government positions.

With the cease-fire holding and the NMOG structures in place, the mediators steered the parties to power-sharing talks sequenced around protocols that addressed various facets of the conflict. By early 1993, the parties had signed a number of protocols, including the rule of law and establishment of democratic rule and power sharing during the transitional period. The mediators faced a major challenge in February 1993 when Habyarimana threatened to withdrawal from the negotiations and unleashed his extremists on Tutsi and Hutu moderates. The threat to the negotiations was averted when the RPF broke the cease-fire and launched a large-scale offensive against government troops, doubling the territory under its control and advancing to within a few miles of Kigali. French authorities again saved Habyarimana from the RPF advance by sending more troops, bringing the number to at least 680, comprising four companies, including paratroopers.

The confrontation in February 1993 was a turning point in the conflict, creating propitious circumstances for the mediators to prod the parties back to negotiations. In a high-level meeting in Dar es Salaam on 7 March 1993, the parties reconstituted the cease-fire and agreed on the mechanisms for the gradual withdrawal of French troops and their replacement with an international monitoring force. As part of these efforts Paris sought a UN force, culminating in UN Security Council resolution 812 on 12 March 1993 that authorized the formation of an international force "under the aegis of the OAU and the United Nations entrusted with the protection of, and humanitarian assistance to, civilian population and support the OAU force for the monitoring of the cease-fire." A UN reconnaissance team recommended that this mission, the United Nations Observer Mission Uganda-Rwanda (UNOMUR), be deployed on the Uganda side of the border to prevent the supply and reinforcement of RPF.

During the final phase of the negotiations between March and June 1993, both belligerents favored a strong but neutral force under UN leadership to implement the agreement. In a joint letter to the UN on 14 June 1993, the government and RPF suggested a rapid UN deployment after the signing of the agreement to "permit its speedy implementation and, in particular, the establishment of a broad-based transitional government thereby avoiding excessively long intervals, which might be detrimental to the peace process."[4]

The Arusha Peace Agreement incorporated six protocols signed by the parties over the twelve months of talks: the N'sele cease-fire agreement, the rule of law, power sharing, repatriation of refugees, integration of armed forces, and miscellaneous provisions. Central to the transition was a multiparty Broad-Based Transitional Government (BBTG) and Transitional National Assembly (TNA) that would be established thirty-seven days after the signing of the agreement. Before their establishment, the Agreement allowed Habyarimana's government to retain power on condition that it would neither usurp the mandate of the BBTG nor introduce new legislation. The transitional institutions would supervise local, parliamentary, and presidential elections in 1995, twenty-two months after the establishment of the BBTG.

UN Interventions

UNAMIR, August 1993–April 1994

The Principal Circumstances That Prompted Third-Party Intervention
The United Nations Assistance Mission in Rwanda (UNAMIR) intervened to implement the Arusha Peace Agreement, an agreement that had been carved out of a deeply polarized society. Most observers correctly saw Arusha as a political rather than a peace agreement.[5]

From the outset, the interveners confronted three major obstacles. First, the Agreement was erected on a moderate multiethnic political center that attempted a power-sharing mechanism against the overwhelming odds of entrenched Hutu power. Second, compounding the Agreement's internal fragility was an unstable regional environment that had a debilitating effect on the implementation process. Third, both the mediators and parties to the Arusha Agreement staked its implementation almost exclusively on international actors who were unwilling and unprepared to expend resources on meeting most of its provisions.

UNAMIR was deployed months after the signing of the Arusha Peace Agreement, but its clearly delineated phases reflected the parties' responsibility to make tangible progress toward implementation. For interveners, deployment was contingent on discernible movement toward peace and the establishment of transitional institutions. For the parties, however, there would be limited progress in key provisions without full UNAMIR deployment.

The Nature of the Intervention Force

In planning for UNAMIR, the interveners were assisted by the existence of a peacekeeping infrastructure, the OAU's NMOG, which had been in place since June 1992, and UNOMUR, which was deployed on the Uganda side of the border and became fully operational in mid-August 1993. On 19 August 1993, the UN Secretary General sent a reconnaissance mission to Rwanda led by General Romeo Dallaire, the chief military observer for UNOMUR (and later UNAMIR's force commander), to examine the functions of UNAMIR and evaluate the human and financial resources required to carry them out. Dallaire's mission recommended a much smaller force than envisaged in the Arusha Agreement and what some UN military experts thought was feasible for effective implementation. UN military experts proposed eight thousand or, at the very least, five thousand troops. In the end, there was agreement on 2,548 troops, of which 2,217 would be staff officers and troops and 331 military observers.

The reconnaissance mission recommended a four-stage progressive deployment. Phase one provided for the deployment of an advance party of twenty-five military personnel, eighteen civilian personnel, and three civilian police after formal authorization by the Security Council. This force would secure Kigali and establish the "essential condition needed to permit the secure installation of the transitional Government," which, the mission acknowledged, "may not be installed until the end of 1993." Slated to take ninety days, this phase was also to lead to the integration of UNOMUR and NMOG in UNAMIR, concluding with a total military force of 1,428.

Phase two, taking ninety days, was to focus primarily on disengagement, demobilization, and integration of the armed forces and gendarmerie. The end of phase two would coincide with full deployment of the 2,548 military personnel. During phase three, which would last about nine months, UNAMIR was to complete the integration of the forces and reduce its staff to approximately 1,240 personnel. In the final phase, lasting about four months, a reduced mission of approximately 930 military personnel would assist in securing the atmosphere required in the final stages of the transitional period leading up to the elections. Three weeks beyond the thirty-seven days (5 October 1993), the UN Security Council passed resolution 872 endorsing the plan of the reconnaissance mission and established UNAMIR for an initial period of six months. UNAMIR's authorizing resolution warned that its deployment beyond ninety days would be contingent on a determination that "substantive progress has been made toward the implementation of the Arusha Peace Agreement."[6]

When it was fully deployed, UNAMIR consisted of military forces and civilian observers from Bangladesh, Belgium, Ghana, and Tunisia. In addition to Force Commander General Dallaire (assisted by Ghana's Brigadier Henry Kwami Anyindoho), Jacques-Roger Booh-Booh, the Special Representative of the Secretary General (SRSG), was the head of both the civilian component and the entire UNAMIR.

There were frictions between the military and civilian components from the start of the intervention. As the SRSG, Booh-Booh was the overall head of UNAMIR, but the delay in establishing his office in Rwanda meant that General Dallaire led the mission for some time, a fact that was to create a gap in command between the civilians and military. With the creation of the civilian administration, the military became subordinated to it; yet as General Anyindoho notes, the administrative support system was weak, incompetent, and uncooperative: "the majority of the personnel in the Administration and Management Division of the mission did not appear to possess the requisite background to give them the necessary confidence for the day-to-day handling of their responsibilities."[7] Furthermore, civilian control of financial resources led to conflicts with the military. According to Anyindoho, "A force Commander who has been given troops to command in an operation must have a say in the financial control of that mission. Why will he not be given assets to control the force? Flexibility, which is a principle of administration, seems to have been ignored in UNAMIR even though our first Chief of Administration happened to be a retired Colonel."[8]

Goals of the Intervention

Conflicting goals about deployment and intervention marked the enterprise from the outset. The Arusha Agreement called on UNAMIR to "assist in the implementation of the Peace Agreement, more especially through the supervision of the implementation of the Protocol of Agreement on the Integration of Armed Forces of the two parties as well as the provision of all kinds of assistance to the competent authorities and organs."[9] The protocol envisaged that demobilization, disengagement, and integration of a new army would be completed between seven and nine months. Under this plan, there would be a new integrated army of nineteen thousand men, divided on a 60/40 percent basis in favor of the government. The demobilization and gradual integration of the rest of the soldiers in civilian life was to start with the voluntary publication of lists of soldiers targeted for demobilization, the establishment of assembly points, monetary payments to individual soldiers, and the formation of a secretariat for rehabilitation and social integration. Throughout this exercise, UNAMIR was to demarcate assembly points, including the establishment of an expanded Demilitarized Zone (DMZ), create the demobilization procedures to supervise the disengagement of forces, and train the new armed forces.

The protocol also provided additional security roles for UNAMIR: guarantee the overall security of the country, especially verifying the maintenance of law and order; ensure the security of distribution of humanitarian aid in conjunction with relief operations and with repatriation and resettlement programs; assist in the tracking of arms caches and neutralization of armed gangs; aid in the recovery of all weapons in the hands of civilians; undertake mine clearance operations; and monitor the observance by the two parties of the modalities for the definite cessation of hostilities. Article 64 of the protocol stipulated that the Neutral International Force shall be "informed of any incidents or violation and shall track down the perpetrators." In its initial role, UNAMIR was to provide security in Kigali, a task that would be linked to the formation of the BBTG and TNA.

Dallaire's reconnaissance mission, however, proposed a more modest mandate for UNAMIR. Thus, instead of "overall security" in Rwanda, the mission suggested that UNAMIR "contribute to" security only in the city of Kigali: "Owing to the presence of several battalions of government forces in Kigali and the introduction into the city of the RPF leadership with a fully equipped RPF battalion, the Mission would establish a weapons-secure area in and around Kigali." Outside Kigali, while UNAMIR's role in monitoring the cease-fire and demobilization of troops was to remain intact, the mission proposed a reduction of the assembly points, cantonment points, and integrated training centers from a total of forty-eight, as suggested by the two parties, to twenty-six. With regard to maintaining civilian security through monitoring the activities of the gendarmerie and communal police, the mission changed the mandate to "investigate and report on incidents regarding the activities" of the police. On the security components that provided for disarmament of militias and civilians, the mission, conscious of the difficulties caused elsewhere, simply ignored them.

These contrasting postures toward the goals of the intervention were captured in UN Secretary General's report following the reconnaissance mission.

> The concern of all parties was that, should the neutral international force not be deployed in a timely manner, a political vacuum might occur if the transitional Government was not established in Kigali. The mission responded by clarifying the decision-making process at the United Nations and by stressing that the dispatch of a peacekeeping force to Rwanda would depend on a final determination by the Security Council.

Members of the Security Council, wary of an open-ended intervention, opposed not just the provisions of the Arusha Agreement but also the timing of deployment. UNAMIR was created in a global context characterized by apprehensions about the wisdom of international peacekeeping. Boutros-Ghali took the lead in presenting the Arusha Agreement as an "opportunity for the international community to contribute to the successful implementation of the peace process," and constantly warned that delays would "seriously jeopardize" the agreement. However, in the Security Council, where it mattered most, Rwanda was not a high priority. Growing U.S. apprehension about funding peacekeeping operations was heightened by the killing of eighteen U.S. soldiers in Mogadishu, Somalia, two days before Security Council debate on UNAMIR began. Following the Somalia debacle, the Clinton administration came out with a new peacekeeping policy, termed Presidential Decision Directive 25, that stressed limiting the costs and risks of peacekeeping.[10]

The first contingent of UNAMIR under General Dallaire arrived in Kigali at the end of October 1993, but it became fully operational at the end of December 1993 after the integration of NMOG into UNAMIR and the creation of a weapons-secure area in Kigali manned by Belgian and Bangladeshi troops. With the deployment of nearly thirteen hundred peacekeepers, four hundred Belgian soldiers ushered the RPF civilian leaders and six hundred soldiers into Kigali, the first move in the establishment of the BBTG.

Lurking in the background of the deployment, however, were domestic and regional power realignments that were unfavorable to implementation of the Agreement. Internally, extremist opponents of the Arusha Agreement organized by Habyarimana's supporters and their militias redoubled their efforts to defeat the implementation of the Agreement at three levels. First, their main propaganda instrument, the Radio Télévision Libre des Mille Collines (RTLMC), began broadcasting in August 1993 by openly calling on the population to reject the Agreement and to prepare to fight against the installation of an RPF-dominated government. Second, the extremists increased the recruitment and training of militias in ostensibly "self-defense" programs and expanded the arming of the presidential guard and gendarmes. At the end of August 1993, amid the escalating levels of violence, Prime Minister Uwilingiyimana warned that growing insecurity did not "augur well for the implementation of the agreement because security is a prerequisite for successful implementation." In November and December reports of escalating ethnic massacres conducted by armed Hutu militias throughout the country clouded the implementation climate.

At the regional level, the Rwandese peace process was dealt a severe blow by the military coup in Burundi on 21 October 1993 in which the elected Hutu president, Melchior Ndadaye, was assassinated and Tutsi-Hutu conflict violence ensued. Ndadaye's death at the hands of the Tutsi military only helped to inflame ethnic passions in Rwanda, giving opponents of power sharing more ammunition that Tutsis were bent on dominating the two countries. Most observers regard events in Burundi as the most important trigger to the unraveling of the Agreement, largely because it undercut the moral and organizational positions of Hutu political parties that previously had been the core of the consensus for negotiations and power sharing.

Stripped of the initial mandate of overall security, UNAMIR operated from the end of 1993 not just on shoestring resources but in a dangerous political vacuum that signatories of the Arusha Agreement had predicted. In mid-December 1993, the SRSG, Booh-Booh, held talks with the RPF and the government in which both sides issued a joint declaration reaffirming their commitment to the Arusha Peace Agreement and the installation of transitional institutions by the end of the same month. The Secretary General's December 1993 report to the Security Council noted that the cease-fire had generally been respected and recommended the early deployment of troops designated for phase two of the operation, thereby increasing UNAMIR to its peak strength of 2,548 military personnel.

Attempts to constitute transitional institutions, however, stalemated in late December 1993 as a result of severe disagreements over representation in the

BBTG and TNA. These disagreements stemmed from Habyarimana's demands for the revision of some of the provisions of the Agreement that barred his supporters from representation in the transitional institutions. Although Booh-Booh crafted a temporary compromise that led to the installation of Habyarimana as the interim president on 5 January 1994, the deterioration of the security situation in the country worsened the implementation process. UNAMIR had the mandate to contribute to the security of Kigali in collaboration with the local police, including enforcing the ban on weapons. Yet, UNAMIR's modest mandate could not meet the flagrant distribution of arms to militias and civilians by roving Hutu death squads responding to the RTLM's call to exterminate Tutsis. In January and February 1994 there was a multiplication of incidences of violent demonstrations, roadblocks, assassination of political leaders, and murder of civilians. In January 1994, responding to a report from a close confidant of Habyarimana about plans by the Interahamwe to exterminate Tutsis in Kigali and the intensified stockpiling of arms, General Dallaire sought permission from the Department of Peacekeeping Operations (DPKO) in New York to use overwhelming military force. The DPKO, however, informed General Dallaire that such action would go beyond the UNAMIR mandate that authorized him to contribute to the security of Kigali in collaboration with local authorities. As violence escalated, the DPKO relented in early February 1994, authorizing the peacekeepers to assist Rwandese police, on a case-by-case basis, to recover illegal arms. In spite of this action, UNAMIR's capacity to seize weapons and provide security was hampered by the rules of engagement that required it to work with local police, which was allied to the Interahamwe.

UNAMIR's glaring impotence forced General Dallaire to send another cable to New York on February 1994 warning that the success of the peacekeeping operation would be in jeopardy without prompt confiscation of arms stockpiled by the militia. He predicted "more frequent and more violent demonstrations, more grenade and armed attacks on ethnic and political groups, more assassinations and quite possibly outright attacks on the UN peacekeepers."[11] When General Dallaire's requests for a robust mandate fell on deaf ears, Belgian authorities made pleas to the Security Council. The United States and the United Kingdom, however, vehemently opposed the enlargement of UNAMIR operation, citing the costs and risks of exceeding the original peacekeeping mandate. In a letter to the Secretary General on 14 March 1994, Belgian Foreign Minister Willy Claes echoed General Dallaire's concerns:

> Current political developments in the situation in Rwanda are not encouraging. . . . As you are aware, the deadlock in the formation of a broad-based transitional government is leading, despite the efforts of your Special Representative, to a deterioration of the political climate. The Rwandese army appears increasingly annoyed by the parties' procrastination, while information on the stockpiling of weapons by the various militias is becoming even more compelling. Even some of the leaders admit that a prolongation of the current political deadlock could result in an irreversible explosion of violence. . . . It seems to me, however, that [the] higher profile of the United Nations on the political

level should be accompanied by a firmer stance on the part of UNAMIR with respect to security. . . . Unless the negative developments we are witnessing are halted, UNAMIR might find itself unable to continue effectively its basic mission of playing a major supporting role in the implementation of the Arusha Peace Agreement.[12]

Frantic efforts by UNAMIR, Western ambassadors, and regional states failed to break the deadlock on the formation of a transitional government throughout the spring of 1994. In February 1994, Booh-Booh issued a blunt warning that unless Rwanda's feuding parties showed seriousness in implementing the Arusha Agreement, the UN forces would be withdrawn: "Rwandese politicians ought to assume their responsibilities before the country sinks into insurmountable hardships. We have made lengthy consultations and efforts to solve the situation, but the UN's patience is running out. If war breaks out again, the UN mandate would be seriously compromised and we would have to pull out." With the impending expiration of the UNAMIR mandate at the end of March 1994, leaders of Rwandan human rights associations and NGOs pleaded to the Security Council "to maintain and reinforce" UNAMIR because its withdrawal "would be interpreted as abandoning the civilian population to the worst of calamities."[13]

The Secretary General's report at the end of March 1994 recommended the extension of UNAMIR's mandate for an additional six months with a new deadline and dire warning: "In the event that the transitional institutions are not installed within the next two months and if, by that time, sufficient progress in the implementation of the next phase of the Agreement has also not been achieved, the Council should then review the situation, including the role of the United Nations." On 5 April 1994 the Security Council resolution 909 extended UNAMIR's mandate until 29 July 1994. The big problem remained lack of movement on domestic reconciliation, a task that regional states shouldered in a last-minute effort to prevent what Tanzania's President Ali Hassan Mwinyi called a "Bosnia on our doorstep." Summoned before his regional peers in Dar es Salaam to explain his consistent opposition to the formation of transitional institutions, Habyarimana promised to honor his word, but all progress was reversed when his plane was shot down on its return to Kigali. Habyarimana's death on 6 April 1994 began the genocide that killed more than eight hundred thousand people in ninety days, mostly Tutsis and moderate Hutus. The genocide triggered the resumption of the civil war until the RPF troops restored order by taking Kigali in July 1994.

International response to the unfolding genocide followed the pattern that had prevailed since the start of the implementation process. Of critical significance was whether UNAMIR, under its constrained Chapter VI mandate, would stay the course following the disintegration of civil authority. Two days after the crisis started, General Dallaire sent a cable to UN headquarters about a "campaign of terror, well planned, organized, deliberate, orchestrated," and directed against opposition leaders and "particular ethnic groups." He called for a revision of the mandate to counter the genocide, but, in secret and informal discussions that ensued in New York, it became apparent that the priority was how to pull out of Rwanda. After the Interahamwe brutally killed ten Belgian peacekeepers, the security of foreign troops took precedence as Belgium withdrew its 420 soldiers and, shortly thereafter, Bangladesh followed suit. The Belgian withdrawal deprived UNAMIR of its best troops and strengthened international pressure for total withdrawal.

Two weeks into the genocide, Boutros-Ghali presented three options to the Security Council on the position of UNAMIR. The first option proposed the immediate and massive reinforcement of UNAMIR, changing its mandate and authority so that it could coerce the opposing forces into a cease-fire. The second option called for the reduction of UNAMIR to about 270 personnel who would remain to "act as an intermediary between the two sides in an attempt to bring about a cease-fire." The third option was a complete withdrawal. Boutros-Ghali claims that he had a strong preference for forceful action, since it would "give UNAMIR the credibility to deal effectively with the situation. . . . I reminded the Council that the consequences of a complete withdrawal of UNAMIR, in terms of human lives lost, could be very severe."[14] On 21 April the UN Council passed resolution 912 to withdraw the peacekeepers, leaving a token force of 270. UNAMIR's withdrawal gave extremists an opportunity to wage the genocide for two more months. Although Boutros-Ghali described the withdrawal as a "scandal," it merely ended a phase that had started with unrealistic expectations enshrined in the Arusha Agreement. As General Dallaire has admitted, "The UN Mission, and those Rwandans it was intended to secure, fell victim to an inflated optimism to which I contributed, thereby creating expectations that the UN did not have the capacity to fulfill."[15]

Scenarios for Improving Goal Attainment

In the preliminary phase of the implementation, the gap between the parties' inordinate optimism and the reality of international bureaucracy centered on the timing of establishing UNAMIR. Conscious of the brittle nature of the settlement, the RPF and government had, in their joint letter to the Secretary General on 11 June 1993, requested an accelerated UN deployment. As a result, the Agreement set a thirty-seven-day timetable (that is, 10 September 1993) for establishing transitional institutions. In setting the timetable, the parties received prior warning about possible delays, according to Boutros-Ghali:

> At the time of the Arusha discussions, the United Nations made clear to the parties that the decision to deploy a United Nations force rested with the Security Council and that, if approved, the deployment could take up to three months. Given their serious concerns that any inordinate delay in establishing the transitional government might endanger the peace process, the parties had none the less decided to adopt the accelerated timetable.[16]

The unrealistic timetable was compounded by the slow and staggered deployment, weakening the implementation process from the outset. Furthermore, intramural UN debates on reducing UNAMIR's meager forces on the ground considerably undercut the legitimacy of the intervention.

Since the report of the reconnaissance mission recommended a reduction of troop levels to what most critics thought was a less credible intervention, the consensus has revolved around the lack of a "robust" mandate for UNAMIR in meeting the challenge of the extremist forces. Although the ability of the UNAMIR to deal with extremism with a Chapter VI mandate is often exaggerated in some of the revisionist accounts of the UNAMIR's role, there is no doubt that dealing early with instances of militia violence would have made some differences. At the decisive moment when the civil war resumed, Dallaire has claimed that, given five thousand troops and an enhanced UN mandate, he would have prevented most of the killings. By 6 April 1994 UNAMIR's strength stood at 2,539, but the number quickly dwindled to 1,705 after the withdrawal of Belgian and Bangladesh troops. UN Security Council's Resolution 912 of 21 April further reduced this number to 270 men with a mandate to secure a cease-fire and assist in the resumption of humanitarian efforts. As the deputy force commander of UNAMIR remarks, "A force that was already under a weak mandate, poorly equipped and suffering from maladministration had had its final blow. . . . We felt abandoned by those who established us and locked between the RGF and RPF protagonists who did not seem to appreciate our presence in their country, and yet both sides said again and again that they needed our presence."[17]

In addition to being lightly equipped and underfunded, UNAMIR was comprised primarily of Third World military units with inadequate training, equipment, and logistics. Deputy Force Commander Anyindoho has pointed to these problems:

> Right from the beginning of the mission, UNAMIR was best with logistics problems. Apart from Belgium, all the contingents came from developing countries with a weak logistics base at home. For example, the country that provided the bulk of the logistics support for the force had many problems with shipment and delivery of vehicles, engineer stores, and drugs for the force. . . . Logistics, engineering and medical support should never have been provided by a typical Third World country. It is my hope that such a mistake is never repeated in the formation of a new mission. The deficiencies in those areas reflected very badly on the force from the very beginning, and served to exacerbate the situation during the early days of the civil war and beyond.[18]

Other revisionist accounts have suggested that the outcome in Rwanda could have been significantly altered with the deployment of a well-trained, equipped, and commanded five thousand troops drawn primarily from a single country.[19] In this scenario, the introduction of a large combat force could have stemmed the violence around the capital and prevented its escalation to the countryside. But in Rwanda, no such country was available.

UNAMIR's Chapter VI rules of engagement were closely tied to the implementation of the Arusha Agreement: the use of force was limited to self-defense or after the authorization of higher echelons; if provoked, the soldiers were instructed to use nonaggressive and cooperative behavior and enlist the help of Rwandese gendarmerie, UNAMIR's designated local partner. General Dallaire redefined some of these rules, but these efforts were either inadequate or too late. In the end, when the civil war resumed in April 1994 UNAMIR as a peacekeeping force had no peace to keep.

Evaluating the Outcomes of Intervention

Both the military and nonmilitary components were insufficient to resolve the conflict. On the nonmilitary side, as Anyindoho has shown, "It appeared everybody at the UN in New York looked at UNAMIR as one of the easiest missions that was going to accomplish its assigned role in twenty-two months, so a team was hurriedly assembled to administer it. Nothing could have been more militarily inept. . . . For sometime, all successive administrators of UNAMIR were unfortunately non-effective."[20] On the military side, the hasty withdrawal at the height of the civil war undermined UNAMIR's relevance and efficacy in the conflict. The failure of UNAMIR has been captured in the postgenocide consensus about the abandonment of Rwanda. The implacable hostility of key Western countries in the Security Council to strengthen UNAMIR's mandate showed a clear absence of international commitment to the implementation process. General Dallaire summed up the central problem of political will: "The United Nations wanted to send me more troops, but sovereign states made sovereign decisions not to do so."[21]

Exit Strategy

UNAMIR had a clear exit strategy staggered over twenty-two months and timed to coincide with the elections that would mark the end of the transitional period.

UNAMIR II, July 1994–March 1996

The Principal Circumstances That Prompted Third-Party Intervention

UNAMIR II intervened in mid-May 1994 at the height of the genocide and the total collapse of order; large-scale massacres of civilians continued unabated throughout the country; and Kigali was effectively divided between the RPF and Rwandese government forces. With no adequate protection, as many as three thousand civilians in Kigali had taken refuge in public places and religious sanctuaries. There were an estimated 250,000 internally displaced persons in the north, 65,000 in the east, and 1.2 million in the south and southwest. In addition, 400,000 Rwandan refugees had fled to Burundi, Zaire, Tanzania, and Uganda.

The Nature of the Intervention Force

With no Western country willing to commit troops to UNAMIR II, Boutros-

Ghali recommended an expanded force made up of African troops with Western logistical and financial support. The UN Security Council resolution 918 of 17 May 1994 agreed to a force of 5,500 troops. UNAMIR II became fully operational in November 1994 with troops from Ghana, Ethiopia, Nigeria, Mali, Tunisia, Malawi, and Zambia. Apart from the African troops, Western nations such as Australia, the United States, the United Kingdom, and India provided medical, engineering, and communication experts to UNAMIR II.

By the time of UNAMIR II there was a large presence of international organizations and nongovernmental organizations (NGOs) engaged in relief and humanitarian work. Following a visit to Kigali by the Under-Secretary General for Humanitarian Affairs at the end of April 1994, there was a decision to establish the United Nations Rwanda Emergency Office (UNREO) that led the overall coordination of humanitarian relief efforts. As a collaborative framework, UNREO drew from the resources and expertise of UN agencies, notably the Food and Agricultural Organization (FAO), the International Committee of the Red Cross (ICRC), the office of the United Nations High Commissioner for Refugees (UNCHR), the World Food Program (WFP), and the World Health Organization (WHO). The UNREO strategic role was in developing basic operating procedures for the humanitarian assistance including the security of humanitarian personnel and the beneficiaries of relief assistance.

The collaboration between UNAMIR II and the UNCHR broke down in September 1994 over the alleged massacre of Hutus by the RPF. Concerned about the paucity of human rights monitors in Rwanda, the UNHCR commissioned a report that concluded that 30,000 Hutus, many of them returning refugees, had been killed by the RPF. These charges reflected negatively on the protection role of UNAMIR II. Although Boutros-Ghali diffused the internecine conflict by quashing the publication of the report, the image of UNAMIR II was dented by subsequent RPF attacks on refugee camps in January and April 1995.

Goals of the Intervention

UNAMIR II was formed to undo the Security Council's precipitous reduction of UNAMIR to 270. Its formation was preceded by Boutros-Ghali's campaign for the UN Security Council to take more forceful action to stop the massacres. Similarly, General Dallaire recommended a force with deterrent capability, preferably a Chapter VII mandate. During informal discussions in the Security Council in early May 1994, however, there was considerable resistance from key members about "forceful action"; instead, consensus coalesced around a mission that would deliver humanitarian assistance and support the displaced persons. Subsequently, the Security Council increased the force levels of UNAMIR II for roles that were largely humanitarian: it would contribute to the security and protection of displaced persons through the establishment of secure humanitarian areas, provide security and support for the distribution of humanitarian supplies and relief operations, and monitor border crossing points.

The leadership of UNAMIR II also continued the frantic mediation between the interim government and the RPF to reach a cease-fire. After the authorization of UNAMIR II, Boutros-Ghali dispatched a high-level mission to Kigali from May 22–27 to support the cease-fire negotiations. But by mid-July, having captured most of Rwanda and with the government's forces in tatters, the RPF declared a unilateral cease-fire.

Scenarios for Improving Goal Attainment

The deployment of UNAMIR II was a slow and painstaking task. Fatigued by the proliferation of peacekeeping operations, the international community was less willing to provide the resources to support the deployment. Moreover, even though African states did offer to participate in large numbers, they possessed neither the financial nor logistical resources. At the end of July, UNAMIR II had less than 500 troops and 124 military observers on the ground. In recognition of the delays in deployment, the UN Security Council accepted Boutros-Ghali's extension of UNOMUR in June 1994 for an additional three months during which time it helped support the buildup of UNAMIR II and coordinated humanitarian assistance. By October 1994, UNAMIR II troop strength stood at 4,270 and 320 military observers. It was not until 25 November 1994 that Boutros-Ghali reported that UNAMIR II had belatedly reached its authorized strength of 5,500. At the same time, its mandate was extended to 9 June 1995 with further authorization to train Rwandese policemen and protect human rights officers for the genocide tribunal that was formed in November 1994.

There was no alternative to the African peacekeepers constituting UNAMIR II. Although resource and logistics problems delayed its deployment, the composition of UNAMIR II was adequate for its limited roles.

Authorized under Chapter VI mandate, the operation's rules of engagement did not include enforcement action but permitted a proactive role to protect civilians. The Security Council also introduced an expanded definition of "self-defense" in the authorizing resolution: UNAMIR II would be required to take action in self-defense against those who threatened protected sites and populations and the means of delivery and distribution of humanitarian relief.

Evaluating the Outcomes of the Intervention

The military objectives of UNAMIR II were modest, geared primarily toward salvaging the sagging image of the UN in the face of its inaction during the genocide. Moreover, the African troops operating on shoestring budgets were not expected to make much difference to ending a war that was almost over. When the full complement of troops and materiel arrived in Rwanda in October 1994, the RPF controlled virtually all Rwandese territory and the genocide had ended.

The nonmilitary aspects cannot be underestimated for their critical contribution to restoring an essential international presence and contributing to the coordination of humanitarian relief efforts. Despite the delays in deployment, UNAMIR II achieved its basic mission of providing a secure environment for humanitarian relief. In collaboration with the French (discussed below), NGOs, and UNREO, it secured some refugee camps, helped the return of IDPs, and assisted the new RPF government in establishing authority in areas previously under government control. Following the expiry of French intervention in August 1994, UNAMIR II assumed most of the security roles in northwestern and southwestern Rwanda. In addition, UNAMIR II adjusted its operational plans to engage in the stabilization and monitoring the situation in all regions of Rwanda so as to encourage the return of refugees and IDPs, to provide security and support for humanitarian assistance, and to promote national reconciliation through mediation and negotiations. In October 1994, UNAMIR II developed broadcasting facilities to provide Rwandese with factual information in the country, assist in explaining the mission's mandate, and disseminate information on humanitarian programs. After the introduction of RPF troops in the HPZ, UNAMIR II conducted a number of joint operations with the government to secure the camps from bandits and armed criminals.

The nonmilitary functions of UNAMIR II enabled it to outgrow from its limited roles of supporting relief to those of reconstruction and rehabilitation of civil institutions and infrastructure. Although UNAMIR II had neither the capacity nor the mandate to stabilize the economy, establish representative institutions, or reconstitute civil society, its presence contributed to the return of normalcy and provided confidence to some of the returning refugees and IDPs. In addition, given the absence of working local institutions, UNAMIR II did lead to their reconstitution.

Exit Strategy

There was no clear exit strategy for UNAMIR II. In an attempt to overcompensate for its previous flaws, UNAMIR II lapsed into an open-ended mandate to the detriment of relations with the RPF government. By January 1995 its force strength of 5,740 peacekeepers and military had exceeded the authorized level of 5,500. From then on, the Security Council reduced its size within an overall policy of scaling down its peacekeeping components in preference for national and confidence building. In June 1995, Security Council resolution 997 extended the mandate of UNAMIR II to December 1995 but stipulated the reduction of its strength to 2,330 within three months and 1,800 within four months. The new mandate reduced the security and protective functions of UNAMIR II, leaving it almost exclusively the humanitarian tasks of relief and rehabilitation. The RPF's discomfort with the continued presence of UNAMIR II grew markedly amidst deepening mistrust between it and the UN in general. In January 1995, the RPF described UNAMIR as "costly, useless, and undisciplined." As the RPF looked for bilateral military support to boost its security needs, it perceived UNAMIR II as an impediment; moreover, since humanitarian agencies were performing the humanitarian functions of UNAMIR II, the RPF saw the latter role as superfluous. Boutros-Ghali, however, insisted on the presence of UNAMIR II to sustain the reconciliation process. In the end, the two sides reached a compromise in which UNAMIR II withdrew in March 1996 to be replaced by a modest UN office in Kigali. Security Council resolution 1050 of March 1996 created the United Nations Office in Rwanda (UNOR) to support the government's efforts in national reconciliation, building the judicial system, facilitating the return of refugees, and rehabilitating socioeconomic infrastructure.

Operation Turquoise, June–August 1994

The Principal Circumstances That Prompted Third-Party Intervention

France's Operation Turquoise launched on 23 June 1994 occurred in the context of two months of civil war. The war, however, had become increasingly asymmetrical: with the capacity of the forces of the interim government crumbling, the RPF intensified its efforts to capture Kigali and seize areas on the Zairian border held by the retreating government forces. The RPF advance led to massive movement of people from the combat areas toward the southwestern portion of the country. Equally significant, the French intervened at a decisive moment when the deployment of UNAMIR II was stalemated in bureaucratic battles about funding and rules of engagement. By this time, the strength of UNAMIR had risen from 44 to 503, consisting of 354 troops, 25 military personnel, and 124 military observers.

The Nature of the Intervention Force

Operation Turquoise comprised 2,555 French and 350 Senegalese troops under the command of General Jean-Claude Lafourcade. To lend it wider legitimacy, nationals of six Francophone states provided supportive services.

Goals of the Intervention

In seeking authorization from the Security Council, France defined Operation Turquoise as a humanitarian mission to secure and protect displaced persons and civilians, notably Tutsi and moderate Hutus, the main targets of government militias. In its authorization of resolution 929 of 22 June 1994, the Security Council called for a "temporary operation under French control and command using all necessary means to achieve the humanitarian objectives of UNAMIR II."

There was no unanimity in the UN Security Council about Operation Turquoise, a fact that was captured in this description: "a reluctant decision of a divided council." In and out of Rwanda, the concern stemmed largely from France's previous support for the Habyarimana government and potential problems of coordinating the mission with UNAMIR II. On the verge of gaining control of the country, the RPF was implacably opposed to French intervention, seeing it as a means to save the faltering regime. To allay these fears, the Security Council specifically mandated cooperation between Operation Turquoise and UNAMIR II even though both were to retain their separate identities. From the outset, therefore, the objectives of Operation Turquoise were inextricably linked to the broader humanitarian efforts of UNAMIR II.

Scenarios for Improving Goal Attainment

Within a day of UN Security Council authorization, French forces intervened from Zaire with the speed and decisiveness that shamed UNAMIR II. Operation Turquoise was established under a Chapter VII mandate allowing the use of force, but in the end, it encountered little opposition on the ground.

Evaluating the Outcomes of the Intervention

Operation Turquoise occurred at the height of RPF advance into southwestern Rwanda, with 1.2 million people from the northern and central regions beginning to move into Zaire and 1.5 million to the southwest. The military capability and ease of entry enabled the French to set up a safe Humanitarian Protection Zone (HPZ) in southwestern Rwanda, despite RPF opposition. Working closely with UNAMIR II, Operation Turquoise saved lives and halted the mass exodus of refugees into Zaire, as had happened in Goma to the north. French intervention and presence stabilized the HPZ, where French soldiers resettled IDPs into refugee camps, provided security, and disarmed some of the militias among the refugees. As the RPF gains led to more Hutu refugees in the HPZ, the French signaled their intention to use force to prevent RPF entry into the protected areas. Overall, it is estimated that the intervention saved twelve to fifteen thousand lives and prevented many more refugees from streaming across the Zairian border. UNAMIR II mediated between the RPF and French forces, allowing RPF representatives to visit the HPZ and reassure wary Hutus about the new government's intention. UNAMIR II also worked closely with Operation Turquoise to develop an operational plan that ensured the orderly transition of the HPZ to UNAMIR II prior to the departure of the French forces in August 1994.[22]

Operation Turquoise has been criticized for granting refuge to Hutu perpetrators of genocide and facilitating their safe exit into Zaire with their arms intact. In addition, French forces never made any effort to stop the inflammatory broadcasts by the defeated government from its security zones. These criticisms reflect the long-standing tensions between the RPF and France, but they diminish the extraordinary humanitarian efforts of saving lives and managing a difficult situation. Moreover, the limited humanitarian engagement in the end disabused opponents of the intervention of the initial concerns that the French would provide military support for the faltering Hutu government. Perhaps as a demonstration of the importance of Operation Turquoise, there were repeated international appeals for its extension to bolster UNAMIR II, but the French stuck to their deadline.

Exit Strategy

The French were authorized to remain in Rwanda for a maximum of two months, with the option of leaving earlier if Boutros-Ghali decided that UNAMIR II had the capacity to replace French forces. Operation Turquoise ended on 22 August 1994, two months after the intervention.

Conclusion

The failures of international intervention in Rwanda have spawned a policy and academic industry. What is often glossed over in all the excellent scenarios about how the world could have arrived at different outcomes is that the belligerents expected external actors to save them from a weak agreement. The history of conflict and mistrust between the parties compelled them to seek stronger international superintendence in the less charitable post-Somalia international environment. The failure was political rather than technical, stemming from an unwillingness to muster the resources to launch a credible peacekeeping effort. UNAMIR II somewhat salvaged the tattered reputation of the UN, improvising in resources and mandate, making good of a bad situation. Similarly, Operation Turquoise gave the French the opportunity to undo some of the consequences of their previous intervention in Rwanda.

Notes

1. For good analyses of the background to the conflict, see David Norman Smith, "The Genesis of Genocide in Rwanda: The Fatal Dialectic of Class and Ethnicity," *Humanity and Society* 19, no. 4 (November 1995): 65–67, 150; Mahmood Mamdani, "From Conquest to Consent: Reflections on Rwanda," *New Left Review* 26, no. 2 (March-April 1996): 15–16; Philippe Platteau, "Land Relations under Unbearable Stress: Rwanda Caught in the Malthusian Trap," *Journal of Economic Behavior and Organization* 34, no. 1 (January 1998): 1–47; and Gerard Prunier, *The Rwanda Crisis: History of a Genocide, 1959–1994* (Kampala: Fountain Publishers, 1995), 88–90.

2. For analyses of the French role, see Alison Des Forges, *Leave None to Tell the Story: Genocide in Rwanda* (New York: Human Rights Watch, 1999).

3. For accounts of this phase of the conflict, see Filip Reyntjens, "Constitution-Making in Situations of Extreme Crisis: The Case of Rwanda and Burundi," *Journal of African Law* 40, no. 2 (1996): 234–243; and Bruce Jones, "The Arusha Peace Process," in Howard Adelman and Astri Suhrke, eds., *The Path of a Genocide: The Rwanda Crisis from Uganda to Zaire* (New Brunswick, N.J.: Transaction Publishers, 1999), 131–136.

4. Boutros Boutros-Gali, ed., "Joint Request by the Rwandese Government and the Rwandese Patriotic Front to the Secretary-General of the United Nations Concerning the Stationing of a Neutral International Force in Rwanda," *The United Nations and Rwanda, 1993–1996*, vol. 10 (New York: United Nations Publications, 1996), 166.

5. See for instance, Howard Adelman, *Early Warning and Conflict Management, International Response to Conflict and Genocide: Lessons from the Rwanda Experience,* vol. 2 (Copenhagen: DANIDA, 1996). For other analyses of the Arusha Agreement, see Gerard Prunier, *The Rwanda Crisis,* 159–191; and Patrick J. O'Halloran, *Humanitarian Intervention and the Genocide in Rwanda* (London: Research Institute for the Study of Conflict, January 1995).

6. UN Security Council, Resolution Establishing UNAMIR for a Sixth-Month Period and Approving the Integration of UNOMUR and UNAMIR, S/RES/872, 5 October 1993.

7. Henry Kwami Anyindoho, *Guns over Kigali: The Rwandese Civil War–1994, A*

Personal Account (Accra: Woeli Publishing Services, 1997), 8.

8. Anyindoho, *Guns over Kigali*, 9.

9. References to protocols in the Agreement are drawn from *The United Nations and Rwanda, 1993–1996*, 170–200.

10. For discussion of this directive and impact on Rwanda see Michael N. Barnett, "The UN Security Council, Indifference, and Genocide in Rwanda," *Cultural Anthropology* 12, no. 4 (1997): 551–578; Bruce D. Jones, "'Intervention without Borders': Humanitarian Intervention in Rwanda, 1990–1994," *Millennium* 24, no. 2 (1995): 225–249; and Alan J. Kuperman, *The Limits of Humanitarian Intervention: Genocide in Rwanda* (Washington, D.C.: Brookings Institution Press, 2001).

11. Dallaire's role is analyzed in Linda Melvern, *A People Betrayed: The Role of the West in Rwanda's Genocide* (London: Zed Books, 2000). See also Romeo Dallaire, "The Changing Role of UN Peacekeeping Forces: The Relationship between UN Peacekeepers and NGOs in Rwanda," in Randolph Kent and Shashi Tharoor, eds., *The Role of Peacekeeping* (New York: St. Martin's Press, 1996), 208.

12. "Letter dated March 14, 1994 from the Minister of Foreign Affairs of Belgium to the Secretary-General Expressing Concern that Worsening situation in Rwanda May Impede UNAMIR's Capacity to Fulfill Its Mandate," in *United Nations and Rwanda, 1993–1996*, 244.

13. John Baptiste Kayigamba, "Rwandan Human Rights Groups Plea to International Community," Inter Press Service Feature, 26 March 1994.

14. *United Nations and Rwanda, 1993–1996*, 43.

15. Dallaire, "The Changing Role of UN Peacekeeping Forces," 208.

16. *United Nations and Rwanda, 1993–1996*, 24.

17. Anyindoho, *Guns over Kigali*, 55.

18. Anyindoho, *Guns over Kigali*, 8.

19. See, for instance, Scott R. Feil, *Preventing Genocide: How the Early Use of Force Might Have Succeeded in Rwanda*, report to the Carnegie Commission on Preventing Deadly Conflict (New York: Carnegie Corporation, April 1998), 37–38.

20. Anyindoho, *Guns over Kigali*, 9.

21. Dallaire, "The Changing Role of UN Peacekeeping Forces," 208, also noted that "UNAMIR suffered several important shortcomings from the very beginning. This was due, in part, to a conscious decision by the Security Council seemingly to classify the crisis in Rwanda as a low risk priority."

22. For balanced analyses of Operation Turquoise, see Arthur Jay Klinghoffer, *The International Dimension of Genocide in Rwanda* (New York: New York University Press, 1998), 82–85; Anyindoho, *Guns over Kigali*, 99–110; and Prunier, "Operation Turquoise: A Humanitarian Escape from a Political Dead End," in Adelman and Surhke, *The Path of a Genocide*, 281–307.

5

Foreign Interventions in Cambodia, 1806–2003

David Chandler

Cambodian history since the 1500s has been one of almost constant and often painful foreign interventions. Some of these have been occasioned by internal conflict. Others have been outright invasions. Still others have stemmed at least in part from humanitarian motives.

I will argue in this chapter that Cambodia is now being perceived by foreign powers in a different way and that interventions are taking a new and very different form. Thus, while as recently as the 1980s it was possible to point to continuities in Cambodia's generally unhappy relationships with Thailand and Vietnam, stretching back over centuries, these continuities are no longer as perceptible or as important as they were. This is because Vietnam and Thailand no longer seem interested in interfering in Cambodian affairs. The same can be said of interventions in Cambodia that had their roots in Cold War priorities and Cold War strategic thinking.

Cambodia is easy to invade. No natural features impede armies from sweeping across its landscape. Perennial invaders, moreover, are easy to identify. Thailand and Vietnam, since the mid-eighteenth century at least, have been powers with large ambitions, sizeable armies, and relatively dense populations. They have intervened repeatedly in Cambodia and did so with special intensity in the 1800s. In more recent times, while continuing to intervene, they have been joined successively by France, Japan, and the United States.[1]

Cambodian leaders, and those opposed to them, have tried with mixed results to contain or encourage these incursions by calling on what James Scott
terms the "weapons of the weak"; that is, playing one side against another. Their
tactics have often fallen into a predictable and dangerous pattern. When a Cambodian ruler or faction sought the intervention and patronage of a foreign power
(call it A), rivals inside Cambodia tended to call for assistance from A's sworn
enemy, whom we can call B.

A vivid example of this pattern occurred in the 1840s when Thailand and
Vietnam, in support of rival Cambodian factions, fought to a draw on Cambodian soil, nearly destroying the country in the process. Similarly, in the 1970s, as
we shall see, the Lon Nol government sought U.S. assistance while its opponents, the Khmer Rouge, looked to America's enemies for help: China and Vietnam.

In a variation on the pattern, Prince Norodom Sihanouk, during his years in
power (1955–1970), performed a dangerous balancing act. He adopted an anti-
American foreign policy stance (and thereby assured a flow of assistance from
the Communist bloc while keeping the Vietnamese Communists at bay) while
also pursuing a vigorous anti-Communist domestic policy, thus assuring continued U.S. assistance until he cut it off in 1964.

Some of the states intervening unilaterally in Cambodia have had a strategic
or humanitarian vision. France in the colonial era and Vietnam in the 1830s,
with their versions of a civilizing mission, spring immediately to mind. So does
Vietnam in the 1980s, when at least part of the rationale for its ten-year intervention was to protect Cambodia from a return of the Khmer Rouge. In most
cases, however, the intervening states have pursued their own objectives without
considering humanitarian issues or collateral effects. Thailand's interference in
1941 and the 1950s, Vietnamese Communist incursions from the late 1940s to
the mid-1970s, South Vietnam's invasion and occupation in 1970–1971, and the
U.S. involvement from 1970–1975 provide examples of intervening nations or
entities whose priorities overrode any consideration of the impact of their interference on Cambodia or its people.

Intervening nations, by definition, seldom respect the sovereignty of the
places in which they intervene. This has been especially true in the Cambodian
case. In May 1970, for example, the United States invaded Cambodia, then its
ally, without informing its chief of state, who had the grace to welcome the invasion after he heard about it on the radio. In the 2000s, disdain for Cambodian
sovereignty has taken the form of pressure, stemming from the UN and the
United States, for an international trial of the Khmer Rouge leadership. Propo-
nents of such a trial have argued with mixed success that it must be run internationally because Cambodia's own judiciary is too incompetent and biased for the
task.[2]

More ambiguous and far less bellicose interventions have recently replaced
the ones that I discuss in this chapter, as we shall see. Interventions by larger

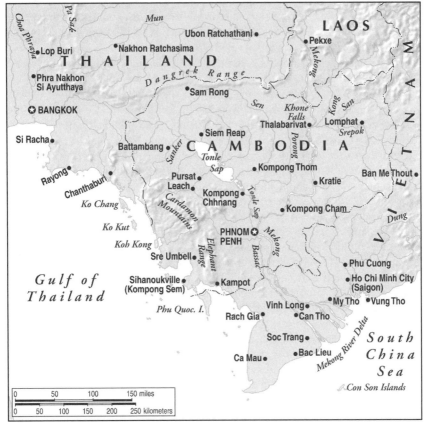

Map 5.1 Cambodia

powers in the 2000s are being set multilaterally by foreign donors with humanitarian or quasi-humanitarian agendas. In this regard, a donor country's political influence over the Cambodian leadership (a crucial objective in the Cold War era) is less important nowadays to the donor than obtaining commercial advantages. In this regard, the Paris Peace Accords in 1991, a watershed in Cambodian history, can be interpreted from one angle as the planned, rational, and quasi-benevolent retreat of patrons from a country where, on balance, most of them had done a good deal of harm. I will return to this point below.[3]

No More Interventions?

The unilateral foreign interventions that scarred Cambodia for centuries seem to have come to an end. I also see no prospect of renewing the internal conflict between the so-called Khmer Rouge and its opponents that devastated the country between 1968 and the late 1990s. The Indochina region, in this respect, has become, for the time being, safer in terms of low intensity conflict than much of Africa or South Asia, although the possibilities of conflict between Myanmar and Thailand to the east cannot be ruled out.

Why have the interventions stopped? Why has internal conflict subsided? Why are they unlikely to recur?

To begin with, the civil war in Cambodia, the involvement of larger powers, and the Khmer Rouge movement were deeply rooted in the Cold War. A civil war between Communists and their opponents broke out in Cambodia in the 1960s, faded between 1975 and 1978 with a Communist victory, and resumed in the 1980s. By the early 1990s, the Khmer Rouge had lost most of its foreign support. The civil war sputtered to an end in 1998 after thousands of Khmer Rouge adherents, including several of its leaders, were amnestied by the Phnom Penh regime whose leader, Hun Sen, urged his compatriots in 1999 to "dig a hole and bury the past." The conflict will not be rekindled.

In a similar fashion, the powers that have intervened in Cambodia in the past, in a politico-military, border-crossing way (Thailand, Vietnam, France, Japan, and the United States) are unlikely to reenact these interventions. The climate of opinion that encouraged them and the priorities they shared at the time have altered, probably for good, and international mechanisms are now in place to discourage such unilateral incursions.

Cambodia itself, of course, has not become stronger or less vulnerable to border-crossing attacks. In fact, alongside Laos, it is probably the weakest state in Southeast Asia. What *has* altered is the zeitgeist or spirit of the times and the relationships and priorities of other nation-states toward Cambodia and among themselves. In Southeast Asia these relationships and priorities have been increasingly subordinated to such globalizing, multilateral concerns as market forces, global communication, and regional cooperation and to such supranational organizations as ASEAN, APEC, the UN, the World Bank, and so on. The field of human rights, also, has assumed an important place in foreign policy formulation that would have been unimaginable even fifteen years ago.

What follows deals almost entirely with the past and with types of interventions that are unlikely to recur. The lessons that these interventions teach us, if any, might well be transposed to other states or situations in the 2000s, but we need to ask, as we attempt these transpositions, whether the interventions were of a generic sort or were so heavily colored by local conditions and the changing spirit of the times as to have little or no applicability elsewhere now or in the future.

Nineteenth-Century Interventions

In 1806, the young Cambodian monarch, Ang Chan, entered into an alliance with the newly installed Nguyen emperor, Gia Long, in Vietnam. He did so, it seems, to loosen the ties that bound him to the Thai king, Rama I, who had placed him on the Cambodian throne. The documentary sources give us no information about Chan's motives, but his decision soon led to the defection of his three brothers to Bangkok and also to thirty years of increasingly systematic Vietnamese protection of the Cambodian court, punctuated by local uprisings and a pair of Thai invasions. In the process, Cambodia was severely damaged. Tens of thousands of people were driven from their homes, towns and cities were burnt down, and the economy was in ruins. In the 1840s it was on the brink of disappearing as a recognizable nation-state. After several years of fighting between Thai and Vietnamese forces, the Vietnamese withdrew, and in 1848 the Thai placed Chan's younger brother, Duang, on the Cambodian throne. The ensuing Thai protectorate lasted into the reign of Duang's son, Norodom (r. 1860–1904) and ushered in the colonial era.

Vietnam's stated motives in intervening in Cambodia were to nurture the Cambodian king and to protect Cambodia from attack. In the 1830s, after a ruinous Thai invasion, protection evolved into outright annexation, a policy that angered Cambodia's disempowered elite and sparked an anti-Vietnamese uprising that soon elicited Thai military support. Thailand's stated motives in their intervention were to protect Cambodian religion and to place a sympathetic ruler on the throne. While Vietnam, like France later on, had embarked on a civilizing mission in Cambodia, the Thai were interested, it seems, in sustaining a similar Theravada Buddhist culture, thereby increasing their own fund of merit.

The unintended consequences of Thai and Vietnamese interference included the near destruction of Cambodia, lingering Thai ambitions to impose a protectorate over Cambodia, and a legacy of anti-Vietnamese racism among Cambodians that has many of its roots in the period of Vietnamese control.

When French naval officers from Saigon visited King Norodom's court in 1863, they offered him open-ended French protection in exchange for timber concessions and mineral exploration rights. They also secured Norodom's permission to explore the Mekong valley, which was then a blank space on their maps. Although these objectives were limited, they had been encouraged to believe that Norodom would be willing to accept more systematic French protection, which he soon did, to use as a counterweight against the Thai.

Cambodia was a windfall to the French, acquired painlessly with the king's permission. Norodom didn't know what he was getting Cambodia into, but because of his complaisance Cambodia soon became France's favorite possession. A French historian refers to the era as "colonialism without pain." Had the French failed to intervene it is arguable that Cambodia would have been divided up by its neighbors and would have disappeared as a nation-state.

Between the 1860s and 1953, the French froze Cambodia's political institutions in place and built cities, roads, and a few schools. They laid the basis for an export economy and quarantined the country not only from further interventions, but also from the forces of pluralism, nationalism, and modernity that were developing at the time in Thailand, Vietnam, and elsewhere in the world.

In the nineteenth century the French, the Thai, and the Vietnamese obeyed their own imperial imperatives whenever they intervened in other countries. None of them was subject to agreed upon standards of behavior or accountable to any international organization. The only restraints on their conduct were self-selected ethical ones, public opinion (in the French case), and limitations of resources. International conduct in those days was largely a matter of, to use two marvelous French phrases, *force majeure* and *raison d'etat.* These terms dominated Cambodia's own governance as well. Not surprisingly, the welfare of Cambodia's people never received much sustained attention either from its own rulers or from foreign powers intervening in the country, except indirectly, in the sense that the French brought more peace and more law and order to Cambodia than it had enjoyed in the past. At a less tangible level, the relations between the French and (nearly all) Cambodians were relatively friendly, unmarked by the bitterness, confrontations, and violence that characterized the French colonial era in Vietnam.

Twentieth-Century Interventions, 1940–1964

Cambodia's colonial calm dissolved in the maelstrom of World War II. Thai forces invaded northwestern Cambodia in late 1940, after the fall of France, and with Japanese help Thailand soon regained two Cambodian provinces in the region, Battambang and Siem Reap, which they had annexed in 1794 and which had been taken back by France in 1907. By mid-1941, Japanese troops were stationed throughout Indochina with French permission, poised for their southward advance. They had no specific politico-military goals in Cambodia and for most of the war the French maintained administrative control over its possessions in Indochina. In March 1945, however, fearing an Allied invasion, the Japanese interned French citizens throughout the region. In Cambodia, they informed the young king, Norodom Sihanouk, that his nation was independent. The five-month interlude that preceded France's return in force brought the Vietnamese Communists to power in Vietnam and demonstrated to some Cambodians, at least, that colonialism might not last forever.

During the first Indochina War (1946–1954) Cambodia was rarely a combat zone. Independence came peacefully in 1953. Vietnamese Communist troops, the so-called Viet Minh, used Cambodian sanctuaries for forays into southern Vietnam, much as they did later on. They recruited thousands of Cambodians, especially along the border, to assist them. Some of these men and women formed the nucleus of Cambodia's Communist movement.

After the Geneva Conference in 1954, Cambodia emerged for the first time in centuries into a wider world whose politics were dominated by the Cold War. After the "loss" of Vietnam to the Communists, the United States was determined to hold the line in the rest of what had been French Indochina. Cambodia's perennial enemies, Thailand and (southern) Vietnam, were closely allied with the United States, and Norodom Sihanouk, Cambodia's volatile, nationalistic ruler, opted for a policy of neutrality whereby Cambodia took no sides in the Cold War but accepted aid from Western powers as well as from the Communist bloc. His "pro-Communist" international position baffled U.S. policymakers and angered the regimes in power in Saigon and Bangkok, which set in motion inept but violent plots to overthrow him, sometimes with the knowledge of the United States. [4]

In the mid-1960s, as the Vietnam War intensified, Sihanouk tried to accommodate the Vietnamese Communists, whose troops were already operating on Cambodian soil, by permitting them, in secret, to remain there in exchange for guarantees that, when the war was over, Vietnam would honor Cambodia's existing frontiers. Soon afterward, he rejected U.S. aid and in 1965 broke off diplomatic relations with the United States. By making friends with northern Vietnam, his enemy's enemy—just as King Chan had done in the 1800s—Sihanouk eventually provoked the United States and precipitated his fall from power.

Interventions by the United States and Vietnam, 1970–1975

Sihanouk's fall was delayed for several years by his lingering popularity among Cambodia's rural poor, his diplomatic skills, and the timidity and disorganization of the Cambodians who opposed him. In the late 1960s, however, his flamboyant style and his seemingly pro-Communist stance, as well as the country's economic decline, angered many in the army and among Cambodia's small elite and encouraged them to plot against the prince. The plotters hoped for U.S. assistance. In arguing against Sihanouk they could also rely on widespread anti-Vietnamese feeling—directed at Communists and non-Communists alike—among the population at large.

A bloodless coup in March 1970 removed Sihanouk from power. Under the subsequent pro-American regime, the Khmer Republic, Cambodia plunged into the Vietnam War and the United States entered a period of intense involvement in Cambodian affairs. For reasons that remain obscure, U.S. president Richard Nixon believed that Cambodia was a key to ending the Vietnam War in an honorable fashion. For his part, the Cambodian head of state, Lon Nol, counted on President Nixon's written professions of friendship to see Cambodia through to victory over what he called the Vietnamese "unbelievers."

The United States had several goals in Cambodia, once its forces had failed to destroy the Vietnamese Communists' headquarters there in an armed incursion in May–June 1970. Primarily, it seems, the United States was interested in using Cambodian troops to draw Vietnamese Communist units out of southern Vietnam where the United States had begun to withdraw its forces. The U.S. president called this tactic "the Nixon doctrine in its purest form," perhaps because no American troops were being killed or wounded in the process. Nixon saw the Khmer Republic as a bulwark against Communist expansion and as a key to America's endgame in Indochina. Lon Nol, for his part, felt that Cambodians were intrinsically superior to the Vietnamese and believed that his poorly led, poorly trained forces could win if they were aided by the United States. As it turned out, Nixon and Lon Nol were both tragically mistaken.

When the cease-fire brokered between the United States and Vietnamese Communists took effect in 1972, the Vietnamese withdrew most of their forces from Cambodia. Three years of civil war between Republican and Khmer Rouge forces ensued. U.S. saturation bombing of central Cambodia in 1973, halted by the U.S. Congress, postponed the Communist victory for two years while probably strengthening the resolve of local Communist forces, popularly known as the Khmer Rouge. When the Phnom Penh government faced defeat in 1975 and the U.S. government was unwilling to provide further funds, the United States abandoned Cambodia, less than a month before being driven out of Vietnam.[5]

The internal conflict in Cambodia in the early 1970s, in which the United States was a willing participant, was not amenable to resolution for several reasons. In the first place, the Communist-led guerrilla forces, like their counterparts in Vietnam, were fighting on their own soil and could play on xenophobic sentiment among the population. More importantly, unlike the Vietnamese Communists, the Khmer Rouge refused to enter into any negotiations at all. Finally, President Nixon and his associates (like the foreign patrons for the Communist side) had become so deeply involved militarily and in terms of "face" that extrication had become contrary to what they perceived as their national interests. Leaders on both sides of the Cold War viewed Cambodia as a crucial battlefield in an ongoing global struggle, but the United States was more heavily committed to Cambodia than the other powers were. Until March 1975 the United States rejected offers by third parties to help to negotiate a settlement.

Above all, U.S. intervention in Cambodia was tightly linked to America's ongoing, diminishing involvement in Vietnam and to President Nixon's supposedly honorable strategy of withdrawal. Vietnamese Communist intervention in Cambodia in the 1960s had its roots in U.S. involvement in southern Vietnam; extricating these troops from Cambodia was not a likely prospect, since doing so would have exposed them to the firepower of the United States.

Cambodia was a sideshow for larger powers. It was also a crucial element of America's (and Vietnam's) endgame in the second Indochina War. Had the anti-Sihanouk coup taken place when it did, but had the Americans failed to intervene, it is likely, as American policymakers feared, that a pro-Communist, pro-Vietnamese government would have been installed in Phnom Penh prior to 1975, jeopardizing America's withdrawal from Vietnam and outflanking the South Vietnamese regime.

U.S. involvement in Cambodia and the bombing campaign of 1973 inflicted enormous damage on the country. They also delayed a Communist victory there and thus in Vietnam as well. Involvement in Cambodia enabled the United States to withdraw its forces from Vietnam in good order. The unassessed collateral damage to a country where the United States had no economic interests, where no U.S. citizens were in danger, and where no American troops were engaged was horrendous. It was also never a factor in U.S. geopolitical calculations.

After April 1975, American attitudes and policies toward Southeast Asia fell prey to the "never again" or "Vietnam" syndrome, which included a large element of resentment against Vietnam and also elements of institutionalized amnesia. The syndrome faded as the Cold War came to an end, but the region never regained the importance it had enjoyed in the two decades following the Geneva Conference.

Democratic Kampuchea (1975–1979) and Its Aftermath

Compared to previous Cambodian regimes, the government of Democratic Kampuchea (DK) was the most self-reliant. Indeed to a large extent DK's passion for independence (from Vietnam) probably induced its downfall. In any case, "independence-mastery" was a cornerstone of DK policy. Pol Pot and his colleagues believed in the overwhelming liberating power of collective revolutionary will. The idea that Cambodia could stand on its own feet and could prosper with little or no assistance from abroad appealed to these leaders and to thousands of ordinary Khmer. So did the idea of cutting the country off from the evils of the outside world while DK's radical policies could gather momentum. It is perhaps "not accidental," as Stalin might say, that Thomas More's *Utopia* was an island.[6]

While DK's leaders admired the radical policies of Maoist China and North Korea and accepted moderate amounts of aid from both countries, they eschewed foreign patronage and alliances. They boasted instead that Cambodia's revolution was the swiftest and most far-reaching in world history and owed nothing to foreign inspiration, money, or advice. At the same time, DK's leaders saw Cambodia's "two thousand year history," accurately perhaps, as a series of humiliating interventions and defeats at the hands of foreign powers. With "independence-mastery" they believed that Cambodia could liberate itself from the past and could also regain the glory of the medieval Cambodian kingdom of Angkor. "If our people can make Angkor," Pol Pot declared in 1977, "we can make anything."[7]

Pol Pot, like Lon Nol, believed that Cambodia was invulnerable. He also believed that enemies surrounded it. In 1978, perhaps counting on Chinese military backing and underestimating Vietnam's military strength, he led DK into a suicidal war with Vietnam, which sparked what may have been the last unilateral, border-crossing incursion by a foreign power onto Cambodian soil.

At the end of the year over one hundred thousand Vietnamese troops swept into the country in a blitzkrieg offensive. DK had been unwilling to arm its people, and its army, while courageous, was no match for the most seasoned combat troops in Southeast Asia.

Cambodia cracked open like an egg, and Vietnamese forces occupied Phnom Penh on 7 January 1979. Ironically, in part because of its policies stressing self-reliance, DK had no allies on which it could call for assistance until it was driven from power in 1979. At that point its government in exile found ample support for its guerrilla army from China (Vietnam's enemy at the time) and Thailand, whose rulers feared Vietnam and believed that its occupation of Cambodia would destabilize the region.

The United States, smarting from its experience in Vietnam, agreed; its enemy's enemies, following the old formula, were now its friends. Because of the "never again" syndrome and the marginality of Cambodia, however, the United States was unwilling to act unilaterally. Instead, claiming to follow the "lead" of the Association of Southeast Asian Nations (ASEAN), the United States supported a UN-sponsored boycott of the new pro-Vietnamese regime in Phnom Penh and supported DK's holding Cambodia's seat at the UN. As a result, the new regime in Phnom Penh was unable to obtain aid from any non-Communist powers except India and was kept out of the UN throughout the 1980s. From a Cambodian perspective, the situation has been aptly described as "punishing the poor"—that is, the long suffering people of the country.[8]

In the meantime, Vietnamese troops, aided by Cambodians, fought against DK forces that had been joined on the Thai-Cambodian border by several thousand non-Communist resistance fighters. Khmer Rouge forces did most of the fighting and inflicted most of the casualties. Throughout the 1980s the Khmer Rouge called the diplomatic tune. Its delegates, ostensibly working on behalf of a Coalition Government of Democratic Kampuchea (CGDK), occupied Cambodia's seat at the UN.

The internal conflict in Cambodia in these years was difficult to resolve for several reasons. In the first place, now that the Indochina War was over Cambodia had little strategic or economic importance. No large powers were willing to intervene to the extent necessary to provide outright victory to either of the contenders. Moreover, Cold War imperatives still prevented larger powers from altering their policies to suit Cambodia's needs. Finally, the Cambodian factions themselves were unwilling to compromise in any meaningful fashion with one another and were receiving sufficient foreign assistance to keep going. The CGDK was a façade that only partially concealed abiding animosities among its component factions, which coexisted with the CGDK's hostility toward the incumbent government in Phnom Penh.

The Vietnamese intervention in Cambodia, the other half of the equation, bore some resemblance to its intervention in the 1830s, some to the French colonial enterprise, and others to the U.S. involvement in the 1970s. Vietnamese motives for intervening seem to have included Vietnam's resentment against attacks from DK in 1977–1978, disdain for Cambodia's headlong Maoist revolution, anger at Chinese support for DK, and, once victory had been achieved, an opportunity to embark on a civilizing mission. Vietnamese involvement in day-to-day Cambodian affairs diminished after 1984. There is no indication, however, that, had the Cold War and Soviet financial support continued, they would have been willing to relinquish their idea of a Vietnam-dominated "Indochina," withdraw all their troops, or allow an anti-Vietnamese government to take office in Phnom Penh.

Despite what can be read as Vietnamese intransigence, the humanitarian motives and outcomes of the Vietnamese interlude need to be considered. Vietnamese efforts to slow down, redirect, and humanize Cambodia's Marxism-

Leninism, however dreary and misguided they appear from a post–Cold War perspective, certainly benefited more Khmer than anything that DK aimed for or accomplished. The infrastructure that Vietnam cobbled together in Cambodia in the 1980s was far more humane in orientation than DK's had been, though the country remained desperately poor and there was no freedom of information or opinion. Fighting against DK and CGDK forces, Vietnam lost more than twenty-five thousand of its own men. Their intervention was the costliest in casualties to the intervening state of any that I have discussed so far. The Vietnamese presence in Cambodia certainly prevented the Khmer Rouge from returning to power. Had that happened, it is unlikely that any other power would have engaged the Khmer Rouge militarily in an effort to drive them from Phnom Penh.

The contrast between the Vietnamese intervention in the 1980s and the U.S. intervention a decade earlier, from a humanitarian perspective, is very sharp.

The Paris Agreements and UNTAC

As the Cold War faded, Cambodia became a minor policy irritant for powers patronizing different Cambodian factions, as well as for the members of ASEAN who had been discussing the Cambodian "problem" ineffectually for several years. When Vietnam withdrew its troops from Cambodia in 1989, the major sticking point for a conclusive settlement disappeared but there were still disagreements among the Cambodian factions and among their patrons about how best to proceed. On balance, Cambodia's patrons came to believe in 1989–1990 that their continuing politico-military involvement with Cambodian factions had become counterproductive, and the factions, which were still at war with each other, were enjoined to share this view.[9]

Behind clouds of humanitarian and face-saving rhetoric, a crucial aspect of the Paris Peace Accords of 1991 was that the larger powers that had intervened for many years in Cambodian affairs wanted to alter or abandon the roles they had been playing for so long. More precisely, they wanted to return the country to Cambodian jurisdiction. From now on, they decided, foreign involvement in Cambodia was to be peaceable, multilateral, and geared to the needs of the country as well as to the peaceable interests of donor nations. In Paris, an enduring pattern of Cambodian foreign relations, namely rivalrous political patronage, died a peaceful death. China, the United States, Thailand, and Vietnam, backed by less proactive powers such as the former Soviet Union, Australia, and France, withdrew their politico-military support from Cambodia's warring factions and agreed to a UN-sponsored solution. Australia and its dynamic foreign minister, Gareth Evans, played crucial roles in brokering this complex set of arrangements. The factions ceased fighting each other for a time. The government in Phnom Penh, still spurned by the UN, was urged to forsake its claims to power (and legitimacy) in exchange for a UN protectorate and the promise of a new constitution (Cambodia's fifth) and "free and fair" elections, an unknown quantity in Cambodia's past.[10]

The United Nations Transitional Authority in Cambodia (UNTAC) was a novel form of foreign intervention in Cambodia and, at U.S. $3 billion, the most expensive operation in UN history to date. It is difficult to imagine another scenario that would have delivered as many benefits, in the long run, to Cambodia. Many of these were unintended, to be sure, and the UN left other legacies which were not as beneficial, but on balance the massive foreign intervention of 1992–1993 needs to be viewed in terms of its successes rather than its shortcomings.

On the positive side, UNTAC encouraged local human rights NGOs to take root in Cambodia and gave millions of Khmer the exhilarating experience of voting in a free and fair election, arguably the first in Cambodia's history. UNTAC also eased the repatriation of some three hundred thousand Cambodians who had been living in refugee camps in Thailand and established a tradition of press freedom in Cambodia that, although occasionally abused, has persisted into the 2000s. UNTAC stood by patiently as the Cambodians hammered together a new constitution that restored the monarchy, honored the notion of human rights, and set rules for a multiparty National Assembly. More importantly, UNTAC set a precedent for the multilateral, relatively benevolent foreign involvement in Cambodia that has been in effect in the country since 1993.[11]

On the negative side, although the elections were indeed free and fair, and although a royalist faction won them and Norodom Sihanouk was crowned king again, the incumbent regime under Hun Sen refused to relinquish power. An uneasy coalition was quickly established with the royalist faction, providing for co-prime ministers. This face-saving but vulnerable arrangement allowed the UN to withdraw from Cambodia on schedule, but it was only a matter of time (in fact, four years) before Hun Sen's Cambodian Peoples Party (CPP), via a *coup de force* that effectively disarmed the royalist faction, came to dominate Cambodian politics root and branch.

It could also be argued, in hindsight, that the lofty language of the Paris Peace Accords had little relationship with political realities in Cambodia at the time. Certainly the provision that the incumbent government should cease to govern while UNTAC was in Cambodia was naïve, and there were no provisions in the accords by which UNTAC could enforce the results of the elections. Moreover, the reluctance of the UNTAC powers to use force or sustain casualties to its military contingent (comprising some thirteen thousand men and women from several countries) meant that the Khmer Rouge retained their weapons and lingered on as a diminishing domestic military threat for several years. Because the Khmer Rouge remained armed, so did government forces, and the bloated, one-hundred-thousand-man army, which has only very recently begun to reduce its ranks, is a negative legacy of the UNTAC period. Finally, the idea that political pluralism and a loyal opposition could be born and reach maturity in Cambodia overnight was totally unrealistic, except in the minds of larger powers whose overriding and understandable priority was to extricate themselves from the Cambodian political process.

The UN intervention in Cambodia, nonetheless, can be seen as a rare case in which a massive, heavily armed foreign intervention achieved its most basic political aims. Moreover, in the process, the UN met no sustained resistance from the "host" country, which had been at war with itself and with foreign powers for over twenty years. UNTAC's success can be traced in part to the flexibility of the incumbent government, the political acumen of Hun Sen, the unwillingness of the royalist faction to resist, and the corresponding brittleness and rancor of the DK faction. By boycotting UNTAC, the Cambodian Communists effectively removed themselves from Cambodia's political scene. The victorious royal faction, for its part, was happy to have gained a foothold in Cambodia after twenty years of exile.

Another factor in the success of UNTAC was the willingness of Cambodian political factions (again, except the Khmer Rouge) to accept UN involvement in Cambodia, in part because the factions' leaders were convinced that substantial multilateral foreign assistance would follow the UN's departure.

Conclusion

Whether the costly UNTAC operation is viewed in hindsight as a "failure" or a "success"—and there are good arguments to be made for both positions—the UNTAC era ended centuries of politico-military involvement by foreign powers in Cambodia. It also opened up a realm of possibilities for Cambodia's beleaguered population, as well as for more and more varied forms of foreign activity inside Cambodia by donor governments and foreign NGOs. As foreign patronage for the various factions ended, it was only a matter of time before Cambodia's civil war, rooted in Cold War thinking and Cold War alliances, came to an end. In 1998, Pol Pot died, the Khmer Rouge dissolved as a fighting force, and, for the first time in over a quarter century, Cambodia was at peace.

In 1999, following relatively free and fair national elections in the preceding year, factional infighting declined, substantial foreign aid resumed, and Cambodia became a member of ASEAN.

For the first time in its history, Cambodia is not a bone of contention between its neighbors or of politico-military concern to even larger powers. Centuries of foreign intervention have ended and forceful intervention of a border-crossing military sort is unlikely to recur. A peaceable, multilateral operation of the sort that occurred in 1992–1993 is also unlikely, because it is hard to imagine Cambodia's ever getting into the same deep trouble or receiving as much sustained international attention as it managed to attract at the end of the Cold War.

From now on, Cambodia will be a small, independent Southeast Asian state suffering from the social, political, and economic maladies of many developing nations. Foreign intervention in the 2000s takes the form of massive and badly needed foreign assistance aimed at improving Cambodia's infrastructure, rebuilding its intellectual capital, and helping with the pressing issues of education, good governance, and public health. Intervention nowadays also takes the form of widespread foreign exploitation of Cambodia's diminishing resources of gemstones, timber, and fish, and the domination of Cambodia's tourist industry by foreign powers, particularly Thailand.

The forces attending globalization, meanwhile, can hardly be expected to benefit ordinary Khmer and will probably prove impossible to control. These forces, which are beyond the scope of this chapter, may also be more harmful in the long run to Cambodia's people and their landscape than more traditional types of foreign intervention discussed above.

Notes

1. For an account of these precolonial incursions, see David Chandler, *A History of Cambodia*, 3rd ed. (Boulder, Colo.: Westview Press, 2000). The early nineteenth century is treated in detail in David Chandler, *Cambodia before the French: Politics in a Tributary Kingdom, 1794–1848* (Ann Arbor, Mich.: University Microfilms, 1974) and by Khin Sok, *Le Cambodge entre le Vietnam et le Thailande* (Paris: EFEO, 1991).

2. On prospects for a trial, see David Chandler, "Will There Be a Trial for the Khmer Rouge?" *Ethics and International Affairs* 14 (2000): 67–82. As this is written (July 2003) the prospects are becoming slightly less bleak for some kind of trial taking place in the future. In some countries the notion of sovereignty as a sacred cause is stronger than ever—in the United States and China, for example—while in others (the European Union comes to mind) it is weakening in the face of federalizing imperatives. The notion that regimes and individuals are subject to international law for their behavior and subject to international jurisdiction is relatively new but seems to be gradually gaining strength. At the same time, in many parts of the world nationalism is as virulent as ever.

3. For a detailed account of Cambodian history in the 1990s, see Sorpong Peou, *Intervention and Change in Cambodia: Towards Democracy?* (New York: ISEAS, 2000). See also Grant Curtis, *Cambodia Reborn?* (Washington, D.C.: Brookings Institution Press, 1998) and McAlister Brown and Joseph Zasloff, *Cambodia Confounds the Peace-Makers*, (Ithaca, N.Y.: Cornell University Press, 1998).

4. For a description of these plots, see David Chandler, *The Tragedy of Cambodian History: Politics, War and Revolution since 1945* (New Haven, Conn.: Yale University Press, 1991), 101–107. The ongoing work of Kenton Clymer of Northern Illinois University on U.S.–Cambodian relations in this period will be invaluable when it is published.

5. The best account of this tumultuous period is still William Shawcross, *Sideshow: Nixon, Kissinger and the Destruction of Cambodia* (New York: Simon and Schuster, 1979). See also Chandler, *Tragedy*, 192–235, and Justin Corfield, *Khmers Stand Up!* (Clayton, Australia: Monash Asia Institute, 1994).

6. Michael Vickery has noted some striking but fortuitous resemblances between life in DK and in More's imaginary state. See his *Cambodia 1975–1982* (Boston: South End Press, 1983), 281: "The rigidly egalitarian communism, identical clothes and houses . . . identical working hours, mass lectures, communal farms and communal dining halls, shifting children out of families."

7. See U.S. Foreign Broadcast Information Service, *Daily Reports*, 7 October 1977 (translation of Pol Pot's speech of 29 September, on the eve of his state visit to China).

Every regime in Cambodia since independence, incidentally, has had a logo of Angkor Wat on its national flag.

8. See Eva Misliwiec, *Punishing the Poor: The International Isolation of Kampuchea* (Oxford: Oxford University Press, 1988). Evan Gottesman's insightful *Cambodia after the Khmer Rouge* (New Haven, Conn.: Yale University Press, 2002) provides an in-depth analysis of Cambodia in the 1980s. See also Michael Vickery, *Kampuchea* (London: Lynne Rienner, 1984), a sympathetic account of the early years of the PRK.

9. See Robert Sutter, *The Cambodian Crisis and U.S. Policy Dilemmas* (Boulder, Colo.: Westview Press, 1990). For a series of essays on the largely successful UN protectorate that followed, see Michael F. Doyle et al., eds., *Keeping the Peace: Multidimensional UN Operations in Cambodia and El Salvador* (Cambridge: Cambridge University Press, 1997), 23–206; also Trevor Findlay, *Cambodia: The Legacy and Lessons of UNTAC* (Oxford: Oxford University Press, 1995).

10. The United States, in spite or perhaps because of its largely unsavory track record in Cambodia, was surprisingly passive in the peace process and in the UNTAC operation, deferring to Australia and the UN and providing no troops or police to the UNTAC forces. See Christopher Brady, *U.S. Foreign Policy towards Cambodia, 1977–1992: A Question of Realities* (New York: St. Martin's Press, 1999).

11. For an astute analysis of Cambodian politics in the late 1990s, see Frederick Z. Brown and David G. Timberman, eds., *Cambodia and the International Community: The Quest for Peace, Development and Democracy* (Singapore: Asia Society, 1998), and especially David Ashley's chapter, "The Failure of Conflict Resolution in Cambodia: Causes and Lessons," 49–78. For a hostile treatment of Western policies in this period, see David W. Roberts, *Political Transition in Cambodia 1991–1999: Power, Elitism and Democracy* (London: Curzon, 2001). Roberts argues that Cambodian "political culture" is intrinsically hostile to democratization and any attempt to alter that culture is tantamount to imperialism in a twenty-first-century guise.

6

Sustaining Peace in War-Torn Societies: Lessons from the Haitian Experience

Chetan Kumar

The U.S.-led intervention in Haiti has often been held up as an example of how not to conduct foreign policy. Ill-defined and open-ended interventions in affairs of other countries for reasons tangential to national security are seen as primarily squandering U.S. military resources and readiness on dubious results and outcomes that only generate more ill will among those targeted for intervention. Furthermore, to the extent that problems in these countries may have been decades or centuries in the making, they are seen as only being fixed through the "n"-word—nation building—whereby expensive ventures are undertaken to rebuild entire polities or economies. For many contemporary experts, such nation building is at best misplaced hubris, at worst sheer folly.

This chapter uses the example of Haiti to propose that efforts to build peace in war-torn societies need not be endlessly expensive or open-ended and, if conducted with precision and moderation, can lead to the achievement of key long-term U.S. foreign policy goals without undermining short-term priorities. These long-term goals include the strengthening of weak or failing states so as to make them less susceptible to becoming havens for drug or terrorist networks, a key objective included in the National Security Strategy released in 2002 in the aftermath of the terrorist attacks on the United States in September 2001. Some pointers toward achieving these goals are presented from the prism of

Haiti's historical and current experience.

The History of Conflict in Haiti

Haiti is the poorest country in the Western Hemisphere. On most measures of economic achievement, it ranks toward the bottom in the region and also in the world. It is perhaps the only country in the world to have had, through the two hundred years of its independence, an economic product that has steadily grown *downward* since its birth. However, the country has never completely collapsed. It has never been a "failed state," in the contemporary international jargon, but is a perennially failing one.

Part of the answer as to why Haiti has acquired such unique historical characteristics lies in the evolution of its political economy before and after its independence. With freewheeling ports and large plantations that grew tobacco, coffee, and molasses for Europe, colonial Haiti was the region's most sought after territory.[1] French colonial rule, however, had certain particularities. Two groundbreaking works—Michel-Rolph Trouillot's study of the Duvalier era, *Haiti: State against Nation*, and Joan Dayan's study of the links between Haitian history, religion, and literature, *Haiti, History and Gods*—point to several of these and their subsequent impact on the course of Haitian history.

An important particularity of the colonial political economy identified by Trouillot and by anthropologist Sidney Mintz was the *gens de couleur*, or people of mixed race, who were the offspring of French plantation owners and slave women. Unlike their English colonial counterparts, the French frequently indulged in conjugal relationships with their slaves, thus giving rise to a class of mulattoes. These colored individuals frequently aspired to and sometimes attained the commercial status and properties of their masters.[2] Another important particularity identified by Trouillot related to land ownership in the colonial economy. The French let slaves farm small vegetable plots on their estates. For slaves who were otherwise horribly repressed, these plots were the only positive elements in their lives. After serving a long day under brutal conditions as members of organized labor gangs, slaves could return to *their* plots where they were "masters of the soil." While the brutal press-gang overseer therefore became the epitome of evil, one's own small plot of land became the pinnacle of good. Hence, when the slaves won their independence from the French and took over their masters' lands, many of them chose not to revive the plantation economy[3] and its forced labor, but instead divided the land into small landholdings geared toward subsistence agriculture and the generation of modest surpluses. Smallholding, however virtuous it was for the freed slaves, held little promise for the *gens de couleur* who had thrived in the plantation economy. Their motives for rebellion against the French had more in common with the burghers who led the American war of independence than with the slaves who sought a rural idyll. They wished to overthrow the French yoke so that they could exploit the riches of Saint-Domingue not as second-class citizens but as

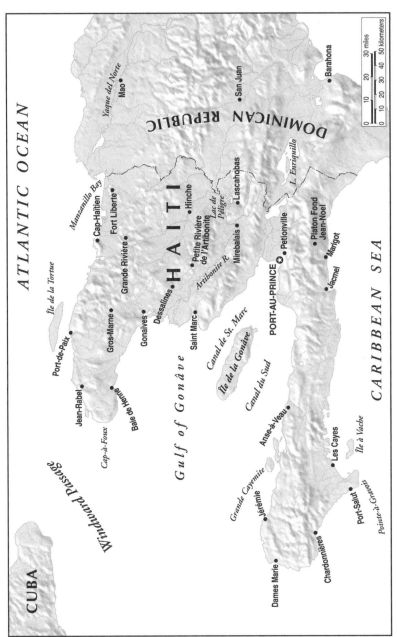

Map 6.1 Haiti

entrepreneurs in their own right. Their conception of land use therefore involved a continuation of the plantation economy rather than subsistence farming. While slaves and the *gens de couleur*, or mulattoes, joined hands to fight the war of independence, their differing conceptions of Haiti's political economy clashed shortly after independence when the country's militantly egalitarian first president—Dessalines—was assassinated in a conspiracy reportedly fomented by his mulatto general Petion, who then became president.

Haiti's mulattoes, however, did not try to force the peasantry back into a plantation economy. Having fought a war against the French together with the freed slaves, they did not wish to undertake coercive actions that would have been tantamount to reestablishing slavery. The peasants were allowed to retain their own plots of land, a right which they had won from the French plantation owners and which defined Haitian nationhood.[4] While a brief attempt was made shortly after independence under the breakaway regime of Henri Christophe in the north of Haiti to revive the plantation economy, the subsequent death of Christophe and the reunification of Haiti paved the way for the institutionalization of a static economic equilibrium.[5]

In this new economic order the mulattoes—both military and civilian—joined hands with the black officer class in the army to form a mercantile elite that dominated a largely extractive state.[6] The primary social division, however, was not between people of different color but between an urban class that derived its income from the export of the modest surplus created by the peasantry and a peasant class who owned their own land but who had their small surpluses expropriated for export by the city dwellers. This primarily economic division was reinforced by a cultural division between a French-speaking urban elite and a Creole-speaking peasantry. While allowing the peasantry to retain their plots of land, the Haitian state continued to levy progressively higher taxes via customs houses on the export of peasant produce. The middlemen who brought this produce to the ports passed these taxes on to the peasants. Eventually, custom house receipts became the mainstay of the Haitian state, which had organized itself not to invest in growing the economy or developing factors of production but to merely collect revenues. The more thorough exploitation of the countryside for commercial purposes was stayed by an informal social pact that arose from the shared legacy of the struggle for independence.

Given the parasitic nature of the Haitian state, Haitian politics became centered on struggles among various urban groups to control the biggest chunk of taxation revenues.[7] Politicians became more obsessed with the ritual and procedure of politics that affected their ability to grab a share of the state's bounty for their constituencies than with larger social and economic questions. Of course, this obsession was frequently couched in a nobler political discourse that mirrored the existing debates in Europe. This situation has not changed much in contemporary Haiti, where the political system remains incapable of articulating a national project that would employ the energies of all sectors in promoting development and remains focused on the appropriation of spoils for political loyalists.

Perhaps the most significant question in Haitian history remains that of the failure of the country's elite to ever create a nationwide development enterprise.[8] Despite the potential for significant commercial earnings from the production and export of cash crops, the state did little to foster the requisite political economy. While the building of common cause with slaves to obtain independence from the French might explain the bourgeoisie's initial reluctance to coerce the peasantry into a massive revival of the plantation economy, it does not explain the subsequent inability of the elite to foster, even given these parameters, the modicum of economic growth or expansion. A partial explanation has been identified by Trouillot, who points out that the sixty-year embargo slapped on Haiti by foreign powers in the nineteenth century for daring to overthrow its colonial masters stunted the development of the Haitian economy by making it more profitable for Haitian and foreign merchants to exploit loopholes in the embargo than to make investments in productive capital.[9] A broader explanation, however, may also lie in the sweep of Haitian history.

Historically, countries that have been able to create economic development and expansion have had either strongly cohesive national identities, such as the United States or the United Kingdom, or have had strong elites that have not, for reasons of ideology or race, hesitated to coerce other population groups within that country into providing the raw material for economic expansion. Guatemala and South Africa fall within the latter category. A third category involves countries such as India and Brazil, where strong national identities have allowed the elite to persuade the rest of the population to bear the costs of economic expansion.

None of these circumstances were to be found in Haiti shortly after independence. The shared affinity between the elite and the masses brought about by the independence struggle did not translate into a cohesive enough national identity. The freed slaves viewed the elite and its wealth with suspicion. Their egalitarian ideals did not sit well with the latter's quest for profit and capital accumulation. The elite, on the other hand, viewed the peasantry's lack of economic yearning and their *voudou* practices with utter disdain. These mutually negative perceptions prevented the formation of any national capital generation enterprise over the next two centuries. The same factors perhaps also accounted for the inability of the Haitian elite to persuade the masses to participate voluntarily in any type of national development. Caught in an almost self-perpetuating equilibrium of mistrust, Haiti's social sectors have historically had only one collective enterprise to their credit—the war of independence that created the country.

Given its chronic inability to develop either a national program or substantive politics, Haiti had seen a considerable devastation of its land and resources by the beginning of the twentieth century. Lack of investment and organization in agriculture, for instance, meant the absence of a system for adjudicating disputes over land titles and also of any long-term attempts to conserve or renew the soil. Little protection or incentive was provided to the peasantry to enable it to develop its land.[10] There were no rural services provided by the state to en-

able the farmers to capitalize on their natural inclination to form instant cooperative work gangs (or *konbite*)[11] to assist each other in times of distress.[12] The
practice of forming *konbite*, a residual albeit voluntary phenomenon from the
colonial days, indicated a strong communal spirit among the peasantry that,
while it may not have led to cooperative land ownership, certainly did augur
well for cooperative investing, marketing, and even profit sharing. These modes
of economic activity, if they had been fostered, would not just have led to rural
development but also have been compatible with peasant aversion to gross individual wealth accumulation.

Following the end of the Civil War, the United States had ended its participation in the Western embargo on Haiti and had recognized the country. U.S.
mercantile interest, waxing rapidly in Latin America and the Pacific, soon
turned toward Haiti, where the growing crisis over land and resources had also
led to a more rapid turnover in governments. The increased instability and levels of violence, and the Chase National Bank's interest in protecting its Haitian
interests, led the United States to intervene in Haiti in 1915. The intervention's
primary objective was to marketize the country's economy and create an outlet
for U.S. investment. The U.S. military commanders, in accordance with the
prevalent racial attitudes at the time, quickly identified the mulattoes among the
elite as their primary intermediaries. This was their first error as far as establishing a market economy was concerned. The system, as it existed, did not yet—
despite ongoing crises—offer the elite enough incentive for change. The U.S.
military commanders also decided that the peasantry was idle and had to be
forced into productive work. This assessment was, of course, quite incorrect.
U.S. attempts to press the peasantry into work gangs to build roads for a market
economy soon prompted a peasant revolt led by Charlemagne Peralte, who kept
American marines distracted from their nation-building enterprise for the better
part of the duration of the U.S. intervention.

U.S. commanders also concluded that the inability of the Haitian state to
spread its mantle throughout the countryside was one of the barriers to economic organization. This conclusion was incorrect, in that it was the balance
between Port-au-Prince and the various outposts of the state in the regional centers that had stayed all-out parasitic repression in the first place. In addition, the
Haitian army still retained the sense of having led its people to independence
and therefore of treating them with a modicum of respect.

U.S. commanders replaced this old army with the Garde Nationale d'Haiti,
which was trained to inflict its will more systematically and which later became
the dreaded Forces Armée d'Haiti (FAd'H). The new guard saw less reason to
be restrained when taxing the common Haitians. In fact, it saw itself as constituting a new praetorian elite and therefore undeserving of any kind of challenge
or balance.

In the aftermath of the U.S. departure from Haiti in 1934, the guard played
an increasingly prominent role in internal repression. Simultaneously, a small
largely black middle class spawned by U.S. military and economic projects
began to espouse views that often clashed with those of the traditional elite. In

the 1950s, this group generated a nationalist movement called Les Griots. Riding this wave of black nationalism, and also the backs of the repressive new army, a physician named François Duvalier ascended to the presidency in 1957. Like all nationalists and populists that preceded him, Duvalier began his presidency by targeting select members of the mulatto elite and even the Catholic Church that had traditionally supported the establishment. He drove several members of this gentry into exile. The remnants quickly adapted to the new order, which consisted of a cult of personality brutally and arbitrarily enforced at all levels of Haitian society by the notorious Volunteers for National Security, or *tontons macoutes*. Like his populist predecessors, Duvalier started out claiming to be able to emancipate the masses but instead created an even more oppressive and dysfunctional version of the system centered entirely on himself. Under his vicious rule Haiti's economy sank even further. And in spite of their apparent persecution, the merchants increased their share of the country's wealth. Social inequities became worse.

After his death in 1971, Duvalier was succeeded by his son Jean-Claude who had a milder temperament than his father. In many ways, he was the kind of benign despot who was seen as a force for growth in the developing world at that time. Foreign donors therefore conceived of a new strategy for Haiti, which was predicated on the assumption that Haiti's only remaining comparative advantage as an economy was the availability of labor at rock-bottom prices for assembling consumer goods primarily for the U.S. market. Under this strategy assembly industries, once established and flourishing, would form the engine for growth that would motor the rest of the economy.[13] International assistance, then, would contribute toward creating state institutions that could guarantee a stable and free market for the assembly manufacturers and providing infrastructure such as power plants and feeder roads for the assembly plants.

While this development strategy was based in sound economic theory, several things went wrong with its implementation.[14] First, to the extent that the strategy was not formulated on the basis of a broad popular or even an elite consensus, it could not mobilize the majority of the Haitians to make it work. Second, the Duvalier state was as lacking in social and economic roots[15] in the rest of Haitian society as its predecessors, even though it had access to a large and decentralized mechanism for inflicting terror in the form of the *tontons macoutes*.[16] Lacking roots, and therefore substance, the state did not make the effort to streamline and modernize itself to run a competitive and productive market economy to benefit the majority of Haitians, as had been anticipated by the foreign donors.[17] Third, Haitian elites who subcontracted and worked for the assembly manufacturers transferred all their earnings abroad and did not reinvest in Haiti to create a sustainable indigenous dynamic of savings, reinvestment, and new production. In the absence of a broader national framework, the elite saw little incentive for keeping their money within the country.[18] Also, while the Duvalier regime's nationalism had helped to create a tiny black middle class, it had done little to diminish the stranglehold of a few large mercantile families on the Haitian economy.[19] These families had little interest in increasing local production.[20] Hence, even assembly manufacturing did not reach its full potential.

An important apparent lapse in these development policies was to not take into account the historic exclusion of the peasantry by the ruling elite.[21] The general assumption was that, as the decline of Haitian agriculture continued to produce an outflow of migrants to the cities, they would be absorbed by the new industries. However, since the latter did not live up to their full potential, the unabsorbed migrants congregated in large slums in Port-au-Prince. Those peasants that still remained in the rural areas had little contact with the state and little access to services with which to develop their considerable artisanal and productive talents.

A focused effort to marketize this peasantry through devices that have been used elsewhere in the developing world, such as rural cooperatives and micro-credit, could have led to some positive engagement between the state and the peasantry. Given the fact that, despite years of massive migration, most Haitians still live rural lives, any engagement between the state and the peasantry might have allowed the former to move beyond parasitism. What was needed was a development strategy that *required* the fullest possible engagement between the state and its people, even if such a strategy made only partial economic sense in the short run, since such engagement might have prompted a more resilient political process better able to deal with internal tensions. Therefore, a state situated within a more substantial national framework might have fulfilled international expectations by providing stable support for a flourishing market that, among other industries, would also have allowed assembly manufacturing to take root.[22] Given the stark divergence of the elite and peasant conceptions of Haitian nationhood shortly after independence, the issue of the peasants' status was not just significant from the economic standpoint, but also from the perspective of defining the nature and the role of the Haitian state in the country's economy and society. Furthermore, enabling the peasants to acquire sustainable and profitable livelihoods in their localities would also have prevented the rapid growth of slums—which continue to be a major source of unrest—in the cities during the mid-1970s to mid-1980s.

Beginning in the early 1980s, a movement for change grew in both urban and rural areas that sought a sometimes violent overthrow of what was seen as a failed system.[23] This movement was led first by the Haitian version of the Roman Catholic liberation theology church, the *ti legliz*,[24] and then increasingly by the progressive members of a small middle class that had grown under the wings of foreign development assistance and *maquiladora* investment. Popular frustrations, accentuated by the massive numbers of Haitians living in slums, often led to violent incidents between the elite and the activists. The state, knowing no other form of response, reacted with brute force. The resulting domestic and international reaction caused Jean-Claude Duvalier to flee into exile in 1986. General Namphy took control of the government.

In the four years following the departure of Jean-Claude Duvalier, Haiti saw a number of coups and ineffective governments as the elite reacted to the popular upsurge. Clearly, Haiti's wholly inadequate political process could neither manage the economic development program of the 1980s nor the consequences that ensued from its failure.

A potentially important moment in Haitian history, perhaps the first opportunity to generate a truly national enterprise since the struggle for independence, was lost in 1987 when a National Congress of Democratic Movements representing Haitians of all stripes—leaders of the peasantry, the business elite, religious organizations, human rights groups, and others—was convened to assist in drafting a post-Duvalier constitution. With their totalitarian repression, the Duvaliers had achieved what other more noble causes had failed to achieve—a uniting of all of Haiti's sectors as had not been seen since the ceremony at Bois-Caiman in 1791 that had launched the country's war for independence. The Congress concluded with support for Haiti's new 1987 Constitution, a Provisional Electoral Council to conduct the next elections, and a plan to keep the various sectors mobilized and coordinated in support of democracy.

Yet this opportunity was soon lost. Haiti's friends in the region, for reasons that are still unclear, chose to ignore what was clearly a democratic and progressive movement, and perhaps the best bet to promote both free markets and democracy, and supported instead the promises of General Namphy that he could guarantee a stable democratic transition and hold fair elections. When the elections were eventually held, the Congress's candidate, Gerard Gourgue, was expected to win. General Namphy's thugs, however, carried out a massacre at a polling station that led to the annulment of the elections. This tragedy was both poignant and ironic. If the Congress had won, the elections might have set the stage for the first significant, and more moderate and progressive, reorientation of the country since its independence. However, the massacre convinced most Haitians that more extreme steps were called for and set the stage for a dynamic of response and counterresponse between the elite and the masses. The lack of strong external support for the Congress was also clearly a failure of preventive action on the part of international actors, in that an opportunity was lost to preempt the conflict that followed and to save the hundreds of millions of dollars spent on keeping peace in its aftermath.

The failed elections of 1987 were followed by rigged elections in 1988 that prompted the international community, with monitors from the UN, the Organization of American States (OAS), the Caribbean Community (CARICOM), and the United States, to intervene to guarantee free and fair elections in 1990—the first of their kind in Haitian history.[25] A former World Bank official, Marc Bazin, headed a coalition of progressive parties and was viewed as a likely winner. Instead, to the elite's chagrin, he lost to the popular priest Jean-Bertrand Aristide, who had proposed a popular upsurge or Lavalas—literally "flood"—against corrupt governance. Traditional political parties affiliated with the elite, however, retained control of the parliament.

The loose movement that coalesced under Aristide's leadership and the Lavalas banner during this period offered a comprehensive cross section of pro-democracy trends in Haiti. It included venerable peasant movements such as the

Hinche-based Mouvman Papaye de Paysan; the remnants of the 1987 CONA-
COM; some representatives of a still small but increasingly larger and progressive middle class; a wide range of human rights and pro-democracy organizations; and a host of discordant "popular organizations" constituted primarily of
slum-based and unemployed migrants. To the extent that they were subsumed
under Aristide's fiery rhetoric and messianic persona, to which they willingly
submitted order to ensure victory in the 1990 elections, Lavalas was seen as a
monolith by many in the international community, and the primary political
split in Haiti, and hence the need for dialogue was also unfortunately seen as
being between Lavalas on the one hand and a handful of small opposition parties representing the traditional elite on the other.

On assuming the presidency, Aristide and his supporters appropriated the
term Lavalas for their government. In the nine months of the first Aristide government in 1991, clashes between the parliament and the presidency were frequent. However, this was not parliamentary politics of a conventional sort. The
Lavalas government and its opponents both brought their supporters out into the
streets to push their positions. This was a frightening time for Haiti's traditional
elite. Many interpreted Aristide's fiery rhetoric regarding the uprooting of the
old system as calling for their physical extermination. However, they only reacted to this situation and did not take measures to challenge Aristide by reaching out to the population on their own or by building agendas and strategies of a
progressive nature. The technocrats in the Aristide government, on the other
hand, were able to come up with an economic plan that won the approval of
international financial institutions.[26] The plan sought to streamline government,[27] collect taxes efficiently, and redefine the role of the state as a net pro-
vider of services and not as a net extractor of value. However, the government
failed to put this plan to public debate, thus forgoing the opportunity to build
consensus around its key tenets. Instead, rowdy demonstrators called for compliance with the Lavalas agenda.[28] For their part, many in the elite saw the plan
as being little more than a vendetta against their interests. In the absence of
attempts to construct a broader, more sober consensus, the plan became a victim of Haiti's perennial theatre of violence and so did the progressive agenda of
the first Aristide government. Fearing extinction, Haiti's elite and the armed
forces allied with it responded with a coup in September 1991.

It is important to note that Aristide was catapulted to power in the 1990
elections not on the basis of a popular desire for the institutions and norms of
democracy but as the vanguard of a new regime that would fundamentally trans-
form the polity in a radical fashion. These expectations, reflected in Aristide's
"flood" rhetoric, contradicted the gradualist approach of both those members of
the Lavalas alliance who belonged to the small but growing middle class and the
few progressive elements among the traditional political and economic elite. The
elected government of 1990–1991, therefore, embodied a fundamental contradiction. It sought to address popular demands for overwhelming social and economic change through the forms and institutions of electoral democracy, which
traditionally postdate such change and are ill-adapted to rapid and radical trans-

formation. This contradiction was perpetuated in 1994 when Aristide was restored to power.

Many have argued that both Gerard Gourgue and Marc Bazin, unburdened by Aristide's apocalyptic visions of cleansing floods and fires and the historical memories these evoked of Dessalines's pogroms, might have been better able to persuade the Haitian elite to accept a progressive program of change. While this question cannot be answered hypothetically, it is quite clear that both the 1987 Congress and the ensuing elections, as well as the economic plan of the first Lavalas government, constituted significant opportunities for Haitians to move forward together as a nation. In both instances, however, Haiti's friends and neighbors displayed great ambiguity toward these historic moments and the moments were soon lost. Subsequently, numerous efforts have been carried out in vain by the international community to re-create the possibilities that these moments represented.

The International Response to Conflict in Haiti

After taking power, the military regime embarked on a campaign of systematic slaughter of Lavalas activists. This campaign, and the resulting outflow of refugees, prompted a concerted international response. The response of the two regional organizations of which Haiti is a member—the OAS and CARICOM—was especially vigorous, spurred by both the OAS's firm post–Cold War commitment to the consolidation of democracy in the Western Hemisphere[29] and the crucial role played by both organizations in facilitating and monitoring the election won by Aristide. The OAS rapidly suspended all aid to Haiti except humanitarian assistance. When the OAS delegation negotiating with the military regime was ordered to leave the country, the organization called on members to impose a trade embargo.

In autumn 1992, the UN authorized a joint OAS/UN envoy to negotiate with the military government.[30] The coup leader, General Cedras, accepted a proposal to establish a joint OAS/UN civilian mission (MICIVIH) to monitor human rights in Haiti and agreed to work under the leadership of the OAS/UN Special Envoy toward reviving Haiti's fledgling democratic institutions.

Efforts to engage the Haitian military in dialogue with Aristide, however, made little overall progress. On 16 June 1993, the Security Council placed an oil and arms embargo upon Haiti. Cedras then indicated a willingness to negotiate. The resulting agreement, signed at Governors Island in New York, committed Cedras to retire from government and allow Aristide's return to Haiti. In the interim, Aristide was to work with the Haitian parliament to restore the normal functioning of Haiti's institutions while the UN was to provide a small peacekeeping force to help modernize the armed forces and assist in the creation of a new civilian police force.

Initial signs were promising, with the Haitian parliament ratifying Aristide's appointment of Robert Malval as prime minister and the Security Council lifting the embargo on Haiti and authorizing a United Nations Mission in Haiti (UNMIH). The promise quickly turned sour, however, when a UNMIH deployment was met by hostile demonstrations, prompting the withdrawal of the deployment and the flight of most members of MICIVIH. The Security Council rapidly reimposed the arms and oil embargo and instituted a naval blockade.[31] On 15 October, the Justice Minister in the Malval cabinet was assassinated. By early 1994 the few remaining MICIVIH personnel reported an alarming increase in human rights violations. Facing intransigence from the military government, the Security Council imposed further sanctions, to which the regime responded by appointing a "provisional" president who formally expelled MICIVIH from the country in July 1994.

By 1994, the deteriorating situation in Haiti had loosed a surge of refugees on American shores, putting domestic pressure on the Clinton administration. The upshot of resulting U.S. activism was a UN Security Council resolution authorizing the formation of a U.S.-led "multi-national force" (MNF) to facilitate the departure from Haiti of the military leadership and the restoration of the legitimate authorities.

In mid-September 1994 President Clinton finally declared all diplomatic measures exhausted and ordered the MNF to use force to remove the military regime. Faced with this impending invasion, the Cedras regime appealed for a last-minute intercession. After skillful negotiation by a distinguished American team, Haiti's military leaders agreed to resign subject to an amnesty from the Haitian parliament. As a result, the MNF was able to move into Haiti on 19 September without opposition.[32] President Aristide returned to Haiti on 15 October 1994. In 1995, the MNF handed over the task of peacekeeping to UNMIH.

Subsequently, in 1998, after three years of peacekeeping, the UN Security Council reduced the UN role in Haiti to supporting the further development of a civilian police force. In 2000 both the OAS/UN human rights monitoring mission and UN peacekeeping in Haiti were brought to a close. A new UN civilian mission, MICAH, commenced with a mandate to assist Haiti in the areas of justice, security, and human rights. This mission was further replaced in 2002 by a civilian OAS mission with a similar mandate and with the additional role of brokering an end to the ongoing political impasses that are detailed below.

Assessment of the International Response to the Crisis in Haiti

Despite numerous criticisms, both the initial international response to Haiti's immediate crisis and the subsequent peacekeeping operations accomplished their key goals. Haiti's elected government was restored and a civilian police force created to replace the repressive army, all without losing a single peacekeeper.[33]

The key deficiencies in the international response to Haiti that became manifest shortly thereafter were not in the conduct of the peacekeeping operation in Haiti but in the international strategy for understanding and dealing with Haiti's long-term political impasse. When Aristide was restored, so was the deadlock that had characterized his previous government. Part of the package for his restoration should have been the institution of a comprehensive multisector dialogue on key elements of political and economic reform, chaired by Aristide as the president but facilitated by Haitian civil society and observed by the international community. In the absence of such an effort, Haiti's weak political institutions remained deadlocked along class and factional lines. The international community did not comprehend that the real divisions in Haiti are not between political parties: the political process does not accurately or substantively represent and embody the country's interest groups. There were no precedents or entities for facilitating gradual change through consensus; this was neither the focus of Aristide's rhetoric nor that of his opponents in the military and the oligarchy.

International actors—led by the European Union and the United States in this instance—have provided some assistance for building democratic practices into Haiti's nascent institutions. Political parties as well as parliamentarians have received training programs targeted at building their understanding of democratic political processes. Civic education programs targeted at inculcating democratic civic virtues have also been launched among the population at large. These tutelary approaches, however, have had little lasting impact. The population demands the radical redress of its more immediate plight and sees little gain from gradual democratization, while the political elite focuses on maintaining control of the limited state institutions.

The divisions between Aristide and his opponents are also reflected in the gradual inability of the new Haitian National Police, created after he abolished the army in 1995, to maintain law and order in a neutral or effective manner. Despite initial successes, primarily in rooting out corruption among its own ranks, the police had a dismal record of following up on crimes, particularly where high-profile political assassinations were concerned. While during a political crisis in early 1999 the police did remain neutral and maintain public order, the protracted political deadlock and the ensuing suspension of international aid have badly affected the police force. Some officers have become involved in drug traffic as Haiti has become the favorite transshipment point for Colombian traffickers, handling 8 percent of all cocaine entering the United States. Drug-related corruption extends through all levels of government and drug-funded construction has become Port-au-Prince's predominant economic activity. Partisan behavior by the police, often under political pressure, has grown. In the aftermath of the first round of parliamentary elections in 2000, a number of opposition candidates were arrested on dubious charges of fomenting political violence. After local and international protest, they were released. The continuing high crime rates and increasing politicization of the police have undermined confidence in the possibility of a democratic and neutral state that is able to provide all sectors with basic security. As a result, the popular yearning for a return to stronger, possibly authoritarian, government has grown.

It is noteworthy that the police would have been less subject to political manipulation had it been better resourced and trained. In the aftermath of Aristide's restoration, however, the bulk of international assistance went toward the actual cost of peacekeeping and the revival of the moribund Haitian economy and not toward the maintenance of a viable police force. Ironically, most of the economic assistance provided by external actors to Haiti remains unused, as a political system populated by politicians fearful for their lives has continued to be deadlocked and incapable of delivering the design and implementation of economic programs. Through practices tantamount to racketeering, the state apparatus has continued to reap benefits from the limited economic activity for those in authority. The line between the private and public sector has been blurred, with both sectors often controlled by the same elements.[34] Debates over privatization mask narrower factional disputes over control of a few state-owned enterprises.

Haiti's 1987 constitution bars two consecutive presidential terms. Hence, in accordance with his promise at Governors Island to assist in building Haiti's frail institutions, Aristide agreed to step down as president at the end of his first term in 1996. His supporters, however, argued that since he had spent most of this term in exile, he should be allowed a second term. The international community informally backed the constitutional position. It helped to finance and monitor the presidential elections in 1995 that led Rene Preval to succeed Aristide as president and has assisted with subsequent national and local elections. While the peaceful, democratic transfer of power from Aristide to Preval through elections was a historic accomplishment, the first of its kind in the country's history, Haitian institutions subsequently became deadlocked.

The governments of both Aristide and Preval had agreed to implement the economic plan first conceived at the beginning of the Aristide presidency in 1991, with the support of international financial institutions. Key elements of this plan were a restructuring and privatization of the small and corrupt public sector and a series of other economic reforms designed to boost the confidence of both Haitian and international entrepreneurs. Aristide argued that this reform package would only benefit a small elite and cause great suffering to the majority of the population. His opposition to this plan from mid-1995 onward halted key components of the reform process. Neither Aristide nor his newly formed Fanmi Lavalas Party sought to promote a multisector dialogue on an alternative path to economic reform that could have addressed what might have been genuine concerns regarding the stringent demands made by international financial institutions. The precoup Lavalas movement had, by contrast, displayed a talent for generating creative solutions and compromises through dialogue. A key difference was that many talented negotiators and functionaries in the Lavalas movement had grown disillusioned with Aristide's assumption of a messianic persona and had either formed splinter parties or moved into the private or nonprofit sectors, leaving Haiti altogether.

The standoff over economic reform was complicated by a dispute over the legislative and municipal elections of 6 April 1997. The electoral process was halted before the second round of voting.[35] In June 1997, Prime Minister Rosny Smarth resigned in frustration, further paralyzing the government.[36] Successive attempts to appoint a prime minister foundered over splits between the two major factions into which Lavalas legislators in parliament had split over Aristide's policies and persona—the anti-Aristide Organization of People in Struggle (OPL) and the pro-Aristide Fanmi Lavalas. In March 1999, after concerted facilitation efforts by international mediators and some civic organizations, certain opposition parties reached an informal accord with the president for appointing an interim prime minister and a new Electoral Council and for holding new legislative elections. The costly consequence of this political wrangling was to delay large amounts of international development assistance. The deadlock also caused an almost complete dissipation of the popular energies and enthusiasm generated by the democracy movement of the late 1980s. Despite international efforts, the Haitian political process thus appeared largely incapable of addressing internal tensions.

In May and June 2000 legislative and municipal elections were finally held to break this deadlock. In the first round, 55 to 60 percent of the electorate voted, the majority for Fanmi Lavalas, perhaps in the hope that having the presidency and parliament under the same party would break the political deadlock. A dispute quickly arose over electoral procedure. International observers demanded a recount for certain seats in the Senate before second-round voting. The Haitian government refused, saying that it could not control the decisions of the Provisional Electoral Council. The latter defended its vote-count formula, saying that it had improvised under highly imperfect circumstances. Controversy grew with the flight of the Council's chairman, who claimed that his life had been threatened. When the Haitian government decided to proceed with the second round of voting without recounting the first round, the OAS withdrew its observer mission. Shortly thereafter, the United States suspended assistance to the country's police force. The opposition parties declared the onset of authoritarianism.

After several failed attempts by the international community to resolve the issue of the vote count in a manner that both Fanmi Lavalas and the opposition parties would find satisfactory, the Haitian government proceeded to conduct the presidential election in November 2000 despite international reservations. All opposition parties boycotted the election, and, as the same flawed Provisional Electoral Council conducted it, the international community did not recognize its results. Haiti's donors declared that they were suspending all official aid to the country until a solution to the political impasse had been found that was acceptable to all parties involved and that future aid would be disbursed through NGOs.

Recently, the OAS has resumed, through its Secretary General Cesar Gaviria, its political role in the country, whereby it has been attempting to mediate between Aristide, who was reelected president in 2000 in a controversial election boycotted by the opposition and an umbrella grouping of opposition parties. However, these and other international attempts at mediation, while laudable and partly successful, have rarely sought to engage the full spectrum of Haitian society so as to keep the primary political protagonists on their toes and accountable for their words and actions. To the extent that all political actors in Haiti make their claims on behalf of the Haitian population, the latter might be in a better position to call them to order than the international community alone. At the time of writing in 2003, the OAS had made little headway in ending the political impasse between the president and the opposition.

This cyclical dynamic of Haitian obstinacy and international reaction could have been arrested at a much earlier stage, when political deadlock first ensued in 1996–1997, through a more creative application of international facilitation efforts to encourage Haitian civil society, particularly the Catholic and Protestant Churches, to play a more active role in bridging political divides. Instead, international mediators undertook informal efforts to negotiate between Aristide and the primary breakaway Lavalas faction, the OPL, and left aside both other political actors as well as key elements of civil society. These mediation efforts did not yield significant or quick results and often left all parties pointing at external actors as unnecessarily meddlesome in Haitian affairs. It is important to note that despite Aristide's incumbency as president, Haiti's small middle class remains apprehensive of runaway populism. Aristide won the popular vote in the parliamentary and presidential elections of 2000 but lacks the confidence of the business and middle classes, a minority whose entrepreneurial and managerial talent is essential for Haiti's economic revival. Elections are not the central issue; the underlying problem is the different social sectors' near total lack of confidence in each others' objectives and intentions.

A starting point for confidence building would be to work toward consensus, with Haiti's small but increasingly active civil society as the intermediary, on a few pragmatic issues whereby the state can direct its limited resources and energies toward providing security and primary capital such as roads, education, and microcredit lending. The provision of such goods should benefit all classes and sectors and allow for real growth in the Haitian economy. Discourse centered on such public goods may also allow for Haiti's national debates to move from the divisive discourse of wealth redistribution to that of more equitable opportunities for wealth creation. Initiatives to provide appropriately targeted credit and convert informal holdings to formal titles have led peasants in parts of the country both to revive and expand market production and could be encouraged. International donors could encourage cooperative farming in order to eliminate the inefficiencies of scale generated by smallholder farming.

In this context, it is important to note that localized schemes have helped to bring parts of the country's sizeable informal economy into the economic mainstream by giving informal entrepreneurs titles to their assets and registering them so that they are eligible for assistance, such as small loans and credit, on easy terms. Prominent examples include a plan developed jointly by the Aristide government and by the Center for Free Enterprise and Democracy with the assistance of economist Hernando de Soto to formalize informal property holdings, and the significant expansion of its loan portfolio by one of the country's largest commercial banks, Sogebank, to include micro-entrepreneurs.[37] Economic purists may argue that this is an inefficient, small-scale approach to poverty reduction, but micro-entrepreneurism has proven to be a workable approach to long-term growth and may be a more realistic option in a postconflict economy than schemes for attracting large industry.

The discourse on public goods could also focus on the country's moribund judicial system, which has not benefited from well-meaning international attempts to reform it (such attempts reportedly having been carried out without any regard for Haiti's special circumstances). Haiti has recently experienced a surge in decentralized social violence. Disputes over land property have increasingly been resolved, in the absence of a functioning judiciary, through violence. In an effort to build nonviolent dispute resolution skills, the government's land reform agency, INARA, has tried to incorporate informal arbitration in its programs, with modest results. Jacques-Edouard Alexis, until recently the prime minister of Haiti, has expressed his interest in a national conflict resolution program to develop appropriate skills among the leadership. Civic actors have also proposed a system that involves traveling courts, whereby judges and clerks spend a day in a locality dealing with disputes before moving on to the next district. In addition, civil society organizations of all stripes have joined a growing chorus for administrative and political decentralization so that the endless deadlocks among the elite in Port-au-Prince do not stymie creative energies at the community level. Both alternative arbitration and decentralization could form important elements of a multisector consensus.

Some of the best prospects for building such a consensus in Haiti may lie with civil society. For instance, the informal 1999 accord that paved the way for elections in 2000, and which also produced an interim government with ministers drawn from both Fanmi Lavalas and opposition camps, arose partly from small-scale efforts toward multisector dialogue supported by the International Peace Academy. This dialogue also assisted in the formation of an autonomous civil society group, the National Council for Electoral Observation, which successfully promoted voter education before the parliamentary elections in 2000 and then performed credibly its primary function of electoral observation. It also convened Fanmi Lavalas and its opponents in informal meetings prior to the elections to obtain guarantees from all sides to ensure a peaceful electoral process. Given the overall level of political tension, the elections were remarkably free of violence. Subsequently, this dialogue also yielded the Civil Society Initiative, which facilitated negotiations to end the deadlock between Aristide and the opposition in January 2001 and which, for the first time, involved both the mainstream Catholic and Protestant Churches in a joint facilitation role. While these negotiations deadlocked, civil society groups were able to ensure that when they did restart, the protagonists resumed discussions from their last known positions rather than reinventing the game all over again. Members of the Initiative have shuttled, with modest success, not just between politicians of various stripes, but also between the Aristide camp and key sectors such as business and the middle class. As a result, Aristide is now backing, for instance, key private sector initiatives to marketize the informal economy. Members of the Initiative have also started, with backing from the European Union, a number of multisector policy dialogues aimed at generating concrete proposals for government action. At the time of writing, however, the Aristide government has accused the Initiative of forming a coalition to topple it, and hence limited its future role as an intermediary.

A hopeful sign is the continued resilience of some long-standing grassroots organizations, which provided the original backbone for the Lavalas movement. These include the Mouvman Papaye Paysan, Haiti's oldest peasant movement, and the Assembly of Popular Organization Power (PROP) that had first organized slum dwellers into a political force on behalf of Aristide. These groups have begun to develop issue-specific agendas critical of the policies of La Fanmi Lavalas. Church movements are also reconfiguring their political alignments. A growing evangelical movement, which subscribes to the populist right-of-center values similar to those held by their Guatemalan counterparts, has begun to challenge both the political establishment and the Catholic Church. The Catholic Church's Commission for Justice and Peace, one of the strongest defenders of human rights in Haiti and long a standard-bearer for Lavalas, has begun to take an increasingly independent stance against human rights violations by all sides. Although the industrial and professional sectors remain small, unions such as the National Federation of Haitian Educators (CNEH) and the Organization of Haitian Industrial Workers (OGITH) have begun to take more consistent and independent positions on key issues. This political activity augurs well for wider democratic participation and representation.

Focused discussion on ways to achieve pragmatic compromises between different sectors is necessary to develop and implement a process of economic and political reform. Several steps can be taken to promote this. Policy dialogues of the kind initially developed by the Civil Society Initiative may assist political discourse in moving beyond one of grievance to an articulation of concrete policy differences and options. They may also serve to build trust and confidence between the various sectors. Haiti clearly demonstrates that, in an atmosphere of fear and recrimination, intersector relations must improve before elections or other trappings of democratic governance can be devised or else electoral or other democratic outcomes will not win the support of those sectors that feel threatened. This does not imply that newly democratic governments should not be launched through electoral means. Elections, however, are only one element in a wider process to alter intersector relations and create genuine participation.

Recently, several civic organizations have proposed the establishment of a center that, with international support, could assist politicians and political parties in acquiring and deploying some of the basic tools of democratic political discourse including coalition building and cooperative drafting of legislation.

In addition to the above, alternative forms of political participation that aid the process of institution building are needed *until* the formal institutions acquire the desired capacity. These alternative forms of participation can be generated within the context of existing policies. For instance, the implementation of specific international initiatives to address the problems of development and the environment in Haiti could be accompanied by broad-based dialogues among the sectors most likely to be affected by them.[38] A process of identifying common gains and of mutual guarantees could be a very powerful tool for building lasting interaction. Such interaction could eventually form the basis for consensual national frameworks for social and economic action. Several international projects of this kind have recently unfolded. A USAID project in Platon Fond Jean-Noel has constituted a federation of eighteen thousand farmers into twenty-five cooperatives to grow and directly market Haitian Bleu coffee for export to U.S. markets, a scheme that has fostered both enterprise and environmental conservation.

Popular participation may also provide the key to better policing. In an effort to reduce police corruption and bring policing closer to the communities, a number of external actors, particularly Canada, have sought to institute community policing practices. However, tense social and intersector relations, land disputes, and vigilantism have hampered the potential for such policing.

Perhaps the greatest threat to law and order remains the increasing use of Haiti as a transshipment point by drug traffickers for drugs flowing from Colombia to the United States. The narco-economy provides both a disincentive to legitimate state activity and an incentive to illegitimate activity—supporting a web of civic corruption. Given the overall dereliction of the Haitian state and the political system, and the international consensus on withholding official aid until the political impasse is broken, the only short-term solutions to controlling the problem lie among Haiti's neighbors. One possibility is to engage private professional security firms from among Haiti's neighbors to perform interdiction duties immediately outside Haiti's territorial waters. Another less politically cumbersome proposal might be to make an exception to the general policy of withholding official assistance by training and resourcing Haiti's small customs force, which has reputedly performed heroically in daunting circumstances.

Political violence has caused some of Haiti's most promising talent to flee the country. Some have suggested creating a special security force, drawn from the police, for protecting senior government officials, leaders of political parties, and other high-profile political personalities. However, this carries the risk of becoming a "praetorian guard." One short-term tactic for combating political impunity could be the revival of a domestic version of the type of human rights monitoring and observation carried out by international groups, including MICIVIH, in the early 1990s. Representatives of civic organizations could accompany personalities considered at particular risk because of their views or political affiliation as a deterrent to attack.

Key Conclusions

Haiti's current crisis demonstrates that there must be change at the level of intersector relations in the country before the formal processes of democracy can be stabilized. The mere existence of such processes does not guarantee the success of democracy. Such a change in intersector relations can be brought about by means of dialogue, as happened in Guatemala and as is being proposed by some for Haiti, or it can be externally enforced as is the case in Bosnia-Herzegovina. However, without this change, the results of elections and other apparently democratic outcomes will not enjoy legitimacy with those sectors that feel threatened.

The Haiti case provides some specific pointers toward how the international community can foster appropriate intersector relations in a society in order to stabilize the formal processes of democracy:

- First, while the primary political factions clearly need to be an important focus of efforts to build and sustain peace in any society, they cannot be the only focus. Such a focus needs to be embedded in a broader process of dialogue and consultation with representatives of different social sectors so as to generate a consensus on policy parameters that is not easily shaken by short-term calculations of the primary factions.

- Second, no postconflict society can deliver immediately on the high expectations that its members may have of democratic government. As attempts are made to stabilize the situation, crises of "social patience" may disrupt the fragile peace. In this context, in addition to ensuring that the most elementary needs of the population are satisfied, local and international authorities should also ensure maximum participation by civic and community representatives in the development and implementation of initiatives designed for their benefit. This participation will not only engender a sense of forward momentum and hope, thereby alleviating some of the crisis of "social patience," but also create a sounder basis for democracy by encouraging local organization centered on such participation.

- Third, the rule of law and the availability of security and justice for the common person are clearly important determinants of the degree to which democracy can emerge and be stabilized in a postconflict situation. Should political factions continue to dominate the political discourse through fear and impunity, then politics will be deadlocked along the lines of their often contradictory interests. The emergence of other voices, however, will open new spaces for compromise. Hence, the establishment of the rule of law, including through interim means such as community policing and alternate dispute resolution, should be a top priority for international and local actors.

- Fourth, the type of economic strategy in a postconflict situation that may support the emergence of viable local political processes often may not coincide with conventional understandings of sound strategies. The demands of fiscal discipline and rapid inflows and outflows of capital may generate stresses and competition of the type that immature political systems are unable to handle. On the other hand, development schemes that are not initially capital intensive, but rather centered on providing the simple means (title, credit, etc.) through which common persons can engage in entrepreneurial activity may generate greater longer-term wherewithal for political stability. Persons engaged in sound productive activity may be less susceptible to the short-term blandishments of various factions.

- Fifth, international efforts should take into account the possibility of significant variation between local and international understandings of the factors that may lead to sustainable peace both before and after conflict. If local understandings of these matters have emerged through open and participatory processes (as has happened on several occasions during recent years in Haiti) or reflect agreement between key sectors, then they should be honored, even if they differ from preferred international courses of action. Only through a genuine process of interaction and learning will the key local actors appreciate the finer elements of democratic participation.
- Sixth, the ideological polarization generated by extended periods of conflict can significantly erode the ability of key actors in a society to bargain concretely around specific policy issues. Great emphasis should be placed on reviving or strengthening this ability.

These arguments also point toward a different road map for conceptualizing and implementing external actions, including those by the United States, for creating and sustaining peace in societies ridden by conflict.

Viable Political Processes Are Central to Peace

While countries may have had long-standing economic, social, or environmental problems that could raise the level of internal tension, the actual eruption of mass violence is contingent on the extent to which existing political processes can manage these tensions. Hence, the key to creating or sustaining peace within a country lies not with economic or humanitarian assistance but with reviving or strengthening political processes that can successfully manage current and future tensions. In the absence of such processes, other kinds of international assistance may even increase the levels of conflict.

Fostering Peace Is Conducive to Long-Term U.S. National Security

Usually when mass violence erupts in vulnerable countries it does not directly threaten U.S. national interests. Even when there is a threat it may only be brief. However, given the increasingly porous nature of national boundaries, such violence may occasionally lead to longer-term threats. Haiti sent waves of refugees to U.S. shores in the 1990s; now it is one of the most significant points of transshipment of drugs into the United States. Similarly, the failure of interested parties, including the United States, to support a viable political process in Afghanistan in the 1990s has now created a significant threat for international peace and security. It is quite likely that without the muscular U.S.-led intervention in Bosnia and Kosovo in 1995 and 1999, respectively, the region would now face greater political instability from radicalized minorities on the one hand and outlaw regimes on the other. Hence, across the board, it is in the U.S. interest to support the revival of viable political processes in weak countries torn by violent conflict or internal tensions. However, to the extent that such conflict is only likely to threaten U.S. security on an uneven basis, this support can be of a very specific and focused nature, rather than open-ended "nation building" that many policymakers fear.

External Interventions Should Focus on Reviving Participatory Political Processes and the Rule of Law

Such focused and specific assistance should involve two components: first, the reestablishment of rule of law and basic security in a manner that allows open political activity to resume and viable political processes to emerge; second, the rapid identification, through dialogue among all relevant parties, of a common consensus on the parameters of a truly participatory and resilient political process. It is critical that this common consensus should be based not just on the views of the leaders of the parties to conflict, but also of representatives of civic organizations and key social sectors such as religious groups (accords signed between leaders are often based on tactical considerations and rarely represent lasting and deep-seated consensus on their own). It is also critical that these two components precede the holding of internationally sponsored elections; otherwise, the continuation of intimidation and the absence of deep-seated political consensus will lead to an affirmation of the fault lines of conflict through the electoral exercise (as happened in Bosnia in 1996). These components should also precede the provision of large-scale assistance for reconstruction. In the absence of a common understanding of the needs of the country, parties to conflict will resume fighting over the division of such assistance (as happened in Somalia and as has happened in Haiti). These important lessons have clearly been integrated into the international approach toward the rebuilding of Afghanistan where, instead of decreeing a blueprint for governance in Afghanistan through the Bonn agreement in 2001, the UN and the United States supported a two-year transitional process—currently ongoing—through which the Afghans develop their own governmental framework. This process has involved the used of traditional means such as the *loya jirga*—a national conclave of traditional and local leaders nominated by their communities and summoned with their consent by the national governing authority of the moment—and has not been limited to the dominant warlords alone. The participation of a wide group of stakeholders has been sought and achieved. Some critics have argued that as the Afghans have taken time to develop their own judiciary, police, army, and other institutions, the rapid reconstruction of Afghanistan has lagged. These criticisms are countered by the discreet but muscular U.S. and international security presence that continues to underpin the transitional Afghan government, and by the fact that the notoriously independent Afghans have not yet coalesced their frustrations against the international presence in their country. More positively, the new Afghan government has acquired significant capacity for developing its own projects and for lobbying for resources to support them. As the old adage goes, a man who receives a fish on a plate has been fed for a day, but one who learns how to fish has been fed for life.

Peace Operations Should Support the Building of Political Consensus and the Restoration of Rule of Law

The plans for any international peace operation (whether it is characterized as "peacekeeping" or "peacemaking" or "monitoring") and for its "exit strategy" should be drawn up to focus on the two components identified above. The civilian side of the operation should prioritize the building of the necessary political consensus. The military side should focus on the rapid restoration of the rule of law. Neither side will be able to carry out its task without active participation from all levels of indigenous leadership—from the national to the local. In this context, it should be noted that the local institutions that provide both genuine political participation and the rule of law may differ greatly from their Western counterparts. In Afghanistan, for instance, local clan leaderships and tribal elders have traditionally provided both genuine and significant political participation as well as rule of law, and sustainable peace in that country will require substantive and continued engagement with these leaders.

Exit Strategies Should Center on Revival of Local Political Processes

A tight focus on the facilitating political consensus and on establishing the rule of law will allow external actors to work within the frame of a definite and achievable "exit strategy." The other aspects of reconstruction—economic, social, environmental, and so on—can be directly handled through negotiations between the newly revived and secure local political process on the one hand and relevant international institutions such as the World Bank, the United Nations Environment Programme, or the UN Fund for Women on the other. These aspects need not be included within the parameters of a peace operation or any other type of time-bound intervention by external actors. The task of "nation building" belongs fundamentally to the nations concerned. In this context, all indications to date are that the types of "transitional administrations" that have been established by international authorities in a number of countries in recent years, where external administrators run entire polities and economies, may stabilize the situation in the short term but may not enable countries to stand on their own feet in the long run. Once again, this important lesson has been incorporated into the UN's "light footprint" approach in Afghanistan, where instead of creating a transitional administration the UN has deployed a small mission to support a reconstruction process led in all aspects by an Afghan government. Similarly, at the time of writing, many analysts were proposing that instead of creating a transitional administration in Iraq led by the U.S. military or by an international body, the United States support instead—in a manner similar to Afghanistan—the formation of an Iraqi interim authority that would lead a two-year transitional process toward a long-term framework for governance. With strong international support, this authority would conduct a national dialogue to build consensus around such a framework and also ensure that Iraqis—and not foreigners—were seen as leading the reconstruction of a significant Middle Eastern state.

External Interventions in Internal Conflicts Should Be Based Only on a Common Strategy

A focused international effort to support the emergence of a viable political process can only work if all concerned external actors operate within the framework of a common strategy. It could be disruptive, for instance, if a large sum of money were made available for reconstruction by one international institution at the same time as another international institution is attempting to facilitate a consensus on the nature of the political process. The parties to conflict, instead of focusing on the long term, may turn their attention to squabbling over how best to use the money without first having developed the political capacity to make such decisions on their own. If international actors then step in and resolve the dispute by imposing a solution, they could undermine the long-term viability of the country's political process and also add years to their "exit strategy." Hence, a common strategy is critical for international actors. However, while most actors appreciate the importance of coordination, no one ever submits to the imposition of such coordination. Most attempts at mutual coordination rarely amount to being more than a degree of information sharing. Under these circumstances, the mapping of a common strategy could be greatly enhanced through the nomination of an authoritative and credible facilitator—a high representative of the international community— for each instance of violent conflict, whose primary task will be to ensure that key actors adjust the timing and extent of their interventions to allow the emergence of rule of law and viable political processes prior to the provision of other types of assistance. For instance, the Special Representative of the UN Secretary General has ably performed this role in Afghanistan. In the near future, the United States may wish to propose the nomination of such a facilitator, preferably a credible international diplomat with strong standing in the Islamic world, for the task of ensuring coordinated international support for a viable political process in Iraq.

External Interventions Should Draw upon Knowledge of a Country's Political Evolution

A key ingredient of any planning aimed at ensuring sustainable peace in a society is a thorough knowledge of the large-scale political evolution of that society through the course of history and of the factors that have driven this evolution. This knowledge need not be of the detailed scholarly variety that focuses on sociological or anthropological minutiae but nevertheless needs to be thorough and grounded in experience gleaned from previous international work in the relevant countries. One of the key tasks of the international facilitator proposed above could be to ensure that relevant international actors have direct access to the collective wisdom of researchers and experts that may have focused on particular countries. Students of Haiti, for instance, have long known that the very circumstances under which the country became independent, as well as subsequent developments, have created a severe social chasm within that country that has constantly derailed its politics. An international strategy for intervention in Haiti should have been premised, therefore, not on the immediate revival of its dysfunctional institutions, no matter how democratic they appeared, but on creating the prior political consensus across social groups that may have allowed these institutions to function more effectively. Similarly, experts on Afghanistan have long warned that the country's national life is the equivalent of the ethnography of Somalia mapped onto the geography of Scotland and has never supported more than the most fragmented or tenuous of polities. The UN's "light footprint" approach in Afghanistan appears to have taken this expert advice into account by shying away from heavy "nation building." Again, experts with deep knowledge of Iraq have suggested that the recent conflicts between the Shias, the Sunnis, and the Kurds in Iraq have resulted not from traditional enmities between these groups, but from Saddam Hussein's heavy-handed oppression of the political autonomy of minority groups that have challenged his rule. This would suggest that, left to their own devices, these groups can cobble together a federal polity with modest international support; faced with a heavy international "nation-building" process, however, they may turn against this presence.

The UN Remains Relevant to the Strategic U.S. Objective of Making Weak States More Resilient

Despite the fracas in the Security Council over Iraq and the resulting public impression of the UN as being "irrelevant" on the part of some Americans, the UN remains the only actor in the international arena with the legitimacy and the accumulated experience of nearly two decades with regard to "nation building." In fact, much of the UN's most significant work in this regard takes place far away from the media glare that surrounds high-profile diplomatic battles in the Security Council or large peacekeeping operations. Most of this work is done by agencies such as the UN Development Programme (UNDP) or UNICEF under the rubric of "capacity building" and involves support for dialogue processes to build multistakeholder consensus; the reform of governance, including the reform of the judiciary and the police; the strengthening of institutions such as parliaments and civil service; training in conflict management for key stakeholders, including civil society; recovery at the community level so that refugees and former combatants can be reintegrated into economic life; human rights education, and so on. This support is provided not just in the aftermath of violent conflict, but also prior to its eruption so that weak states could be more resilient before internal events threaten their security as well as that of their neighbors. For instance, at the time of writing, UNDP is supporting a program to "build social cohesion" in Guyana which aims at preventing internal tensions from leading to a further breakdown within the country. In this context, the high diplomatic drama in the Security Council does not affect the UN's overall "relevance," and U.S. policymakers should take note of that.

Notes

1. Sidney Mintz, "Can Haiti Change?" *Foreign Affairs* 74, no. 1 (January-February 1995): 74.
2. Mintz, "Can Haiti Change?" 76.
3. Mintz, "Can Haiti Change?" 79–81.
4. See Michel-Rolph Trouillot, *Haiti: State against Nation: The Origins and Legacy of Duvalierism* (New York: Monthly Review Press, 1990), 49–50.
5. Mintz, "Can Haiti Change?" 79.
6. Trouillot, *Haiti: State against Nation*, 44–48.
7. Trouillot, *Haiti: State against Nation*, 85–86.
8. Trouillot, chapter 2, "A Republic for the Merchants."
9. Mintz, "Can Haiti Change?" 78–79. See also Trouillot, *Haiti: State against Nation*, 50–58, 64–69.
10. See Alex Dupuy, "Free Trade and Underdevelopment in Haiti: The World Bank/USAID Agenda for Social Change in the Post-Duvalier Era," in Hilbourne A. Watson, ed., *The Caribbean in the Global Political Economy* (Boulder, Colo.: Lynne Rienner, 1994), 100.
11. "Haiti—Building Democracy," *Comment* (London: Catholic Institute for Inter-

national Relations, February 1996), 23.

12. Perhaps the most authentic account of the potential of Haiti's peasantry is provided by Haitian author Jacques Roumain in his classic 1944 novel *Masters of the Dew.*

13. Dupuy, *Caribbean in Global Political Economy,* 93–95.

14. For arguments in support of an assembly manufacturing-led growth strategy for Haiti, see Clive Gray, "Alternative Models for Haiti's Economic Reconstruction," and Mats Lundahl, "The Haitian Dilemma Reexamined," in Robert Rotberg, ed., *Haiti Renewed: Political and Economic Prospects* (Washington, D.C.: Brookings Institution Press, 1997).

15. See Robert Maguire et al., "Haiti Held Hostage: International Responses to the Quest for Nationhood, 1986 to 1996," occasional paper 23, Thomas J. Watson Institute for International Studies, Brown University, Providence, R.I., 1996, 8.

16. For a brief outline of the thirty-year reign of terror of the *tontons macoutes* and the possibly irreversible scar it has left on Haiti's national psyche, see Michel S. Laguerre, "The Tontons Macoutes," in James Ridgeway, ed., *The Haiti Files: Decoding the Crisis.* (Washington, D.C.: Essential, 1994).

17. Dupuy, *Caribbean in Global Political Economy,* 95–96.

18. Dupuy, *Caribbean in Global Political Economy,* 97.

19. Dupuy, *Caribbean in Global Political Economy,* 98. Also see Trouillot, *Haiti: State against Nation,* 158.

20. For a detailed account of the role of big mercantile families in Haiti's economy, see "Haiti's 'Economic Barons': Memo from Congressman Walter E. Fauntroy," in *The Haiti Files.*

21. According to Trouillot, "By ignoring the problems of the rural world and the relationship between it and the urban classes, the light industry strategy in the end complicated them." Trouillot, *Haiti: State against Nation,* 210.

22. A review article by Peter M. Lewis that surveys several recent volumes which draw lessons from the experience of promoting development and economic reform in Africa points to the nature of governance in a society—the institutions of the state, the relations between these institutions and the people, and the social coalitions that engender these relations—as key variables in determining the path of economic reform. "Economic Reform and Political Transition in Africa: The Quest for a Politics of Development," *World Politics* 49 (October 1996): 92–129.

23. See Marx V. Aristide and Laurie Richardson, "The Popular Movement," in *The Haiti Files.* Also see Alex Dupuy, *Haiti in the New World Order: The Limits of the Democratic Revolution* (Boulder, Colo.: Westview Press, 1997), 97–98.

24. For a summary of *ti legliz* activities, see "Haiti—Building Democracy," 7.

25. For an account of the international community's role in these elections, see David Malone, *Decision-Making in the UN Security Council: The Case of Haiti, 1990–1997* (Oxford: Clarendon Press, 1998), 50–54.

26. See Donald E. Schulz and Gabriel Marcella, *Reconciling the Irreconcilable: The Troubled Outlook for U.S. Policy toward Haiti* (Carlisle, Pa.: U.S. Army War College, Strategic Studies Institute, 10 March 1994), 12.

27. Robert Maguire et al., "Haiti Held Hostage," 18.

28. Schulz, Marcella, *U.S. Policy toward Haiti,* 9–11.

29. The increasing vigor of the OAS's commitment to democracy was dramatic: in 1985, the Protocol of Cartagena de Indias incorporated democracy-promotion in the OAS charter; in 1989, the Organization began to observe elections in member states when requested; in 1990, it created a "Unit for Promotion of Democracy" and launched addi-

tional programs to bolster democratization; in 1991, its General Assembly adopted a mechanism to respond when democratic order is interrupted in any member state; and in 1992, it strengthened its several instruments for promoting democratic government in the Protocol of Washington.

30. David Malone's authoritative and detailed work, *Decision-Making in the UN Security Council: The Case of Haiti, 1990–1997*, provides the best available account of the complexities of international decision making on Haiti in the aftermath of the overthrow of President Aristide in 1991.

31. The most comprehensive and critical analysis of these sanctions and their impact is offered by Elizabeth Gibbons in *Sanctions in Haiti: Human Rights and Democracy under Assault* (Washington, D.C.: Center for Strategic and International Studies Press, 1999). For another comprehensive review of the initial impact of these sanctions on Haiti, see G. Berggren et al., "Sanctions in Haiti: Crisis in Humanitarian Action," working paper, Harvard Center for Population and Development Studies, Program on Human Security, Harvard University, Cambridge, Mass., November 1993.

32. A critical assessment of the role of the Multinational Force in dealing with insecurity in Haiti is provided in Bob Shacochis, *The Immaculate Invasion* (New York: Penguin Books, 1999).

33. The successes of both MNF and UNMIH are detailed in David Bentley, "Operation Uphold Democracy: Military Support for Democracy in Haiti," *Strategic Forum*, no. 78, Institute for National Strategic Studies, National Defense University, Washington, D.C., June 1996.

34. See Jean-Germain Gros, "Haiti's Flagging Transition," *Journal of Democracy* 8, no. 4 (October 1997): 104.

35. On 19 August 1997, the United Nations suspended electoral assistance to Haiti until the Provisional Electoral Council could establish that it was capable of holding free and fair elections. Michael Norton, "UN Suspends Election Aid in Haiti," Associated Press, 22 August 1997.

36. An interesting explanation for disputes among current Haitian politicians, many of whom once supported Aristide, has been offered by Andrew Reding, who suggests that Haiti's winner-take-all electoral system, as opposed to the kind of proportional representation system that prevails in South Africa, is putting heavy stress on a nascent democracy. "Exorcising Haiti's Ghosts," *World Policy Journal* 13, no. 1 (Spring 1996): 21.

37. The bank, which currently has as clients seven hundred street-side sellers of a variety of goods, plans to raise its roster to ten thousand by 2002, a sign of the commercial success of this program. See David Gonzalez, "Port-au-Prince Journal: A Haitian Bank Takes to the Streets," *New York Times*, 17 April 2001.

38. Some USAID projects in recent years have begun to show a laudable trend toward more participatory project implementation in Haiti. See Mimi Whitfield, "Clean Water, Garbage Pickup Slated for Cite Soleil Slum," *Miami Herald*, 3 November 1997.

7

Intervention in Sierra Leone

Kwaku Nuamah and I. William Zartman

Sierra Leone is a case of state collapse in which the conflicts of the 1990s were not an independent event but merely the work of maggots on a dead body. Thus, no intervention could have done anything more, at best, than remove the momentary parasites taking advantage of the situation. It would require a longer, deeper, and more sustained effort of the Sierra Leoneans, necessarily with help from the international community, to restore a functioning political, economic, and social structure necessary to prevent a recurrence of conflict. At the same time, it is noteworthy that this internal conflict was not an ethnic conflict, despite some secondary ethnic ramifications.

The collapse of the Sierra Leonean state, already a weak creation of colonization and decolonization, took place under the long reign of Siaka Stevens (1968–1985) and his All Peoples Congress (APC), drawing primarily on the interior Temne and Limba people from the northern part of the country reacting against the previous predominance of the coastal Mende people from the south and east. Collapse was consummated under Stevens's handpicked, inept successor, General Joseph Momoh, overthrown by dissatisfied junior officers, led by Captain Valentine Strasser, in April 1992. The main rebel groups operated under the name of the Revolutionary United Force (RUF), led by ex-corporal Foday Sankoh and Samuel Bockarie and operating with the active support of the rebel movement and then the government of Liberia under Charles Taylor. The rebellion expanded into neighboring countries and then wore down under the falling away of external and internal support.

The subsequent decade after the first coup saw a seesaw of controls over the capital, Freetown, and the rest of the country by various loyal and dissident military and rebel groups, interrupted in 1996 by the free and fair election of Ahmed Tajan Kabbah. Strasser's colleague, Captain Maada Bio, took power in January 1996 to prevent Strasser from delaying a planned transition to the elected government. Bio relaunched negotiations with the rural rebellion and handed over power to Kabbah in March 1996. Kabbah continued negotiations begun by Bio and made substantial concessions to the rebels that paved the way for the Abidjan Agreement of November 1996. In the third attempt since the elections, junior officers led by Major Johnny Paul Koromah overthrew Kabbah in May 1997 and promptly made common cause with the rebels. Kabbah was restored to power ten months later and again chased out of the capital for several months in early 1999 before being restored once again. During this ten-year period, a legitimate civilian government was in place (scarcely in power) only from the March 1996 elections until the May 1997 coup, from March 1998 until the end of the year and again after the spring of 1999—four years.

External intervention to contain the conflict was practiced by three agents: the essentially Nigerian force of the Military Observer Group (ECOMOG) of the Economic Community of West African States (ECOWAS), the United Nations Observer/Armed Mission in Sierra Leone (UNOMSIL/UNAMSIL), and the British Army. Three peace agreements were signed as a result: the Abidjan Accord of November 1996, the Conakry Peace Plan of October 1997, and the Lomé Peace Agreement of July 1999. All failed. Rebellion, intervention, and state collapse all continue to cohabit in Sierra Leone, against new government efforts to rebuild.

Conflict

The tinder for the conflict began to gather under the Momoh regime when the government stopped paying salaries, notably to its schoolteachers and military.[1] Structures of authority disintegrated, unemployed youth wandered the streets of Freetown and the interior and took to drugs and petty crime, and soldiers turned to brigandage. Disaffected soldiers were the political entrepreneurs who took the match to the tinder. The actual outbreak of the Sierra Leone conflict began as an offshoot of the Liberian civil war and evolved into a full-fledged internal conflict over power and resources with heavy regional undertones. The rebellion began in March 1991 when ex-corporal Sankoh, formerly jailed for his participation in a coup against Stevens in 1971, led his ragtag band of Sierra Leonean dissidents, backed by Liberian fighters and mercenaries from Burkina Faso, to invade Sierra Leone from Liberia.[2] Sankoh had met Taylor of Liberia in the 1980s during guerrilla training in Libya; Taylor supported the RUF in order to

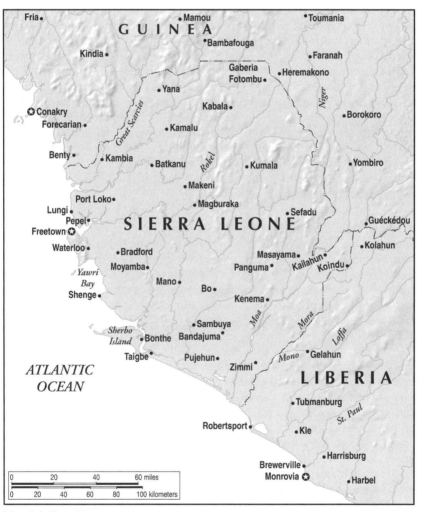

Map 7.1 Sierra Leone

force the Freetown government to change its Liberia policy, which included a contribution of five hundred troops to ECOMOG, the use of Lungi airport as a base for ECOMOG operations, and provision of sanctuary for the United Liberation Movement of Liberia for Democracy (ULIMO), a group of former Liberian President Samuel Doe's followers, as they opened a front against Taylor's rebellion from Sierra Leone.

Sankoh's stated aim was to fight the corruption of the Momoh regime. However, when Momoh was overthrown by his junior officers a year after the RUF rebellion broke out, the rebellion continued against the new government. Twenty-seven-year-old Strasser (who promised to end war and restore economy within a short time) overthrew Momoh on 29 April 1992. This latest coup d'etat prompted the use of force by ECOMOG and following talks in Conakry, Kabbah was restored to power several months later. Many different factors combined to aid the spread of the conflict and rendered it intractable. These can be grouped as contextual aspects related to state collapse, the dynamics of the conflict, and the nature of the conflict resolution efforts.

The Context of State Collapse

While state collapse is recognized as providing the basic opportunity that leaders and their followers seized to carry out the conflict, it also subdivided into a number of specific areas where the state no longer performed its core functions, leaving them up for grabs by diverse agencies. Not all these agencies were hostile to the state, but the fact that they performed state functions further weakened the state as much as did the rebellion itself. These functions include general order, territorial control, population control, control over armed forces, and provision of security.

A weak state system and economic decline hampered the government's ability to respond effectively to the rebellion. By the early 1990s, Sierra Leone's economy was in decline and plagued by official corruption that was generating mass discontent and political instability. Political uncertainty and economic decline undermined effective policymaking and diminished public confidence in the state's ability to secure its interests and lives. Coup plots were rife as Momoh's sole legal party struggled to negotiate a long-delayed transition to a multiparty system. The state's security apparatus was also in a complete shambles as wages failed to keep up with inflation or remained unpaid for weeks. Army morale continued to sink to new lows; soldiers began moonlighting as rebels and joined in looting and harassing the peasantry. The net effect was a government that had to turn to foreign actors for security assistance.

Involvement in the Liberian Civil War increased from 1991 until Sierra Leone became simply a theatre in that conflict, with little control over its own territory.[3] Military units from Nigeria and Guinea joined the Sierra Leone army in mid-1991 and helped to recapture several towns from the RUF. This infuriated Taylor who threatened attacks on Lungi airport and launched cross-border raids in support of the rebels. Sierra Leonean troops responded with their own attacks on rebel bases inside Liberia. Sierra Leone by default had become a new front of the Liberian war, and so by May 1992 the Nigerian and Guinean presence was transformed into a regular ECOMOG mission.

On the other side were ULIMO and other Doe loyalists who had fled to Sierra Leone and joined in counteroffensive measures against Taylor's forces. The government's failure to exercise control over such elements provided an excuse for Taylor's retaliations that fueled escalation and occasionally tipped the scales in the RUF's favor. ULIMO's attacks were sporadic and disrupted attempts to bring the conflict under control. Early efforts by ECOWAS to broker a peace agreement in 1991, for instance, were interrupted by ULIMO's forays into Liberia. The RUF then also used the foreign presence as an excuse for reneging on agreements reached with the government.

Refugees have had a complex effect on the conflict. As thousands of Liberian refugees fled to the eastern part of Sierra Leone, equal numbers of Sierra Leoneans fled into Guinea and Liberia. Refugee populations served as recruitment pools for the rebellion while adding to the economic hardships of the host communities. In Sierra Leone, the crisscrossing of refugees added to the fluidity of the crisis. Guinea became a new front in the conflict, as did several other states in the West Africa subregion that played host to Liberian and Sierra Leonean refugees, notably the Casamance dissidence in Senegal and neighboring Guinea-Bissau drew rebels of fortune from the Sierre Leonean conflict. Refugees attracted internal humanitarian aid workers whose presence invited hostage taking by the RUF; the RUF also took peacekeepers hostage for use as leverage in negotiations. This strategy sometimes backfired when it occasioned the entry of other parties on the side of the government. The RUF also launched repeated attacks on the peasantry and took ordinary people (as well as nonmilitary foreigners) hostage as a way of forcing the government to make concessions. Government compliance with such demands weakened it substantially, but noncompliance led to deadlocks and escalation in the conflict.

Privatization and alienation of security functions have been a specific result of state collapse.[4] With the collapse of the army, the government increasingly relied on private and foreign security agencies for protection, many of which were also affiliated with mining firms. These actors "privatized" the conflict and introduced the ethos of commercial profitseeking as a major current underlying the conflict. The government's need to elicit the help of private security was exacerbated by two additional factors: the inadequacy of assistance received from ECOMOG and UNAMSIL and the imposition of a UN arms embargo on all parties to the conflict. The effectiveness of ECOMOG and UNAMSIL was hampered by the absence of a UN Security Council authorization to use force. The foreign forces also lacked adequate knowledge of the terrain as well as the capacity to deal with the guerrilla tactics employed so efficiently by the RUF. Fluctuations in numbers caused by periodic troop withdrawals by some contributors also meant that the peacekeepers were not a reliable security force for the Sierra Leonean government. Private security firms therefore had to be employed to supplement the peacekeepers and provide strategic training for the Sierra Leone army. The UN arms embargo, on the other hand, meant the Sierra Leonean government could not obtain the ammunition and weapons it needed to pursue the war and had to rely on private groups such as Executive Outcomes and Sandline International for arms shipments.

Private specialty groups have also taken over other state functions. The government needed to continue extracting whatever resources still available from the diamond mining sector to finance its war operations. The RUF's presence in some of the diamond regions posed a security problem which was resolved through cooperation with another category of private specialty entities willing to provide security for mining operations and to pay the government in cash or in kind for a role in the diamond fields. Groups such as Diamond Works and its subsidiary, Branch Energy, had to find their own security for mining operations in the Koindu area. Other commercial mining operations secured assistance from a wide array of private specialty groups (examples include British companies such as Lifeguard, Defense Systems Ltd., Sky Air, and Occidental, and American companies such as Military Professional Resources Inc. [MPRI] and International Charters Inc.). Most of these commercial and security firms also had important connections with major players in the conflict and this further complicated the roles of those players in the search for a solution.

Conflict Dynamics and Escalation

The very dynamics of the conflict provide another element that contributed to its intractability and hampered the search for a negotiated settlement. As the conflict evolved, the proliferation of parties on both sides and the RUF's resort to unconventional warfare thwarted efforts at resolution.

Proliferation of parties, particularly on the side of the government, characterizes the Sierra Leone conflict. Political instability fed uncertainty and often benefited the rebels who took the opportunity to form alliances with supporters of removed regimes. Sierra Leone had five different governments in the decade since the outbreak of violence. Each of the post-Momoh regimes came to power promising a swift end to the war and proceeded to reach out to the rebels with upgrades in offers that yield no corresponding dividends. The RUF also suffered its share of political uncertainties, so that it became difficult to know with whom to negotiate and on whom to rely for implementation of an agreement. A rift between Sankoh loyalists and followers of Sam Bockarie unsettled peace agreements in 1996, although it did little to weaken the RUF. Attempts in March 1997 to remove Sankoh (who had been detained in Nigeria) from the RUF leadership weakened negotiations but not the RUF. Such political uncertainties disrupt peace efforts, delay the implementation of agreements, and provide opportunities for escalation.

Use of unconventional tactics in the conflict frustrated the government army and its supporters, many of whom lacked training and experience with guerrilla warfare. The RUF knew the terrain and on two occasions, late 1994 and late 1998, executed the same swing westward and then southward from their bases to the outskirts of Freetown. Well-planned guerrilla attacks also helped the RUF seize hundreds of pro-government peacekeepers and relief workers at will. In May 2000, they took about five hundred UN peacekeepers hostage, and two months later they seized another 233 peacekeepers (mainly from India) at Kailahun. As a precondition to negotiations with the Sierra Leonean government and British officials, the RUF demanded diplomatic recognition, armaments, and medical supplies from London as well as an end to British military assistance to the Strasser government. The RUF also seized eight foreign nationals and several local employees during attacks on mining installations owned by the Sierra Leone Ore and Metal Co. and Sierra Rutile Ltd. as well as seven catholic nuns (Italians and Brazilians) in the Kambia area. These and other hostages were used as leverage during talks brokered by the International Committee of the Red Cross (ICRC). The RUF also often demanded the withdrawal of all foreign troops from Sierra Leone in exchange for releasing its hostages.

Conflict Resolution Efforts

Resolution efforts were also misguided in important aspects. Inadequate diagnosis, inappropriate agreements, and the premature exit of peacekeepers undermined crucial dimensions of the peace efforts and contributed to prolonging the conflict.

Diagnosed as merely an extension of the Liberian conflict, the Sierra Leone conflict was not understood in terms of its own causes and dynamics. While the conflict may have begun, in part, as an auxiliary of the Liberian war, it took hold because of the ready context within Sierra Leone and it soon became a full-fledged civil war with its own dynamics and issues. The international community, however, continued to perceive it as a subset of Liberia until the mid-1990s. As a result Sierra Leone did not receive any substantial international attention until much later when the conflict had grown in scope and become complicated and intractable. International interventions were therefore late in coming and often inadequate.

Unbalanced agreements have been the result of all mediation attempts. The conflict has witnessed three major attempts at finding a negotiated settlement. Each was based on the principles of power sharing, amnesty for the RUF, and removal of foreign forces in the conflict. The first, the Abidjan Peace Agreement of 30 November 1996, was brokered by Ivorian Foreign Minister Amara Essy with the active involvement of Special Envoy Berhanu Dinka. It stipulated the establishment of a Neutral Monitoring Group (NMG) to oversee general disarmament; removal of all foreign troops from the country; transformation of the

RUF into a political party; and a general amnesty for RUF members suspected of war crimes. Government compliance weakened it so much that the RUF could afford to renege on its promised demobilization. The Abidjan "bad deal" cost Kabbah the presidency six months later when Johnny Paul Koromah exploited its weak position to launch a successful coup d'etat that eventually drew escalation from ECOMOG.

The second agreement, the Conakry Peace Plan of 23 October 1997, was negotiated by ECOWAS to restore the Kabbah presidency, but it ended up granting legitimacy to the Koromah junta that had gone into partnership with the RUF. After Conakry, the junta began asserting itself as a legitimate government with a mandate to rule until the 22 April 1998 handover date when President Kabbah was to return to Freetown. It accumulated weapons and exhibited signs of noncompliance with the terms of the agreement. Eventually ECOMOG had to employ force to expel it from Freetown.

The third accord, the Lomé Peace Agreement of July 1999, was brokered by a team led by Togolese Foreign Minister Kokou Koffigou and Special Representative of the UN Secretary General in Sierra Leone Francis Okelo. The RUF (now negotiating in tandem with the AFRC) demanded inclusion in a four-year transitional government as well as blanket amnesty, expulsion of all foreign troops, and the establishment of a neutral peacekeeping force along the model agreed at Abidjan.[5] External pressures and other dynamics[6] forced the Kabbah government to agree to a final package that included major power-sharing concessions for the RUF. Kabbah became very unpopular among ordinary Sierra Leoneans who expected Sankoh to be put on trial for war crimes. In addition, Lomé created the false impression that the conflict's end was near and therefore hastened the withdrawal of some ECOMOG contingents that, once again, strengthened the rebels and encouraged noncompliance. The agreement's endorsement by U.S. Secretary of State Madeleine Albright was an additional blow to government legitimacy and prospects.

Premature troop withdrawals and announcements of withdrawals also prolonged the conflict by signaling to the RUF that depreciation in government capacity was near. This discouraged the rebels from making concessions and instead fueled sporadic attacks aimed at recovering lost ground. Nigerian president Abdulsalami Abubakar's January 1999 announcement of an imminent withdrawal of his country's troops, for instance, strengthened the RUF's bargaining position at the Lomé talks in May of the same year. Though the Nigerian pullout was delayed indefinitely, the announcement restored the RUF's hope of a unilateral victory and therefore reduced the incentive for them to comply with the terms of Lomé. The withdrawal of the Indian contingent from UNAMSIL in August 2000 was yet another blow to the effort to end the conflict.

Interventions

Each of the three major intervention missions had its strengths and weaknesses. None could have been expected to end the conflict, which is deeply embedded in Sierra Leonean society. Any of them could have been expected to bring the military situation under control, although stopping there and confusing military control for conflict end would guarantee the reoccurrence of the conflict. As it is, none of them even brought the military conflict fully under control. The reasons are as political as they are military, but on the military side, appropriate numbers, tactics, rules of engagement, and simple command and control over one's own troops were lacking at crucial times and sometimes throughout the entire operation. On the political side, appropriate mission, financing, commitment, and strategy were required, plus a willingness to engage in a long-term, well-conceived plan to revive the Sierra Leonean economy, society, and state.

The ECOMOG Intervention

The ECOMOG intervention in Sierra Leone evolved out of ECOWAS's role in neighboring Liberia and also out of previous commitments of two key member states, Nigeria and Guinea, to assist the government of Sierra Leone in its fight against the RUF rebels. Sierra Leone's active role in ECOMOG brought retaliation from the National Patriotic Front of Liberia (NPFL) with cross-border raids and support for the rebels. ECOMOG's initial deployment along the Sierra Leone-Liberia border in May 1992 was therefore prompted by the dual need to assist the Sierra Leone government in holding off RUF attacks and to combat NPFL gunrunning and offensives in the border region. Deployment came at the beginning of violent conflict. The ECOMOG intervention involved troops from ECOWAS members, but almost all of them were Nigerian. By March 1998, its strength stood at ten thousand with Nigeria contributing the largest contingent. Air force and naval units of member states backed the troops occasionally.

The intervention has undergone several metamorphoses as peacekeepers, combatants, and peace enforcers. Unlike the UN intervention, ECOMOG was unambiguous in its support for the government of Sierra Leone and willfully used force to compel the rebels to comply with agreements. Throughout the several phases, ECOMOG's principal goal remained the restoration of peace and stability to Sierra Leone, a key supporter of Nigeria's leadership role in ECOWAS and key contributor to the peace enforcement mission in Liberia. That goal has remained largely elusive even though major aspects have been realized. The intervention did succeed in restoring President Kabbah to power, as the first step is restoring the state, through the application of force when negotiations and sanctions proved ineffective. ECOMOG's other goal was to help the state of Sierra Leone develop its own security apparatus sufficiently to manage the peace and provide a stable environment for national reconstruction efforts. This long-term goal has also not been realized. The intervention has also not reduced the possibility of future conflicts in Sierra Leone.

The ECOMOG intervention could have been improved in many ways. The early mistakes were associated with ECOMOG performance in Liberia, where ECOMOG came in order to save Doe and beat Taylor, rather than to restore the state that Doe had destroyed. Thus, an early operation in 1990–1991 to bring Taylor to power under controlled conditions, before his rebellion had broken down into internecine warfare and his forces had disintegrated into child soldiering and moneymaking, would have precluded the creation of a rebellion in neighboring Sierra Leone. Thereafter, an early use of force against the rebels could have averted some of the escalations that followed the Strasser coup. ECOMOG could also have benefited from proper coordination and better management. Many of its offensive missions were carried out by the Nigerians, whose determination to use force whenever possible was not evenly matched by other contingents. In some instances, poor strategy cost the mission dearly. The 2 June 1997 standoff with the RUF-backed Koromah Junta at the Mammy Yoko Hotel, for instance, resulted in the capture of ECOMOG troops and led to civilian casualties in neighboring Murray Township.

The central role played by Nigeria, a country whose terrible human rights record was attracting international condemnation and sanctions, also hurt ECOMOG's ability to attract much needed international financial support.[7] It also prevented Britain, a key actor in the Sierra Leone situation, from working together with ECOMOG in the search for a negotiated settlement. Had the United States, for instance, provided direct financial support for the essentially Nigerian force of ECOMOG at the end of 1998, the return of the AFRC/RUF and the pressure for a Lomé Agreement would have been avoided.[8] On the other hand, ECOMOG depended on Nigeria, the only country willing to finance and man the operation. The intervention could have benefited from a joint-leadership arrangement involving a neutral state such as Senegal or Mali. Such an arrangement could have enhanced ECOMOG's credibility while allowing Nigeria to play its dominant military role, although it would have posed major problems of coordination and command, since the two armies were based on different colonial military systems and different languages.

The ECOMOG mission was essentially military. ECOWAS members assumed state sovereignty and reckoned that when the rebellion was suppressed, a full and effective state would remain; to question this assumption would have been to question their own existence. This assumption underlay the one effective accomplishment of the ECOMOG intervention, the 1996 presidential election. ECOMOG offered the rebels several opportunities to concede peacefully and even held back to give peace agreements—such as Conakry and Lomé that "rewarded" the rebels—a chance to succeed. The rebels continually reneged on the agreements, forcing ECOMOG to continue the use of force as the primary mode of transforming the conflict. That strategy did not always work well but when it did work, it forced the rebels to comply and contributed to the search for peace.

The ECOMOG intervention had no credible exit plans. It was initially conceived as a mission creep from Liberia that would cease when that conflict was resolved. However, the Sierra Leone problem grew in scope and transcended the Liberian war. ECOMOG's exit therefore became linked to successful resolution of the war. This was an untenable situation for several contributing states that faced financial crisis and security problems of their own. The largest and wealthiest contributor, Nigeria, announced its intent to withdraw from the intervention on the eve of Lomé, before negotiations were completed or the conflict was over. That announcement was prompted by rising costs and a transition to democratic governance in Nigeria following the sudden death of Sani Abacha, the dictator who had kept Nigeria in Sierra Leone and Liberia for several years. In the end the Nigerians delayed their exit; however, the cost of the intervention forced them to seek a partnership with the UN intervention that had had an appalling record in Sierra Leone.

The UN Intervention

The United Nations Observer Mission in Sierra Leone (UNOMSIL/UNAMSIL) was first established by UN Security Council resolution 1181 of 13 July 1998 as a disarmament monitoring force of seventy military observers for an initial period of six months. Its deployment was prompted by optimism that followed the successful expulsion of the Johnny Paul Koromah/RUF junta from Freetown by ECOMOG and the restoration of the Kabbah regime. The intervention was to monitor ECOMOG's efforts to disarm the RUF combatants and to help restructure the government's security forces. It also hoped to document reports of ongoing atrocities and human rights abuses committed against civilians by both ECOMOG and the rebels. The mission failed to accomplish any of its goals and was hurriedly evacuated when the RUF relaunched its offensive to retake Freetown. Only the Special Representative and the Chief Military Observer remained in the country. However, on the eve of the Lomé talks, the UN agreed to station some 210 military observers[9] in the country upon the request of the government.

The second wave of UN presence (UNAMSIL) was authorized by UN Security Council resolution 1270 of 22 October 1999 under Chapter VII following the "success" of Lomé, when both parties had agreed to a cease-fire in order for the rebels to disarm. It was prompted by Nigerian announcements of an impending withdrawal from Sierra Leone, as Sierra Leone and ECOWAS requested an increased role by the UN to ensure that all parties fulfill the terms agreed upon at Lomé. It was therefore perceived as a postconflict monitoring mission. The RUF favored a UN presence because it did not trust Nigeria and ECOMOG to be impartial in the execution of the intervention mandate. However, sporadic violence continued and led to a quick abandonment of several of the terms agreed upon at Lomé. The consequences for the UN were dire as the mission's troops became prime targets for abduction by the rebel alliance. Key contributing parties withdrew their troops, causing the mission great embarrassment and limiting its effectiveness. This second UN intervention involved a much larger force of six thousand troops, consisting of six infantry battalions and a helicopter-borne rapid reaction force, half of the troops coming from ECOWAS (again, mainly Nigeria) and the rest from India, Kenya, and Zambia.

The principal goal of UNAMSIL was to ensure that all parties adhered to the terms of the Lomé Agreement. Toward this, it planned to monitor the disarmament process, facilitate the resettlement of Sierra Leonean refugees in Guinea and Liberia, and assist the government to develop its security apparatus. The intervention also investigated human rights abuses committed by both government loyalists and the rebel alliance. On a less formal basis, the intervention hoped to facilitate further talks on the power-sharing deal agreed upon in Lomé. In the end it spent most of its resources negotiating the release of its own troops taken hostage by the RUF.

The greatest improvements would have required a different set of rules of engagement appropriate to the situation. The UN did not authorize the intervention to use force in its operation, even though it was established under Chapter VII. It was also concerned about cooperating too closely with ECOMOG troops, who were considered to be biased toward the government.[10] These were issues that limited the effectiveness of UNAMSIL. It is likely that a proper identification of the rebels as the villains in the conflict could have helped to authorize an intervention whose sole purpose was to help the legitimate and democratically elected government of Sierra Leone regain control of its territory and population, restore its state, and end the rebel insurgency. After the UNOMSIL debacle at the end of 1998 and the authorization of UNAMSIL in 1999, the UN should also have authorized a change in mandate to peace enforcement. Such a move could have averted the embarrassing episodes of hostage taking that continue to plague the mission.

The UN intervention in Sierra Leone was instrumental in legitimizing the Lomé Agreement that endorsed the RUF as a partner in government. That agreement was largely unpopular among civil society as it banned ongoing efforts to put the RUF leadership on trial for human rights violations. The presence of UNAMSIL, however, facilitated the repatriation of some refugees and helped the government's effort to raise funds for reconstruction. Despite its ineffectiveness as a military force, the intervention helped bring much needed credibility to the peace process. Eventually, implementation efforts after 2000 bypassed the objectionable aspects of the Lomé Agreement and enabled the government to restore its operations and begin to rebuild the state.

The first UN intervention had a clear exit plan. It was mandated for a period of six months, subject to review as necessary. When the conflict intensified to a point where the intervention considered its mandate untenable, it quickly withdrew. The second installment, on the other hand, entered with an open-ended commitment to monitor the implementation of the Lomé Agreement. The UN Security Council did not modify its rules of engagement even as its forces came under persistent RUF attack. Contributing states such as India therefore withdrew their troops when they perceived the intervention as unhelpful to their interests. Such unilateral withdrawals hurt the overall purposes of the mission, although it was the only way contributing states could exit the process in the absence of a general UN policy on collective exit.

The mission's principal goal of facilitating the implementation of the Lomé Agreement was largely unattained until the British intervention restored order and handed over a more secure situation to the reinstated government.

The British Intervention

The British intervention—"Operation Palliser"—was triggered by the "disappearance" of five hundred United Nations Peacekeepers in Sierra Leone. The withdrawal of ECOMOG troops in late April 2000 created a huge security vacuum that UN peacekeepers, under force commander Vijay Jetley of India, were unable to fill. The RUF exploited the situation to escalate its attacks on the UNAMSIL. Five hundred UN troops were taken prisoner by the RUF in May, prompting the UK to dispatch a "rescue" force to the country. The British deployment came in the aftermath of the major clashes of the war and as Liberia, a major backer of the RUF, was seeking international legitimacy and therefore had become less visible as a threat. The presence of the UN force (UNAMSIL) also eased the British entry by helping to legitimatize the intervention. The intervention comprised eight hundred paratroopers with strong air force and naval support.

The British intervention sought to realize several immediate and long-term goals. In the short term, the mission sought to reverse RUF gains and change the conflict structure in favor of pro-government forces. To accomplish this, it launched an operation to rescue the five hundred "missing" UN peacekeepers and also to repel the imminent RUF capture of Waterloo and possibly Freetown. To save Freetown, troops were dispatched to secure the local airport and then deployed throughout the capital and its environs as a buffer to the RUF offensive. The long-term goals were geared toward capacity building assistance to help pro-government forces consolidate the gains of peace and security. To this end, the British troops provided technical training and assistance to the Sierra Leone army that had been in complete disarray following the sudden death of its Nigerian chief of staff, General Maxwell Khobe, in April 2000. British experts also assisted the UN in tactical planning and strategic deployments as well as with logistics such as helicopters to transport Jordanian peacekeepers to defensive positions.

Earlier deployments to help ECOMOG and UNAMSIL could have averted some of the more dangerous dynamics that necessitated the British entry in May 2000. There were several occasions where British intervention could have deterred the RUF from employing abductions as a concession-seeking tool. In January 1995, the RUF seized several employees (including eight foreign nationals) during its capture of the mining installations of the Sierra Leone Ore and Metal Co. and Sierra Rutile Ltd. The rebels also captured seven Italian and Brazilian nuns and several Sierra Leoneans in a later raid on Kambia. British intervention as in May 2000 could have achieved similar goals at that stage of the conflict. Another point where a British presence could have positively impacted conflict dynamics is February 1997, when the Kabbah government was most vulnerable after sending home all mercenaries in fulfillment of RUF conditions for disarmament. Under the terms of the agreement, the RUF was ready to accept foreign observers to monitor its disarmament exercise. The British mission could have constituted the core of such an international presence and helped raise the cost of defection for the RUF. As it turned out, the RUF failed to disarm and continued to violate the peace agreement leading to newer levels of escalation on both sides. When UNAMSIL was first deployed on 22 October 1999, a British intervention could have altered the negative trends of the conflict. Since the first battalions of Kenyan and Indian troops were largely unprepared for the task bequeathed them by the withdrawing ECOWAS troops, a British presence could have fortified their strategic operations and helped the UN better handle escalations by the RUF, which demanded that the UN pay for surrendered arms. This was also a period when Foday Sankoh's grip on the RUF began to weaken and so a better-equipped unit, such as a British intervention, could have hastened a breakup of the RUF and the demise of the rebellion.

The British mission was short-lived and geared toward the accomplishment of relatively limited goals that gave a much-needed boost to government forces but nevertheless produced little lasting effect. Its capacity development program was crucial to the emergence of UNAMSIL as a credible force in Sierra Leone; however, long-standing operational difficulties as well as the UN's reluctance to authorize the use of force robbed the UN mission of opportunities to reverse RUF gains in the conflict. The military and nonmilitary balance remained constant over the period of intervention even though the intervention evolved into a technical support group later and its size was drastically reduced to 251 members.

It is certain that the British originally intended the intervention to be a "rescue mission." It was supposed to be a short, precise, troubleshooting mission that would avoid mission creep, deliver quickly, and exit as soon as possible. However, events on the ground convinced the British to tackle capacity building as a way of ensuring that their exit would not create an imbalance similar to the one created by the ECOWAS disengagement.

The immediate goals were better defined and hence easier to achieve than the long-term goals. As a direct result of the intervention, the RUF was forced to release the five hundred UN hostages. The British impact was felt again in late August 2000 when the West Side Boys (a pro-AFRC faction originally supportive of the government) abducted eleven British soldiers and a Sierra Leonean as leverage for the release of their leader. The British troops intervened to secure their release just as the United Nations was dealt a heavy blow by India's announcement of a pullout. British assistance was also directly responsible for the successful deployment of the Jordanian contingent in Sierra Leone. Without their helicopters and operational cover, the Jordanian troops could have become stranded or restricted to uncontested terrain while the RUF continued to devastate the diamond-rich northwest.

In terms of long-term goals, the impact of the British intervention was quite muted, above all because of the advanced stage of disrepair into which the government army had fallen before the intervention. Poor training and lack of adequate equipment was exacerbated by petty quarrels among the ranks and with allies such as the Kamajor militias. British capacity-building efforts yielded better results for UNAMSIL, which became more professional and superbly handled the rescue of 233 peacekeepers (mainly from India) held hostage by RUF in Kailahun soon after the British intervention.

Conclusions

The conflict in Sierra Leone dropped in intensity in 2001 for a number of different reasons mainly unrelated to the interventions themselves. RUF members agreed to join programs of Disarmament, Demobilization, Resettlement, and Rehabilitation (DDRR), at least in the first phase, although there is still little economy into which to integrate. The RUF has lost much of its appeal as its various experiences in Freetown and in the countryside alike have shown it to have no goal, no program, no electoral support, and no governing ability. Under international pressure, Taylor pulled back Liberian support. The evolution toward collapse in neighboring Ivory Coast also reduced support for Liberia and introduced distracting complications as the forces of General Guei, reputedly close to Taylor, predominated in the western part of the country bordering on Liberia, and then erupted into open rebellion.

There are many lessons from the Sierra Leone case of multiple interventions. The first double lesson is that military intervention is not enough to end a conflict whose basic cause is state collapse, but that military intervention is a necessary ingredient in engaging the road to conflict's end. The conflict began in the failure of governance, the dissolution of the economy, and the breakdown of the social tissue in Sierra Leone, and will only end when these elements are restored. That is a statement of shocking realism, and while it may sound like a counsel of perfection in an imperfect world, it does stand as a guideline for the sustained, broad-based, committed efforts needed to restore Sierra Leone. Violent conflict, even in the outrageous form practiced by the RUF, is a symptom of a deeper malaise.

If such conditions are not dealt with, the cancer in the region, only in remission, will again emerge to eat away at the countries around it. One cannot isolate Sierra Leone and tow it out to sea; it is part of a regional rot and, to broaden the challenge even further, needs to be handled in its context. As seen, early and late the interventions needed to be conducted in relation to the Liberian conflict and its aftermath, and as the conflict continued, it had its own spillover into Guinea and its secondary effects on Guinea-Bissau and Senegal. The latter is not an object of control measures, but the Guinean extension poses its own Sierra Leonean-type problems: reinforcement of the Guinean military reinforces the autocratic tendencies of Guinean president Lansana Conte and creates conditions for a similar type of rebellion in Guinea, a state on the way to its own form of collapse.

On the other hand, the military intervention is an important element in the process of bringing the conflict under control. When the RUF arose, it was necessary to take adequate measures to stop it in its tracks. These measures would have been best taken by the regional organization or a single country acting in its name, and secondarily by a UN operation (squarely under Chapter VII, not shakily so or under Chapter VI), but in fact it took a British intervention to show the necessary military commitment and centralized strategy and command. Appropriate measures should necessarily have begun in Liberia, in the context of the Liberian war, in early 1991.[11] The need for decisive military action continued in 1992 with a focused strike against the RUF by ECOMOG early on; realistically, it needs to be noted that ECOMOG in 1992 was in deep trouble in Liberia and there was no Sierra Leonean army to rely on. Thereafter, there were moments, particularly after 1996 when the Liberian civil war was officially ended, in late 1998 and early 1999, and in early 2000, when ECOMOG or UNAMSIL needed to act as a unified military force with an enforcement mission and active rules of engagement. The longer one waits, the larger the force commitment required.

The Sierra Leone experience raises enormous questions about the non-military side of the conflict management operation. Conflict management "doctrine" indicates that one can only end a conflict by negotiating with one's enemy and that any party to the problem must be a party to the solution. Yet there are limits, if not on the participants, at least on the conditions under which their participation can be envisaged. Some enemies are beyond the pale, incapable of making and holding an acceptable agreement. Which enemies is a judgment call, not easy to make: the deliberate atrocities of the RUF, whose hallmark was amputation, made them appropriate objects of punishment, not power sharing, but what about Renamo in Mozambique or UNITA in Angola or Taylor's NPFL or for that matter either the Palestinians or the Israelis in the Middle East? It is too easy to qualify one's enemy as beyond the pale and not worthy of negotiation.

Suggestions for an answer to the conundrum come out of the Mozambican experience. Despite its vicious past, Renamo was not only a necessary participant in negotiations if the conflict was to be ended, but also an organization which had already made a good deal of progress from a guerrilla movement toward a political party when the negotiations started. As such, it was not only organizationally coherent, but also began to see a stake in electoral participation and in transformation of the conflict to political means. No such indications were available from the RUF, and when the RUF-P (political wing) did take part in the 2002 elections, almost no one voted for it.

The other side of the answer returns the analysis to the military situation. In cases where the enemy does not seem capable of transforming its struggle into a political contest by the rules, military control is necessary. As noted, this is not to be confused with elimination of the broader and deeper causes of the conflict, which if not treated will give rise to a new insurgent expression, but it does indicate that in some cases, if any negotiation is to take place, it will be between victors and vanquished, not equals.

Notes

1. Fred Hayward, "State Consolidation, Fragmentation and Decay," in *West African States*, Donald Cruise O'Brien, John Dunn, and Richard Rathbone, eds. (New York: Cambridge University Press, 1989); David Fashole Luke and Stephen P. Riley, "The Politics of Economic Decline in Sierra Leone," *Journal of Modern African Studies* 27, no. 1 (1989): 133–141.

2. Ibrahim Abdullah, "Bush Path to Destruction: The Origin and Character of the Revolutionary United Front / Sierra Leone," *Journal of Modern African Studies* 36, no. 2 (1998): 203–235; Abdul Koroma, *Sierra Leone: The Agony of a Nation* (Freetown: Andromeda Publications, 1996).

3. For analysis of Sierra Leone's role in the Liberian conflict, see Robert Mortimer, "From ECOMOG to ECOMOG II: Intervention in Sierra Leone," in *Africa in World Politics, The African State System in Flux*, J. Harbeson and D. Rothchild, eds. (Boulder, Colo.: Westview Press, 2000).

4. John Hirsh, *Sierra Leone: Diamonds and the Struggle for Democracy* (Boulder, Colo.: Lynne Rienner, 2001); Adekeye Adebajo, *Building Peace in West Africa: Liberia, Sierra-Leone and Guinea Bissau* (Boulder, Colo.: Lynne Rienner, 2002); William Reno, *Corruption and State Politics in Sierra Leone* (New York: Cambridge University Press, 1995).

5. Kofi Annan, United Nations Security Council, "Sixth Report of the Secretary-General on the UN Observer Mission in Sierra Leone," S/1999/645, 4 June 1999, 2.

6. Adebajo (*Building Peace,* 98) reports that the Reverend Jesse Jackson, U.S. Special Envoy for Africa, pressured Kabbah to accept the deal. With his main backer Nigeria signaling its intent to withdraw and Sankoh's backers (Ivory Coast, Burkina Faso, and Togo whose president, Gnassingbe Eyadema, had a special interest in the RUF on account of his daughter's marriage to Sankoh) urging him to work out a deal, Kabbah had little options except to sign on.

7. Nigeria's atrocious human rights record under Sani Abacha led several would-be ECOMOG donors to impose various forms of sanctions. With the exception of the United States (which channeled initial contribution through military contracts with private security firms like Pacific Architects and Engineers and their subcontractor, International Charters Inc.) and the World Bank (which announced $100 million in emergency aid for Sierra Leone in May 1998), no major external aid came to ECOMOG until the exit of the Abacha regime. As a result, Nigeria had to carry a major portion of the funding burden, rumored in Abuja to cost $1 million per day, with substantial portions of the money allocated finding its way into the pockets of various military commanders.

8. I. William Zartman, *Cowardly Lions: Missed Opportunities to Prevent State Collapse and Deadly Conflict* (forthcoming), part II, case 2f.

9. As of 30 July 1999 there were only forty-nine military observers and two troops, supported by a two-person medical team. The civilian component of UNOMSIL, as of 4 June 1999, was twenty-nine international civilian personnel and twenty-four locally recruited staff (UNOMSIL website, www.un.org/Depts/DPKO/Missions/unomsil.htm).

10. Abiodun Alao, "Sierra Leone: Tracing the Genesis of a Controversy," briefing paper no. 50, Royal Institute of International Affairs, London, June 1998; Hirsh, *Sierra Leone: Diamonds.*

11. I. William Zartman, ed., *Preventive Negotiation: Avoiding Conflict Escalation* (Lanham, Md.: Rowman & Littlefield, 2001).

8

Intervention in East Timor

Eric Schwartz

In the wake of East Timor's transition to full sovereignty and independence on 20 May 2002, it is useful to consider what lessons might be learned from the Australian-led intervention beginning in September 1999. Although almost 80 percent of the East Timorese voted for independence on 30 August 1999, armed militia groups sought to reverse the popular decision through massive violence and killing. In response, the UN Security Council authorized the deployment of the International Force East Timor (INTERFET) on 15 September 1999, to restore order in the territory.

The following observations are preliminary perspectives of a former U.S. government official, designed to contribute to the evolving analysis of this intervention by other practitioners and scholars.

Factors That Gave Rise to the Intervention and to U.S. Involvement

The September 1999 military intervention in East Timor came after widespread violence that followed a UN-sponsored referendum on independence in East Timor. In that referendum the people of the territory opted, by a margin of 78.2

percent, not to accept incorporation into Indonesia. Threatened by this vote for independence, East Timor-based militia, supported by important elements of the Indonesian military, went on a rampage throughout the territory, destroying much of its infrastructure, threatening the small UN election monitoring mission, and killing up to one thousand or more people.

There was a range of factors that led to the Australian intervention in East Timor. It is unclear whether any one, by itself, would have been sufficient to result in the intervention, but taken together they clearly were decisive.

First, the magnitude of human rights abuses taking place in East Timor, combined with extensive media attention, played an important role in encouraging Australian government action. In particular, the Australian public was appalled by reports of widespread abuses in East Timor and made clear that they would support robust Australian government action. The Australian public even supported a proposal for a tax increase that Australian government officials thought would be necessary to finance Australia's military operation in East Timor.

From the Australian government and official international community perspective, a second critical factor was the perception of legitimacy surrounding the possibility of the intervention. The Indonesian annexation of East Timor in 1975 had never been recognized legally by the international community as a whole, though ironically, it had been so recognized by Australia. In addition, it was Indonesia itself that put East Timor on the road to independence with the decision of Indonesian president Habibie to permit a referendum in the territory. Once the East Timorese voted overwhelmingly for independence, there was clear justification for the international community to protect the democratic process against illegal opposition and violence. In that context, other governments that might otherwise have been reluctant to consider intervention were prepared to press the government of Indonesia to permit entry of an international force at the direction of the Security Council.

A related factor was the acquiescence of the government of Indonesia in the decision to intervene. Of course, there was enormous diplomatic pressure put on the government of Indonesia, including U.S. suspension of military-to-military ties just before President Habibie agreed to the intervention, as well as reported prodding from within Southeast Asia. But Indonesian government acquiescence was not inevitable, and it was unlikely that either the Australians or other governments from within the region could have been persuaded to support an intervention—let alone participate in it—in the absence of agreement by the Indonesian leadership (which was an essential requirement for obtaining a Security Council resolution authorizing the intervention).

Another important factor, not only to the Australian government, but also to the United States, was the impact of continued unrest in Indonesia on Indonesia's ability to conduct normal relations with much of the rest of the world. Even if the Clinton administration had been prepared to argue that the critical importance of Indonesia demanded that the United States look the other way in East

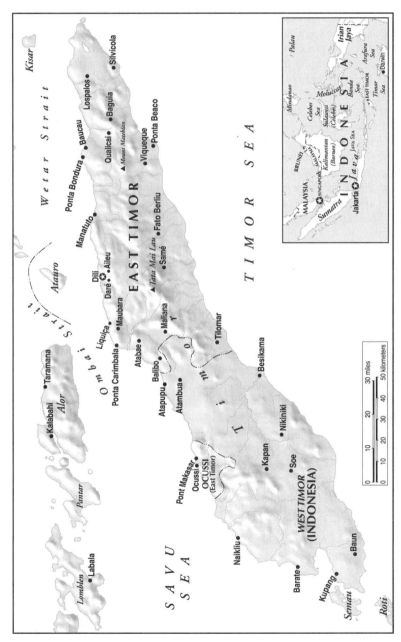

Map 8.1 East Timor

Timor, as the Ford administration essentially had done in 1975, U.S. officials might well have been disregarded by an American Congress prepared to sanction Indonesia for abuses in East Timor.[1]

The strong diplomatic support for Australia by the United States was very important in facilitating the intervention, and all of the factors described above influenced the administration's decision to provide and sustain such support. In addition to those factors, at least some U.S. government officials were concerned that continued turmoil and repression in East Timor could have provided the Indonesian military with a pretext to assert political control in Jakarta. Finally, there was some concern that East Timor represented a major test of UN credibility—and the credibility of the Security Council, in particular. If, after debacles in Somalia and Rwanda earlier in the decade, the Security Council did not act with effectiveness in East Timor, the institution would have suffered stinging criticism for ineptitude.

While these factors resulted in strong U.S. support for the intervention in East Timor, they may not have been sufficient to spur U.S. military participation in the Australian-led INTERFET operation. For U.S. decision makers considering a possible role for U.S. troops, a critical additional element was the simple desire to be responsive to a request for such help from Australia—a trusted and valued ally with a highly capable military.[2] Whatever the Clinton administration would have done in the absence of Australian leadership, the Australian dimension helped to ensure the relatively rapid decision to deploy a small but important contingent of Americans to East Timor and to Darwin. In fact, as the final papers describing the detailed nature of the U.S. commitment went to the president in mid-September, a key question from the national security advisor was whether the U.S. package of military support addressed Australia's concerns.

Moreover, in the transition from INTERFET to the "blue-helmeted" UN Transitional Administration for East Timor (UNTAET), U.S. decision makers focused on this very question of Australian expectations as the administration considered how a small U.S. military contingent (known as the U.S. Group East Timor, or USGET), operating outside the UN mission, might support the East Timorese in the period prior to independence. Of course, this willingness to assist a treaty ally was greatly facilitated by U.S. appreciation of the capabilities of the Australian military (which continued to play a major role in East Timor during the two-year UNTAET phase), and the resulting confidence that U.S. troops would not be drawn into combat or extended involvement in the operation.[3]

The U.S. military contribution to the INTERFET operation was small, but critical. The United States reached its maximum ground presence in East Timor on 11 November 1999, when there were 235 U.S. troops in the territory. In addition, U.S. troops were deployed in Australia in support of the Timor operation, and the troop numbers there went as high as 353 (on 27 November 1999).[4] The maximum regional complement of U.S. troops, which included a marine expeditionary unit offshore, was just over three thousand in early October. The United States provided strategic and tactical fixed wing airlift, tactical helicopter airlift, intelligence, communications support, a civil-military operations center, a logistics planning cell, and other support. The Australians particularly valued the offshore presence of an amphibious readiness group, which included the marines and served as an important demonstration of U.S. interest and resolve as well as alliance solidarity. In fact, some Australians referred to the U.S. offshore deployment as the "strategic reserve." By all accounts, the U.S. contribution significantly enhanced INTERFET capabilities as well as credibility.

In sum, key elements that resulted in the intervention were a gruesome human rights situation that caught the attention of the world's media; an interested and capable regional government operating with strong support of its public; the existence of a clear remedy combined with a high degree of legitimacy surrounding international action; agreement by the Indonesian government to accept international assistance; high perceived regional stakes; and concern about the credibility of the United Nations. For the Americans, a crucial additional element was the request of a treaty ally, combined with an appreciation that the ally was capable of playing an effective lead role over time.

Timing and Goals of the Intervention

The intervention came upon the heels of a UN Mission in East Timor known as UNAMET that was essentially a UN electoral assistance operation with military liaison officers. UNAMET operated under the guidance of the UN's Department of Political Affairs (DPA). As an election-monitoring effort, UNAMET was not a peacekeeping mission and did not have any military troops dedicated to security, as this was to be provided by the Indonesian military.

The UNAMET mission was the steward of a very fragile prereferendum process. UNAMET's role reflected the 5 May 1999 Agreement between Indonesia and Portugal on the Question of East Timor, as well as an associated agreement between the UN, Indonesia, and Portugal regarding modalities. The provisions made clear that the government of Indonesia would be responsible for security, and that arrangement—as troubling as it may have been—was widely believed to be an essential precondition for Indonesian support of the referendum process.

Even as security conditions deteriorated in the period following the May agreement, the Indonesians made it clear that only they would retain responsibilities for security in the territory.

Thus, in the months before the referendum, as acts of violence continued by militias supported by elements of the Indonesian armed forces, the UN, and the international community sought to use diplomatic suasion to urge Indonesian authorities to protect citizens in East Timor and to ensure at least enough security to permit the referendum to go forward. While the threat of larger-scale, postreferendum violence was always present, there was some optimism within the diplomatic community in the days preceding the referendum that violence following the vote might be short-lived.[5]

Of course, in the aftermath of the 30 August 1999 ballot, with the Indonesian military authorities proving either unable or unwilling to stop the carnage in the territory, there was no alternative to military intervention to preserve East Timor's democratization process and safeguard the lives and well-being of the people of the territory.

The goals of the intervention—a green-helmeted "coalition of the willing" led by Australia—were clear and were described in the UN Security Council resolution: "to restore peace and security in East Timor, to protect and support UNAMET in carrying out its tasks and, within force capabilities, to facilitate humanitarian assistance operations."

There was a general unanimity of objectives among all interested governments, from Australia, the United States, and Europe, to the governments in Southeast and East Asia. To be sure, there was some uneasiness within the region about the strong role being played by Australia, but this did not undermine the general consensus in support of international action.

Assessing Several Aspects of the Intervention

It is useful to consider three stages of outside intervention in assessing international community involvement in East Timor: first, the initial deployment of UNAMET in the spring of 1999 leading up to the 30 August referendum; second, the INTERFET military intervention itself, beginning in September; and third, the transition of the multinational INTERFET to a UN peacekeeping operation in early 2000.

The Decision to Deploy the UNAMET Mission without International Military Forces

The understandings reached between the Portuguese, the Indonesians, and the UN in May 1999 did not envision an international force with the capacity of deterring and suppressing violence. Rather, they envisioned the deployment of UNAMET as an electoral assistance mission operating within a very compressed time frame leading to a referendum. The obvious question is whether the governments involved made an error in agreeing or acquiescing in arrangements that put Indonesia in charge of security for the referendum.

It is not clear, however, that this situation could have been easily avoided. First, with respect to whether the United States should have pressed for a different arrangement, American officials were not the central players in these negotiations. The agreements on the referendum process were essentially between the governments of Indonesia and Portugal and the United Nations. Moreover, this seemed consistent with U.S. policy, which sought to encourage the parties to resolve their differences taking into account the sentiments of the people of East Timor. Second, the Indonesian government, and particularly its military, seemed unprepared to relinquish control over security. Moreover, having agreed to the referendum in the first place and with a proud military that had a fair amount of capability when it chose to use it, the government of Indonesia had at least a defensible (however questionable) claim to retaining responsibility in this area.

Should foreign governments have pushed harder for a more robust international presence when the agreement was negotiated, even if doing so would have threatened Indonesian government willingness to agree to the referendum process itself? Could interested governments have generated enough diplomatic pressure to convince the Indonesians to permit an outside force capable of deterring violence? And even if they were able to do so, in the absence of a clear and present threat, would the Australians and others have been prepared to land such a force?

There was no international consensus for a military deployment, and it is far from certain that the obstacles described above could have been overcome. Given the choice between what occurred, including the killings and destruction, the resulting entry of INTERFET and the progress toward independence, on the one hand and, on the other hand, the continuation of the political status quo in East Timor, most of the people of East Timor may have chosen the former. But however realistic the predicament, this is a very unsettling assessment given the grave human rights abuses that did take place prior to the INTERFET deployment. Moreover, whatever the accuracy of the assessment, it is difficult to escape a post hoc conclusion that a serious and concerted effort should have been made to establish an international military presence in the run-up to the referendum.

Speed of International Response When Postreferendum Violence Began: Were Planning and Coordination Efforts Adequate?

Given the possibility of postreferendum violence as understood by Australia, the United States, and other governments, a more pertinent question may be whether there was adequate contingency planning for responding to a bad-case scenario.

This is a complex issue, as planning can take place in many ways and at several levels: at the policy level in Washington and other capitals,[6] between governments and at the UN, and at the military operational level. Moreover, without access to documentation and additional information, an assessment of this issue is further complicated by the difficulty, in retrospect, of distinguishing between general planning for a postreferendum UN presence—which was occurring at several levels—and planning for worst-case scenarios.[7] In any event, a broad review of this issue is beyond the scope of this chapter. What follows are tentative observations about Australian and U.S. efforts in this area.

On the military side, Australia appears to have made preparations for alternative scenarios in the wake of possible referendum outcomes. Late in 1998, the

Australians reportedly realized they needed to take concrete measures to enhance infantry readiness. Moreover, prior to the events of early September, then-Major General Peter Cosgrove led a limited access contingency planning effort,[8] though I do not know its level of detail. Apparently there were also discussions at the U.S. Pacific Command about forces that might be necessary to implement a robust operation in East Timor. Although I have not obtained precise information on the timing of these latter two sets of actions, they seem to have taken place within months prior to the outbreak of postreferendum violence.

At about the same time (and perhaps even earlier), an Australian paper envisioning a three-brigade postreferendum peacekeeping operation had been shared with the U.S. State Department, and a senior Australian military officer had been encouraging UN Secretariat officials to think about follow-on, more robust peacekeeping options.

On the policy side in Washington, National Security Council (NSC) deputies had met on the referendum process in East Timor on two or three occasions within the several months leading up to 30 August. Moreover, U.S. officials at the working level had been engaged in planning and discussion about a post-election UN presence in the territory. According to one former State Department official I interviewed, the State Department, in mid-July, began a quiet internal political-military planning effort in anticipation of possible "worst-case" scenarios that could emerge following a referendum. Also in the summer of 1999, efforts were made elsewhere within the U.S. government to alert senior U.S. foreign and defense officials to the possibility of widespread violence after the referendum. NSC deputies, just prior to the crisis, requested planning information from the U.S. military on possible military options. However, this occurred late in August, and there was not early and detailed interagency planning at the policy level for a worst-case scenario, either within the U.S. government or between the United States and other governments interested and involved in the issue.

A key question is whether U.S. policymakers ought to have undertaken such interagency pol-mil contingency planning and whether they should have been more aware of, and involved in, whatever military planning for contingencies was under way in the summer of 1999. Perhaps such actions would have made for a more rapid response in early September. On the other hand, given the generally slow pace of international action to address man-made conflicts elsewhere around the world, the international response in this case was arguably swift—at least in relative terms. The Security Council resolution authorizing the INTERFET deployment came on 15 September and was the result of aggressive diplomacy in the context of postreferendum violence. Moreover, the arrival of the first INTERFET troops began on 20 September, about five days after the UN vote.

It is also worth noting that the "bad-case" scenario that unfolded after 30 August may not have been the one that most officials expected. For many, the fear was a more ambiguous referendum outcome, which would have given Indonesian authorities a rationale to maintain control in the territory. Planning for a military intervention under this scenario would have been extremely difficult.

Whatever the most likely worst case, extensive early discussion and debate about an intervention option, especially between governments, could have had two adverse outcomes. First, if intergovernmental discussions on contingencies (and response options) took place in the run-up to the referendum, it would have been difficult to have such discussions quietly, and—if they became known to the government of Indonesia—they could have provided a pretext to cancel (or postpone) the referendum. Second, without the reality of a crisis and a trusted ally asking urgently for help, the Department of Defense would have resisted the presentation of meaningful options for U.S. military involvement. Moreover, early presentation of such options in the abstract to senior policymakers might well have been unproductive. In the absence of the high-level representations from Australian allies that only came with the crisis, senior U.S. officials— presented with options in a nonemergency setting and prior to Indonesian agreement to permit an international force—might have foreclosed the possibility of responses that ultimately became U.S. policy.

These obstacles to planning were compounded by the fact that the United States, while ultimately prepared to play actively on the East Timor issue, was not eager to take a leading role in a military operation. And with a proliferation of national security issues that have a claim on the attention of U.S. officials, it is not possible to prepare pol-mil plans against all contingencies. In this particular case, any detailed (and early) contingency planning for a worst-case scenario might well have required a joint effort with the government of Australia.[9] Moreover, the overall process played out while U.S. officials were deeply engaged in Kosovo, which almost certainly had an impact on the attention accorded East Timor.

Nonetheless, it is hard to argue against the proposition that a higher degree of interagency pol-mil contingency planning would have created the possibility of a more rapid international response after 30 August. In addition, it might have helped to avoid some misunderstanding between the United States and Australia in the first part of September 1999 when Australia's political leadership expressed irritation about the perceived ambiguity of the American commitment and level of participation in INTERFET.[10]

Finally, on the issue of coordination, it is important to credit the successful Australian effort at building support for and encouraging participation in the multinational force. This not only enhanced the credibility of the INTERFET effort, but demonstrated that a strong regional actor can engage effectively in coalition building for multilateral peace operations.

The Size of the INTERFET Force

During the week of 5 September, there was some concern among senior U.S. officials that the size of the force being contemplated by the Australians— about three brigades and up to about ten thousand troops—could be inadequate.

At one high-level policy meeting at the White House, one or more officials suggested that, to avoid getting bogged down, the Australians ought to have far more troops, given the uncertainty of the threat picture. (While this meeting took place before the administration had received a detailed Australian concept of operations, it did occur after the Australians made clear they would not deploy to East Timor without the consent of the government of Indonesia.)

Of course, it quickly became apparent that a highly disciplined force, robust rules of engagement, and a willingness to use deadly force when necessary were all force multipliers, making the deployment, initially at only several thousand but growing to as many as ten thousand, adequate to do the job.[11]

According to the government of Australia, by 29 September, ten days after the first INTERFET troops landed, the force had about thirty-seven hundred personnel in East Timor.

The initial plan was to build out carefully from Dili and, by early October, Baucau airfield toward the east had been secured and troops had carried out patrols and operations in a number of provincial towns and cities. According to the Australian Defence [*sic*] Force, INTERFET ultimately included twenty-two nations. At its peak, it consisted of about ten thousand personnel, with the Australians contributing just over half of the force. This included three infantry battalion groups, headquarters and support units, and maritime and air assets. (As it turned out, the Australian and New Zealand forces of INTERFET conducted most of the combat operations and sustained most of the INTERFET casualties.)

The Transition from INTERFET to a UN Peace Operation

It is clear that the military component of the UNTAET operation that evolved out of INTERFET was very much informed by the experience of early September. Where before September it was far from clear that the Indonesian government would permit a robust peacekeeping force to operate in the territory in the transition to independence, after the crisis and the intervention there was no question that the UNTAET force would need peace enforcement authority and capabilities similar to INTERFET, at least in the near term.

A key to the successful transition was the willingness of Australia—and the Australian military leadership—to continue to play a decisive role in transitioning the force and for the government of Australia to continue to serve, in many respects, as the backbone of the operation—although with a somewhat reduced profile.

In fact, the INTERFET-UNTAET transition strategy began prior to the initial INTERFET deployment. In developing the INTERFET intervention option, the Australians made clear that they envisioned a four-phase approach that included establishing the preconditions for deployment, inserting INTERFET, restoring peace and security, and transferring INTERFET to a UN peacekeeping operation to carry the independence process forward.

U.S. officials resisted the Australian desire to put into the Security Council resolution that established UNTAET on 25 October 1999 a target date for the INTERFET-UNTAET handover. Instead, the resolution called for a handover "as soon as possible." Indeed, such transitions have to be based on the circumstances on the ground and not predetermined dates. Thus, the U.S. position was the right one. At the same time, with or without a target date, the Australians were committed to ensuring the success of the follow-on UN force and thus were probably unconvinced that a prescribed target for the transition date signaled any lack of resolve.[12]

In any event, very shortly after INTERFET had stabilized the situation, the Australians moved forward on plans for a progressive handing over of control of the operation to UNTAET in a series of stages, moving over time from the least contested and least dangerous part of the territory to the areas of greatest potential for sporadic conflict with rogue militia groups crossing from West Timor. The continued role that Australia envisioned for itself undoubtedly gave it much greater credibility and authority in dealing with the UN in the planning for the progressive withdrawal of INTERFET.

The Role of the Military Intervention: Creating Space for Transitional Activity

There was overwhelming support for an independent East Timor among inhabitants in the territory. And although peacekeeping troops may have been engaged in civic action projects, the role of both the INTERFET and the UNTAET peacekeeping forces was to deter and suppress militia and any others who might seek to challenge the process leading to independence. Both INTERFET and UNTAET created political space for a broad range of civic institution building, from repair of infrastructure, to stabilization of the economy, to establishing representative government where none had existed.

As a result of the combination of UNTAET sustaining a suitably secure environment, the absence of ambiguity about the territory's future, and the near-absolute absence of local infrastructure and capacity, East Timor provides analysts with an unusual opportunity to examine the challenges and potential for nation building.

James Traub, writing in the July-August 2000 issue of *Foreign Affairs*, provided a graphic description of the task in an interview with a legal scholar in the UNTAET mission.[13] The scholar remarked, "[i]n Kosovo, we had judges, lawyers, prosecutors; the trouble was finding one who didn't have a Yugoslav past or a Serbian collaborator past. Here you don't have a single lawyer. . . . It did not help matters any that the militias had burned or stolen every single law book in East Timor."

Traub alludes to the pervasiveness of the UN transitional administration with his description of the new bureaucrats of the East Timor Authority, as the state administration is called, [who] work out of an auditorium located right behind the Governor's House [with] . . . the names of the nascent ministries taped to the back of computers: Civil Service, Water Supply, Agriculture, Judicial Affairs, and so on. Their job . . . is to supply the Timorese with what they don't have, but also to train them to take over the work themselves.

Though it will be the task of others to evaluate these efforts, the transition assistance process evolved considerably during the two-year period leading to independence on 20 May 2002, as the UN's Special Representative of the Secretary General (SRSG) progressively transferred authority for governance to East Timorese leaders. That process resulted in successful elections for a constituent assembly in the summer of 2001 and the formal transition to independence a year later. To their credit, UN Security Council members established a post-independence UN presence as well,[14] to ensure the continuation of political progress and stability in the newly created nation-state.

Conclusion

On balance, the INTERFET intervention is rightly characterized as a success. Unquestionably, the intervention alleviated death, suffering, and massive violation of human rights and guaranteed that East Timorese independence would not be derailed by militant obstructionists. It also significantly reduced the likelihood that internal conflict would recur in the future. Similarly, the stability provided by both the INTERFET and the UNTAET military forces provided the space necessary for postconflict peace building, while the international community developed not an *exit strategy* but a strategy for the transfer of power to the people of East Timor. It is now up to the citizens of that new country, assisted by the UN and the international community, to create the political, economic, and social conditions that will best ensure long-term peace and stability.

Notes

I was senior director for multilateral and humanitarian affairs at the National Security Council during the East Timor intervention in 1999. This chapter is based largely on my experiences in that position. I would like to thank three individuals who were involved in East Timor policy during the Clinton administration and made very useful comments on initial drafts of this chapter. They are Len Hawley, who served as deputy assistant secretary of state for peacekeeping in the summer of 1999; Jame Schear, who served as deputy assistant secretary of defense for peacekeeping and humanitarian operations; and Matt Vaccaro, who served as a director at the National Security Council.

1. Of course, the issue did not arise, as the Clinton administration was disposed to advance the democratic process in East Timor.

2. The president was also lobbied by world leaders from outside Australia, which undoubtedly helped to encourage his support for a U.S. military role.

3. This point about Australian capabilities is critical to consider as one assesses the likelihood of similar U.S. involvement in peace operations led by other governments.

4. These figures come from unclassified records drawn from my personal files.

5. At the time, discussions were under way at the UN on the nature of the follow-on UN presence that would be required in a transition following a vote for independence in East Timor.

6. In using terms such as "policy level" and "pol-mil planning" in this section, I am generally referring to Washington-based, interagency planning that seeks to integrate civilian and military dimensions.

7. And in fact, planning for the former could include efforts to anticipate the latter.

8. My discussion with General Cosgrove, August 2001. Cosgrove, who commanded the INTERFET operation, served as Commander First Division and Deployable Joint Force Headquarters (Australia).

9. This is not to understate the considerable interaction that *did* take place between U.S. and Australian officials. In any event, it would be very valuable to explore the degree of pol-mil planning for a worst-case scenario that may have occurred within the government of Australia.

10. Despite this conclusion it is worth mentioning that, from the U.S. perspective, the response was a relatively quick one, as National Security Council "principals" first met on the crisis on Monday, 6 September. When they next met informally on Wednesday morning, 8 September, principals made a firm decision to recommend to the president that the United States contribute militarily to the Australian-led effort.

11. The adequacy of the force also was the result of the weak resistance presented by the militia groups, though the militia's disinclination to fight was almost certainly informed by the capabilities that INTERFET brought to bear.

12. Frankly, U.S. opposition to a target date for withdrawal was probably informed by the U.S. experience in setting such target dates for U.S. troop withdrawals in other peace operations (such as Bosnia). In the U.S. case, such targets often have suggested an ambivalence about "staying the course."

13. James Traub, "Inventing East Timor," *Foreign Affairs* 79, no. 4 (July-August 2000).

14. UN Security Council Resolution 1410, on the establishment of the UN Mission of Support in East Timor (UNMISET), 17 May 2002.

Military Intervention: Lessons for the Twenty-First Century

William J. Lahneman

This chapter offers several broad observations and recommendations about military intervention in internal conflict to help inform policies toward current and future cases of this complex undertaking. It also summarizes the major lessons from each case study. It does so not only by tapping the wealth of detailed information in chapters 1 through 8, but also by drawing upon the contributions of the many scholars and other nongovernment experts who participated in the *Project on Internal Conflict.*[1] Their insights and expertise are gratefully acknowledged and, when possible, specific contributions have been noted. The chapter frames its recommendations in terms of their relevance for U.S. policymakers, but they have value for policymakers in any state contemplating military intervention.

The observations contained in this chapter must be considered within the tapestry of the cultural norms, political dynamics, and economic backdrop that make each case of intervention unique. The cases in chapters 2 through 8 amply demonstrate the reason for this caveat. For instance, in Cambodia, little chance of conflict resolution existed until the foreign parties who sponsored the warring factions stopped providing aid. When this came to pass, prospects for successfully concluding the conflict rose significantly. But in Sierra Leone, while foreign actors had a role in sustaining internal conflict, there could be no lasting peace until a meaningful plan for running the country and for stabilizing its economy was developed.

The chapter focuses on factors that affect military intervention because it is this type of intervention that is most complex, most costly, most contentious, and has the most potential for complications and error. Intervention does not have to possess a military dimension. It can, for example, consist only of diplomatic or economic measures designed to bring about the desired results. When nonmilitary forms of intervention succeed, they prevent or end conflict at a cost far lower to all concerned than military intervention.

However, military intervention is required to halt violence and restore order in some cases. In the absence of military intervention in Bosnia and Rwanda, for example, "peace" would have been restored only when the power of the Bosnian Muslims and Hutus, respectively, had been destroyed through sustained ethnic cleansing and genocide. A similar outcome might have occurred in East Timor if intervention had not occurred promptly. In Haiti, antigovernment forces could not hope to restore the elected government of Jean-Bertrand Aristide without foreign military assistance. In Sierra Leone, the government would have been unable to bring the rebels under control without the intervention of foreign troops. Since the rebels had no agenda for bringing about a sustainable peace and viable economic program, their defeat, or at least their neutralization by an intervening military force, was necessary to make a lasting peace possible.

While military intervention is sometimes necessary to stop violent internal conflict and impose stability, it is rarely sufficient to bring about a sustainable peace. This is because military intervention is a tactic, not a strategy, and the improvements it generates are temporary. As noted above with regard to Sierra Leone, while foreign military intervention was necessary to stop the civil war, a lasting peace will not be possible until the government develops a plan that will effectively put enough fighters back to work in the civilian economy to deplete the ranks of the rebel movement.

Accordingly, if one overriding generalization can be made from the case studies in this volume, it is that some degree of reconstruction or "nation building" is necessary pursuant to a military intervention to enable sustainable governments, economies, and civil societies to emerge from the destruction wrought by internal conflict. Somalia is a case in point. It demonstrates the dangers of abruptly terminating military intervention before any real progress has been made toward restoring government institutions and providing law and order. Today Somalia remains a stateless nation in which warlords continue to fight for control and rule using the power of the gun.

This chapter organizes the lessons learned from the *Project on Internal Conflict* into themes, which can be expressed as key questions. These are:

1. Why do most military interventions provide "too little too late?" (Why do military interventions occur only after significant death and destruction have occurred and usually with too little force to make an immediate difference?)

2. What makes a military intervention legitimate and why is legitimacy important?
3. What constitutes a "successful" military intervention?
4. How does military intervention relate to nation-building strategies?
5. What are some of the challenges to successful nation building (or reconstruction)?

Lessons learned by studying military interventions in internal conflict during the 1990s have relevance for the current U.S. interventions in Afghanistan and Iraq, despite the fact that these operations began as interstate wars rather than as military interventions in internal conflicts. While some will choose to emphasize the differences between the interventions discussed in this volume and the interventions in Afghanistan and Iraq, it is important to recognize the many similarities. The U.S.-led military operations in Afghanistan and Iraq were both interstate wars *and* military interventions in internal conflict. Afghanistan under the Taliban and Iraq under Saddam Hussein were both multinational states in which minorities were brutally suppressed and human rights were systematically and significantly violated. Even under these conditions various factions continued to engage in internal conflict against the government and against other factions.

In Afghanistan, violent internal conflict had been a way of life for several generations. The Taliban never controlled the country's entire territory because it never completely defeated the various other armed factions that continued to fight for control. In fact, several of these factions, under the banner of the Northern Alliance, ultimately became principal allies of the United States and constituted a decisive factor in defeating the Taliban. In Iraq, Shiite Muslims in southern Iraq rebelled following the 1991 Persian Gulf War and were brutally suppressed by Saddam Hussein's regime. The enforcement of a northern "no-fly" zone following the war also allowed a Kurdish shadow government commanding armed fighters to emerge in northern Iraq.

By defeating organized resistance and overthrowing the governments of both Afghanistan and Iraq, the United States and its coalition partners essentially created failed states with all of the problems that accompany this condition. Thus, while U.S. and coalition troops are operating in Afghanistan and Iraq as the result of interstate wars, the postconflict situations in both states are strikingly similar to those in many of the cases studied in this volume. Accordingly, achieving successful outcomes in Iraq and Afghanistan will depend upon many of the same factors, demand the same actions, and involve potential pitfalls similar to those encountered in the military interventions of the 1990s.

"Too Little Too Late"

The majority of interventions in the 1990s tended to fall into this category. They were "too little" in the sense that intervention was performed by military forces that were insufficiently configured in numbers, equipment, and command-and-control capabilities to prevail in combat operations. These characteristics also rendered them inadequate, at least in the opening phases of military intervention, to reestablish law and order in the wake of internal conflict so that reconstruction could begin in earnest. They were "too late" in the sense that military intervention occurred only after violent internal conflict had been under way for some time and had caused widespread destruction and human rights abuses. Since it is more difficult to stop violence once it has begun than to prevent it in the first place, why has military intervention tended to follow this suboptimal pattern? Will this pattern continue in the future? Have the terrorist attacks of 11 September 2001 and the subsequent war on terrorism affected it?

One school of thought argues that intervention could be initiated before horrific casualties have occurred if better early warning indicators of impending violent internal conflict could be developed. Better early warning would give policymakers more time to debate the merits of a proposed intervention and deal with the various domestic hurdles to intervention listed below. In cases where a multilateral response is preferred, better early warning of violent internal conflict gives international organizations such as the United Nations more time to organize intervention before widespread death and destruction occur.

Others take the view that, while better early warning indicators would reduce response time, interventions in internal conflict would still be late and inadequate because of the domestic and international dynamics associated with deciding to intervene. As I. William Zartman has commented, it is often a question of failure to pay *early attention* to impending violent internal conflicts rather than a lack of *early warning* indicators.[2]

In chapter 1, John Steinbruner summarized the domestic and international dynamics surrounding military intervention as an ongoing debate between the realist and globalist worldviews.

> Those who believe that the prime cause of civil conflict is usually indigenous to the society in which it occurs are also inclined to believe that the responsibility for settling it properly and practically remains within that society. . . . That perspective emerges from the traditional realist view of international relations. In contrast, those who take a globalist view of international relations see both the sources of conflict and the interests at stake in broader perspective. Globalist assessments of the specific conflicts emphasize the significance of endemic economic austerity in generating them and trace the determinants to faulty connections to international finance and commodity markets. . . . Those assessments see greater reason for direct international intervention to control civil conflict—most notably, to counteract market defects that might undermine the emerging global economy and to defend the basic legal provisions that are necessary to sustain it.[3]

An American subscribing to the realist view might look at a proposed case of military intervention and ask, "What U.S. interests are at stake to warrant intervention?" Someone subscribing to the globalist perspective might argue that it is not a question of national interests. Rather the important point is that no breakdown of legal standards can be tolerated in a globalizing world, because these areas create safe havens for both international terrorist groups and transnational criminal organizations that can disrupt and distort globalization.

It is useful to note a third motive for military intervention, a purely humanitarian one. Americans and others advocate military intervention because they want to see the killings, human suffering, and human rights violations associated with internal conflict stopped. This view contends that U.S. intervention must be based on moral and legal considerations in addition to traditional national interests and concerns about the viability of globalization.[4] Certainly idealism and human rights have been pillars of American foreign policy since the beginning of the republic.[5] Are they a sufficient motive for intervening in internal conflict?

Case analyses show that policymakers in developed countries leaned decidedly toward the realist motivation for intervention during the 1990s but, in the absence of threats to national interests, sometimes intervened for humanitarian motives instead. This fact appears to have created domestic and international political dynamics that help explain the "too little, too late" effect.

Domestic considerations help explain the "too late" effect. For example, during the 1990s, U.S. elected officials needed time to debate the need for U.S. military intervention to halt specific internal conflicts when they perceived that calls for intervention were driven more by humanitarian motives than clear threats to national interests in most cases. The fact that U.S. elected officials held certain views about how the U.S. public regarded intervention further complicated the decision-making process. For example, elected officials typically believe that the American people are resistant to military intervention and that the public has no tolerance for seeing U.S. forces suffer casualties. Policymakers also believe that Americans are opposed to situations in which foreign officers command U.S. troops.[6]

These beliefs bias policymakers against intervention when no clear national interest is threatened and further complicate the domestic policymaking process. As a result, during the 1990s, policymakers often waited until public opinion demanded that something be done to halt human rights abuses before moving toward intervention. However, public demands for action are reactive. They normally arise only after widespread media coverage of human rights abuses has raised public awareness of these situations. Under these circumstances, preemptive intervention and intervention in the initial phases of an internal conflict are all but precluded, since large-scale human rights violations must first have occurred, and the media must have covered these events widely before public opinion in wealthy countries—the countries most likely to intervene—pushes for intervention.[7]

Extensive polling data has shown that, in fact, the public is willing to see U.S. troops engage in military intervention if there is a moral basis for intervention. While the American people do not have a zero tolerance for casualties and do not strongly oppose the use of foreign officers to command U.S. troops, the public has less tolerance for casualties in the case of nontraditional military missions like peacekeeping operations (for example, monitoring a cease-fire agreement or providing police functions as part of restoring law and order following internal conflict) than it has for more traditional ones (such as engaging in combat operations to neutralize threats to American national interests). Moreover, public support for peacekeeping operations may erode if casualties mount during an intervention.[8] So the fact that policymakers tend to be more biased against intervention than the general public is understandable. Public support for intervention can change rapidly, but, once troops are committed and American lives and national prestige are on the line, withdrawal becomes difficult.

It thus appears that lack of political will on the part of potential intervening states is the primary reason why interventions during the 1990s occurred "too late." (The next section describes how a desire to ensure that military intervention is perceived as legitimate also biases policymakers to intervene only after internal conflict has raged for some time.) This lack of political will stemmed from the fact that most cases of intervention did not seriously threaten the national interests of the states concerned, but ongoing human rights abuses required that some action be taken.

Why did most military interventions also provide "too little" in that intervening forces proved inadequate to achieve their mission? The answer is best understood in terms of the international dynamics of intervention. In chapter 2, David Laitin argued that the general lack of will on the part of individual states resulted in a desire to spread the risk and costs of intervention. Accordingly, states preferred to intervene as part of a coalition of like-minded states, but such an approach required multilateral coordination. The United Nations became the principal organization to coordinate multilateral military interventions during the 1990s, although not the only one. Laitin offered a number of generalizations about how the attitudes of individual states toward military intervention for predominantly humanitarian reasons played out in the multilateral decision-making process in the United Nations Security Council. Several of these observations are particularly helpful in explaining the "too little" effect.

First, the psychological effect of the media coverage of civil wars encourages leaders of wealthy states to want to be seen by their constituencies as being responsive to the unfolding human tragedy. Second, the wealthy states usually prefer to obtain a United Nations mandate to intervene. This imparts legitimacy and provides a mechanism for a degree of multilateral participation and burden sharing. Third, the United Nations seeks to achieve a peace agreement among the warring parties prior to intervention because the existence of such an agreement increases the legitimacy of the use of military forces. However, with a peace agreement in place, intervening forces are expected to serve as peacekeepers rather than combatants and thus are sized and configured for noncombat duties. Fourth, wealthy states want to avoid casualties to national troops during military intervention and thus favor the use of troops from developing world countries.[9]

This dynamic created problems during the 1990s. The strong preference to achieve a peace agreement prior to military intervention tended to result in agreements that were quite fragile. A weak peace agreement increased the probability that internal conflict would resume despite the presence of intervening forces, particularly when these forces were composed of a relatively small number of lightly armed peacekeepers. In addition, common peacekeeping practices such as disarming the population inevitably produced violent reactions among local groups. Since the troops used for intervention often came from developing states, they lacked the command-and-control capabilities of developed states' forces, a weakness that was further exacerbated if they operated under an ambiguous UN command structure. These factors reduced their effectiveness if the need for combat operations became necessary, even for purposes of self-defense. The result was that, in the 1990s, intervening forces often found themselves in combat against better organized, more heavily armed, and more numerous local forces. Intervening forces proved ineffective in such circumstances and, in some cases, actually became a liability that complicated attempts to end the conflict. For example, peacekeepers were taken hostage in Bosnia and Sierra Leone.

The interventions in Afghanistan and Iraq could not be more different from this pattern. Why? Primarily because Americans and U.S. policymakers believed that intervention was necessary to protect the most vital of U.S. interests: the security of the American people and of the U.S. homeland. As a result, in both Afghanistan and Iraq, the United States and its coalition intervened with overwhelming force and declared ambitious goals that included toppling the ruling regimes and rebuilding both countries along market economy, democratic lines. However, each case differed from the other in important ways.

The intervention in Afghanistan appears to be the exception that proves the rule about why interventions in the 1990s were too little too late. After the terrorist attacks of 11 September 2001, many states—including all of the major powers—perceived that the Taliban regime threatened their vital national interests by aiding the al Qaeda terrorist movement, which had just demonstrated its capability to commit devastating attacks anywhere in the world, but particularly in the U.S. homeland. Thus, agreement on intervention was swift, a UN Security Council resolution authorizing intervention was readily produced, and high-intensity combat operations employing overwhelming force were conducted. The United States provided the lion's share of military forces and assumed a clear leadership role in a manner reminiscent of the way Australia assumed control of the East Timor intervention.

Events in Afghanistan underscore a basic premise of international relations: when one state's actions pose a clear and present threat to the national interests of other states, intervention will be swift and powerful and there will be no lack of political will. The United Nations will authorize decisive action. This pattern is essentially the very opposite of the pattern of intervention in the 1990s, which lends support to the argument that it is a lack of political will that delays intervention in internal conflicts and that this lack of will stems from the belief that an internal conflict does not clearly threaten national interests. Of course, the rapidity of the response in Afghanistan should not obscure the fact that significant death and destruction in the form of the September 11 terrorist attacks had already occurred prior to intervention, just as in the other cases studied in this volume. Intervention in Afghanistan was reactive.

The recent war with Iraq also reinforces the basic premise that states will react forcefully when they perceive their vital interests to be threatened. However, intervention in Iraq was preemptive. The U.S. administration asserted that the Iraqi regime either possessed or would soon possess weapons of mass destruction (WMDs), Iraq would soon transfer WMDs to al Qaeda or other international terrorist organizations, and these groups would use these weapons against targets in the United States. However, many other states—including France, Russia, and China, who wielded veto power on the UN Security Council, and other powerful states like Germany—did not share this perception of imminent threat. At the time of the intervention, a majority of the American people supported it, but the world community was divided and remains so. As a result, U.S. attempts to achieve UN authorization for intervention failed and some normally staunch U.S. allies, such as Turkey, refused to let U.S. forces use their territory as a staging area.[10]

The result was a rapid intervention with a strong military force, but one that was composed almost exclusively of British and American troops. This fact was not inherently problematic. Intervention in the 1990s included several cases— the Australian force that intervened in East Timor, the American force in Haiti, and the French and British forces that intervened in the final stages of violence in Rwanda and Sierra Leone, respectively—in which the forces of one country served in the predominant role. In fact, as David Laitin and Eric Schwartz contend in chapters 2 and 8, respectively, this kind of approach has come to be considered preferable in most instances of military intervention.

However, in this case the force was composed predominantly of two countries' forces because of a lack of consensus about intervention, which, by the time intervention occurred, had translated into the absence of UN authorization (further attempts by the United States to achieve an additional UN Security Council resolution authorizing the use of force against Iraq would almost certainly have resulted in a formal UN rejection of intervention as an option).[11] Only time will tell if the lack of consensus about intervention will translate into a lack of support for nation-building efforts in this case. At this time, agreement concerning postconflict reconstruction has been elusive, and international offers of financial support for reconstruction have lagged.

In summary, interventions in the 1990s were not efficient: they took place after internal conflict had raged for some time and usually employed inadequate forces. However, they did prevent significant additional death and suffering, participation and costs were dispersed among several states, and they generally had the endorsement of the United Nations, which imparted legitimacy in the eyes of the international community. Events in Afghanistan and Iraq have shown how forceful and swift interventions can be when policymakers believe that intervention is required for traditional reasons of national security. However, they also present an interesting contrast in international legitimacy and provide important insights into this concept.

The Legitimacy Factor

Afghanistan and Iraq present an interesting contrast with regard to legitimacy. Military intervention in Afghanistan has continued to possess a large measure of international legitimacy while that in Iraq has not. Why is this so? How important is international legitimacy?

The establishment and preservation of international legitimacy for cases of military intervention is extremely important because it is in the long-term interest of all countries—particularly the wealthy, developed nations that profit most from the current international system—to strengthen international regimes that regulate the use of force and thus foster the rule of law. As described above, it became customary in the 1990s to achieve legitimacy for a case of military intervention by securing the endorsement of the UN Security Council, regardless of what state or group of states ultimately conducted the intervention. In the absence of a Security Council resolution authorizing intervention, it was desirable to operate under the authorization of a regional intergovernmental organization such as the Organization of African Unity (OAU) or of an alliance such as the North American Treaty Organization (NATO). In the absence of such an endorsement, some form of multilateral action by "coalitions of the willing" was preferable to unilateral intervention for purposes of achieving legitimacy as well as to spread the costs of intervention over many states.

The existence of a UN Security Council resolution authorizing military intervention is most desirable because it implies that all UN member states consider the intervention legitimate under international law. Such a resolution is a substantive matter under the UN Charter, which means that at least nine out of the fifteen members of the Security Council voted in favor of intervention. This number must include all five permanent members of the Council—the United States, Russia, China, France, and the United Kingdom—any one of which could have exercised its veto power to prevent passage of the resolution (permanent members can also choose to abstain when voting on a substantive matter, which is not considered a veto). The passage of a resolution authorizing military intervention also signifies that all UN member states implicitly support the intervention since, under the Charter, all members of the United Nations agree to accept and carry out the decisions of the Security Council.[12]

Decisions to conduct military intervention have been—and should continue to be—contentious ones. The principal reason for this condition is that any decision to intervene violates a state's sovereignty, the concept that each state does not recognize any legitimate authority higher than its own national government. The traditional view of sovereignty holds that other countries should not interfere with what a national government does within its country's borders because these activities are essentially internal matters. The recognition of and respect for the sovereign equality of its members is the UN's first stated organizing principle.[13] However, the preservation of peace, support for human rights, and the promotion of economic and social advancement are also central themes of the UN Charter, and achievement of these goals is sometimes incompatible with traditional respect for sovereignty.

During the 1990s, a majority of the international community came to regard as legitimate military intervention to relieve human suffering and protect human rights.

> Under Chapter VII of the UN Charter, the UN Security Council can impose co-ercive measures and disregard the general principle of non-intervention in the domestic affairs of states if it determines that a particular problem poses a "threat to international peace and security." In the 1990s, the Security Council showed great creativity in defining such threats. It increasingly deemed internal conflicts and gross violations of human rights to be legitimate reasons for inter-national action. By the end of the 1990s, the idea that states should not be al-lowed to hide behind the shield of sovereignty when gross violations of human rights take place on their territory had firmly taken root.[14]

Moreover, the members of the international community generally acknowledged that military intervention often is a *necessary* tactic for stopping the internal conflicts that are so harmful to attaining these goals. The role of military forces in this regard includes their use in peacekeeping and peace enforcement (com-bat) roles, which are the kinds of intervention that this volume emphasizes. However, military intervention also includes the use of military forces in a de-terrent role by means of forward deployments and participation in regional train-ing exercises.

This new doctrine (or "metadoctrine," since it is far from fully developed and not universally accepted) consists not only of strategies for military inter-vention, but also of multilateral strategies of diplomatic, political, and economic inducements for belligerents to stop internal conflicts. Military intervention is thus considered a multidimensional tactic that is part of a larger strategy of con-flict containment.

The current metadoctrine concerning intervention is primarily a Western concept and its application has been restricted to intervention in relatively small countries. For example, the considerable territory, large populations, and power of India and China currently make their internal disputes off-limits to military intervention and, to a lesser extent, other forms of intervention as well.[15] India and Pakistan's emergence as nuclear powers demonstrates this limitation. When India and Pakistan declared that they were nuclear powers, no country or group of countries seriously considered military intervention to disarm them. Simi-larly, no degree of human rights violations by the Chinese government would prompt serious calls for military intervention. On the other hand, intervention to disarm Iraq and eliminate its imputed weapons of mass destruction was another matter entirely. While countries disagreed about the legitimacy of intervening in Iraq for a number of reasons—a lack of proof that such weapons existed or that Iraq was passing them to international terrorist groups, belief that the U.S. stated motives for invading Iraq masked more self-serving motives—there was wide-spread agreement that military intervention would be a legitimate response if

Iraq were found to be producing weapons of mass destruction and selling them to terrorists.

The emergence of the metadoctrine is significant because it constitutes a clear change in the definition of what constitutes acceptable state behavior. Governments no longer have absolute control over what they can do inside their own borders. Specifically, grave violations of human rights by a government provide sufficient grounds at least to invoke the threat of intervention even if the abusive government's actions have no repercussions beyond its borders.

Thus, the legitimate desire to uphold some minimum standard of human rights clashes with the legitimate goal of preserving state sovereignty where military intervention is concerned. No country wants to authorize violations of sovereignty lightly, since all countries want to reinforce sovereignty whenever possible so that their own will be respected. At the same time, military intervention for humanitarian purposes has become increasingly legitimate. How has this tension been reconciled in practice? One way is to conduct military intervention after internal conflict has produced significant death and destruction. In this way, the need to act to reduce human suffering clearly takes precedence over concerns about sovereignty. Thus, the tendency of countries to intervene "late" is influenced by concerns about legitimacy as well as by considerations of national interest and policymakers' desires to satisfy public calls for action to halt human rights abuses.

Experiences in Afghanistan and Iraq shed light on another potential reason why it remains difficult to legitimize intervention before violent internal conflict has begun. This is the difficulty of distinguishing preemptive interventions from acts of aggression. When policymakers send military forces into another country and those forces either engage in combat or threaten to engage in combat, there are six potential motives for doing so.

- First, military forces could be conducting military intervention in the internal conflict of another state to halt widespread human rights abuses, which is legitimate under the metadoctrine discussed above.
- Second, military forces might be conducting a *preemptive intervention.* In this case, violent internal conflict was about to ignite and other countries conducted military intervention to prevent it and avoid large-scale death and destruction. Such action would be legitimate under international law and is arguably the ideal form of military intervention in internal conflict.
- Third, military forces could be responding to an act of aggression from the other country (or agents within the country). This would be a case of *defensive war*, which is another legitimate reason for employing military force under international law (when certain criteria are met).
- Fourth, military forces might be conducting a *preemptive war.* Preemptive war refers to war initiated because an adversary's attack is thought to be imminent. By attacking first, the country that is the target of the

planned attack preempts the other state's ability to perform it. Preemptive war is generally considered a legitimate form of warfare because the motive for initiating the preemptive attack is defensive.

- Fifth, military forces might be conducting a *preventive war*. A preventive war occurs when a country perceives that another country will pose a serious threat to it sometime in the future even though it does not pose a threat at the present time. Perhaps the second country has begun an extensive arms program that will give it clear military superiority in several years. Perhaps it has begun to develop a new category of weapon that will give it a decisive advantage several years from now when the new weapons have been produced in large numbers. Under these circumstances, the first country initiates an attack on its perceived future adversary to defeat it while victory is still possible. Preventive wars are considered wars of aggression and violate international law.
- Sixth, military forces might be engaged in a clear *war of aggression* to conquer territory or obtain resources. International law forbids all forms of aggressive war.[16]

The interventions studied in this volume were clearly cases of legitimate interventions in internal conflicts, according to the evolving metadoctrine. They only occurred after significant death and suffering had occurred. While it is unfortunate that intervention did not occur sooner, it is precisely this lateness that clarifies the issue of legitimacy beyond reasonable debate. Of course, the mere fact that an intervention is responsive rather than preemptive does not rule out illegitimate behavior by an intervening power. For example, a country could use intervention in internal conflict as a pretext for aggression against a neighbor. For instance, the Nigerian intervention in Sierra Leone had elements of predatory behavior because Nigeria's desire to take possession of Sierra Leone's diamond resource was one of the goals of the intervention.[17]

What about Afghanistan and Iraq? The intervention in Afghanistan was a response to the terrorist attacks of September 11. A clear connection had been established between al Qaeda and the Taliban regime, at least in the minds of the major powers, and these countries and many others viewed the subsequent military intervention as a defensive war without elements of preemption or prevention. When the United States intervened in Afghanistan, it did so with UN authorization and as part of a coalition composed of several states. While its actions were still criticized in some quarters, particularly by factions in Muslim countries that accused the United States of waging war against the Muslim world, the fact that many countries supported the intervention and even provided troops made it extremely difficult for these negative interpretations to gain wide acceptance internationally.

In the case of Iraq, the U.S. administration argued that Iraq's program to develop weapons of mass destruction posed an imminent threat to the security of the United States and other countries. Iraq had already or would soon pass these weapons on to al Qaeda and other transnational terrorist groups, which would use them to perform devastating attacks against the United States and other countries. Accordingly, the United States argued that it was justified to initiate preemptive war. Many countries, spearheaded by three permanent members of the UN Security Council with veto power—France, Russia, and China—along with Germany, objected to the proposed intervention on the grounds that Iraq did not constitute the imminent threat to security necessary to legitimize preemptive war. The debate revolved around the existence of proof that a grave and imminent threat existed, the so-called "smoking gun" that would validate the assertions of the United States, the United Kingdom, and the other countries that argued for preemption.[18]

The inability to resolve the strong disagreement over the use of force against Iraq meant that many states considered the subsequent U.S./British invasion of Iraq to lack international legitimacy. Legitimacy can arguably only be restored if evidence discovered following the war proves the U.S. administration's claims. UN authorization after the fact is desirable but can only partially repair the damage to U.S. legitimacy unless U.S. prewar claims about Iraqi transgressions are confirmed. In the absence of such vindication, an aura of illegitimacy will continue to surround this action and claims that the United States behaved improperly—for example, invaded Iraq to steal Iraq's oil reserves or to persecute Muslims—might gain greater acceptance. Importantly, suspicions about the legitimacy of U.S. motives are likely to surface when new cases of U.S. military intervention are being considered.

In summary, imbuing a military intervention with legitimacy is important because it strengthens adherence to the rule of law in the international community. While a strong rule of law is in the interest of all nations, the wealthy countries stand to profit most from such a regime because they tend to be the largest trading nations and are the largest recipients of the benefits of globalization. In the 1990s, a metadoctrine legitimizing military intervention in internal conflict under certain circumstances emerged. However, its current stage of development rules out military intervention in the internal conflicts of large, powerful countries and arguably *requires* that violent internal conflict already be well developed before military intervention becomes a legitimate option. Understandable concerns about sovereignty and the rule of law lead states to demand a high level of proof before they are willing to confer international legitimacy on preemptive actions. Intervening preemptively accordingly runs the risk that the intervening states will be accused of violating international law by engaging in aggression, an accusation that can be difficult to disprove beyond reasonable doubt. As a result, concerns about legitimacy arguably incline policymakers of wealthy nations to allow violent internal conflict to rage for some time before intervening unless they perceive that significant national interests are at stake. Events in Afghanistan and Iraq seem to indicate that, when policymakers perceive that important national interests are threatened, military intervention will be swift, powerful, and even preemptive. Concerns about international legitimacy will be of secondary importance in such cases.

Defining Success

Discussions about motivations and legitimacy deal primarily with when, why, and how to initiate military interventions. It is just as important to address how to terminate them. Development of such a termination or "exit strategy" should occur before military intervention takes place. Ideally, policymakers decide on a set of goals that the intervention must achieve. Then they establish a method for measuring progress toward these goals. Next, they determine the point at which progress toward the goals would be sufficient to declare the military intervention a success. The specific steps for achieving success form the exit strategy.

At a minimum, a successful exit strategy should produce conditions under which the military phase of intervention can be terminated without rekindling instability and internal conflict. To achieve this important result, an effective exit strategy must address nonmilitary aspects of intervention as well as military ones. For example, if military forces have been providing law and order following internal conflict, it stands to reason that the occupying troops cannot leave (and declare that the intervention has been a success) until an appropriate civil organization has been groomed to take over this function. If steps are not taken to ensure that this organization can perform effectively while the intervention force is still in place, then it is likely that law and order will decay once again following troop withdrawal.

These kinds of practical considerations are not the most important reason to include nonmilitary factors in exit strategies. The events of September 11 have underscored what can happen when law and order are allowed to deteriorate anywhere in the world. The unstable states that result are breeding grounds for terrorists and can serve as their bases for waging war on the United States and other countries. The international community should therefore have a strong interest in preserving fundamental legal order because a violation of law and order anywhere in the world can cause problems for all other states in this era of globalization. When viewed in this way, the principal purpose of military intervention in internal conflict is to preserve, restore, or establish for the first time the rule of law within a country. Minimizing the death and destruction caused by internal conflict is certainly an important goal in itself, but it is not the principal reason for states to conduct military intervention. Accordingly, bringing a halt to internal conflict should not be a sufficient reason to declare that an intervention has been successful. Exit strategies should also include nation-building elements.

Setting appropriate goals and developing realistic exit strategies are necessary steps for a successful military intervention, but they are not sufficient to guarantee success. Policymakers must also provide the appropriate resources to achieve them. Haiti, for example, appears to be an example of an ambitious exit strategy that has not been properly supported. Similarly, the goals of the interventions in Afghanistan and Iraq are quite ambitious, even explicitly including the need for the occupying powers to engage in reconstruction or nation building. However, so far U.S. policymakers have proven unwilling to match these ambitious goals with adequate resources. As a result, there currently is a real danger that the corresponding exit strategies will fail to be accomplished.[19]

Each case of intervention possesses different situational dynamics and therefore will have a unique exit strategy. Should territory remain integrated or separated? Should intervening forces avoid changing the local balance of power? Should intervening countries want to influence the behavior of only one side in the internal conflict? Should the intervening force try to remain impartial or should it back one of the warring factions? Should the population be disarmed? Should only one faction be disarmed? The answers to these and a host of other questions will vary according to the situation.

Bosnia and Cambodia provide a useful contrast of the diverse roles that military forces can play depending on the situation. For example, large-scale military intervention with combat-ready forces was required to bring an end to organized ethnic cleansing in Bosnia. Military strategies using lesser amounts of force were not successful. In Cambodia, on the other hand, military forces had a much smaller role to play. Cambodia's warring factions were exhausted from years of fighting and were ready for peace. In addition, the foreign powers that had traditionally funded Cambodia's internal conflict had not only ceased providing support, but were also pressing Cambodia's factions to make peace. Thus, there was little chance that the formerly warring parties would resume large-scale combat operations. As a result, the initial goals of the intervention and the accompanying exit strategy did not need to include an ambitious military component.

Once an exit strategy has been determined, how can the intervening powers track progress toward success? There are two main considerations in this regard. First, it is important to remember the baseline from which any assessment should be made. It is all too common to ask whether things are worse now than they were prior to intervention. The implication here is that, if conditions have worsened since the intervention was initiated, then the intervention must be in danger of failing and is, at the least, moving further from success. The correct question is, rather, "Are things worse now than they would have been in the absence of intervention?" In other words, "What if intervention had not occurred?" In this context, the fact that things might be worse now than before intervention was initiated becomes irrelevant.

Second, it is important to identify valid indicators for tracking progress toward the goals of the exit strategy. It is very difficult to measure progress toward some goals that are widely thought to be important elements in any long-term solution to internal conflict. These include, for instance, a reduction in ethnic or racial hatred, democratization, and the establishment of a functioning economy. Since progress toward these goals is difficult to measure directly, policymakers must rely on proxies that measure them indirectly and whose values can be estimated with some degree of precision. For instance, a decrease in the number of attacks on members of one ethnic group by members of another ethnic group might be used as an indicator that racial tensions are decreasing. A large turnout for an election might signify that democracy is taking hold. An increase in per capita income could mean that the economy is revitalizing. However, there could be other reasons for these developments. A reduction in racially motivated violence and large turnouts at elections could be the result of a large troop presence by intervening forces. If these troops were to be removed, racial violence and election fraud could ensue. Similarly, an increase in per capita income could be the result of the infusion of aid and investment by foreign powers as part of the intervention. While these actions have caused per capita income to increase, the increasing trend might be a temporary effect of the intervention that will vanish if it is terminated.

Other common indicators for assessing the success of an intervention include the number of refugees being generated, the number of casualties sustained by intervening troops, a reduction in the time the media devotes to an internal conflict, success at confining a conflict within an area, relative and absolute costs of the intervention, reductions in operating tempo of intervening forces, and a reoccurrence of conflict. The point is not that all are invalid indicators and should be discarded, but rather that one should exercise due caution when using them to assess progress toward a successful intervention. In most cases, such indicators will be the only kinds of quantifiable information available.

Even under the best of circumstances, it is unlikely that any exit strategy determined in advance will remain completely intact once intervention has begun. Day-to-day events will change the situation in unforeseen ways and will probably require changes to the original exit strategy. However, comprehensive and realistic planning prior to intervention offers the best chance for ultimate success at the lowest cost in lives, material, and national prestige.

In the 1990s, planning a successful exit strategy at the beginning of an intervention was the exception rather than the rule. (Of the cases studied in this volume, the intervention in East Timor is generally considered the best example of proper initial exit strategy design.) Rather, the original limited goals of an intervention were expanded incrementally as events indicated that they were not realistic. Then exit strategies were revised accordingly. This phenomenon is known as "mission creep." Mission creep has been particularly evident in the military interventions in Somalia, Bosnia, Rwanda, and Sierra Leone. In all of these cases, the intervening powers expanded their initial exit strategies to include measures for restoring law and order and bringing about some degree of political, social, and economic stability. By contrast, the exit strategies for East Timor, Haiti, and Cambodia included some nation-building measures and have required little adjustment.

Why this pattern of incremental expansion of goals and the corresponding adjustment to exit strategies? One reason has already been discussed. It is the tendency of the UN Security Council to authorize military interventions that provide "too little." This practice means that military interventions authorized by the Council produce operations with goals that are too limited and initial exit strategies that will not work given actual situations. This kind of approach virtually guarantees that intervening forces must either be reinforced or withdrawn when they prove unable to cope with actual conditions and become a liability rather than a positive factor in ending the internal conflict.

A second reason for mission creep is that the fundamental dynamics of internal conflict incline one or more of the warring factions to resist limited military interventions. Thus, it is likely that policymakers who initially attempt limited military intervention will have to expand the size and mandate of the intervention later on. Essentially, warring factions realize that they can always give in before all is lost in a conflict, which encourages them to experiment with ways to discourage intervening forces from staying their course. In addition, parties to an internal conflict perceive that their interests in the conflict are more vital than those of the intervening states and perceive, once limited military intervention has begun, that the intervening powers will not bring overwhelming force to bear to halt the internal conflict. Warring factions will also try to capitalize on intervening powers' preference to use coalitions by attempting to use weaknesses in such coalitions to their advantage. Thus, local forces have several incentives to resist intervention forces and to believe that they can defeat the intervening forces. Given these motivations, any intervening force that is not capable of engaging in combat operations to defeat warring factions will probably be challenged. The only way to overcome such challenges is to ensure that military intervention is conducted with overwhelming force and with the clear intention of using force without hesitation if necessary.[20]

A third reason for mission creep is that there can be several plausible ways in which military forces can be employed in military intervention to reduce the effects of internal conflict. However, once intervention has occurred, unforeseen developments can escalate an internal conflict and render inadequate a force that initially was appropriate. Such developments would result in mission creep even though the initial planning for the intervention was sound. This reason for mission creep is best examined by reviewing the seven stages of intervention described by Steven Burg in chapter 3. These stages, which describe both military and nonmilitary responses of increasing intensity, are:

1. *Diplomatic peacemaking.* Diplomats look for solutions without the need to intervene militarily.
2. Military intervention in the form of *peacekeeping operations to support humanitarian relief efforts.* The intervening forces provide security for relief workers.
3. *Peacekeeping operations to monitor peace agreements.* In this setting, military forces "intervene" in another country but act as monitors of a peace agreement already in place. Their use in a combat role is not envisioned
4. The imposition of *economic and other sanctions* under the authority of the UN Security Council.
5. *Acts of deterrence.* Military force is employed in a limited fashion to induce desired behavior in local groups.

6. *Coercive diplomacy.* Military intervention occurs and the intervening forces engage in combat operations to halt ongoing internal conflict.
7. *Military occupation and nation building* intended to implement the settlement imposed on the warring parties.[21]

Each of these phases was viewed as a sufficient exit strategy when initially enacted. However, the initial effort by the international community to define success at the lowest of these levels failed. Attempts at incremental expansion of goals also failed. The result was extensive mission creep that ultimately expanded the goals of the intervention through all seven levels.

The first military intervention was designed to solve the problem politically while establishing humanitarian relief objectives such as providing safe havens. However, without a peace agreement, the warring factions soon attached partisan motives to both the involvement of UN peacekeepers in the establishment of safe havens and the crossing of battle lines by humanitarian relief workers. The result was that the lightly armed international peacekeeping forces became pawns of the warring parties. This development forced the intervening countries to consider options of deterrence. Burg described five examples of deterrence in Bosnia. These operations ranged from vague threats of future action against those who attacked UN forces or obstructed humanitarian aid, to limited air attacks against Bosnian Serb military installations. These strikes provoked the Bosnian Serbs to seize UN personnel and use them as human shields against further attack, a tactic that compelled NATO to cease its use of force. As deterrence failed, the United States was compelled to consider a more comprehensive strategy of coercive diplomacy that explicitly linked the use of force to Serb political concessions.

Mission creep should be avoided if possible. When it occurs, actions that seemed appropriate early in an intervention might actually impede the success of subsequent actions that become necessary when the goals of intervention are expanded. For example, in Bosnia, the attainment of initial goals, such as the creation of "safe havens," actually increased the difficulty of achieving the expanded goals that later became necessary. Each time intervention forces acted against one side to enforce a safe haven, it arguably lengthened the conflict by stiffening the other side's resistance. It also eroded the reputation of the intervening forces as impartial agents. A similar effect occurred when initial goals were expanded for the military intervention in Somalia. "Success" in the first stage of the intervention—supporting the delivery of humanitarian assistance—undermined the subsequent goal of creating some form of legitimate self-government. In addition, in both Somalia and Bosnia the limited initial goals of military intervention prevented the resulting UN peacekeeping force from being properly structured for operations in a combat environment. As a result, both situations presented the warring factions with irresistible targets once they no longer perceived intervening forces to be impartial.

By contrast, military intervention in East Timor did not exhibit mission creep. Although the initial intervention force was relatively lightly armed, the

Australians kept a heavily armed combat force standing by and inserted it when it became appropriate. Using a relatively small, lightly armed force at first helped to minimize feelings of resentment within local groups and the general population, but the presence of a large, heavily armed force sent a clear signal to the warring factions that they could not prevail.

Mission creep adds to the costs of intervention, beyond what would have been the case if an appropriate engagement strategy had been determined at the outset. Interventions that experience mission creep also tax public support for such endeavors, particularly when they are not perceived to affect vital national interests. Even if the public believes that an intervention does affect vital interests, it is always harder to maintain high levels of support over long periods. Both of these effects make it less likely that states engaged in military interventions experiencing significant mission creep will take on additional interventions, particularly those that do not impact vital interests, even if consensus exists that intervention is warranted.

In summary, policymakers should identify and prioritize the objectives associated with a proposed military intervention as completely as possible prior to initiation. In particular they should identify cases in which achieving limited goals might impede the attainment of other objectives later on. Unfortunately, several factors incline policymakers to set limited initial goals that are unrealistic. Additionally, events following military intervention can render even realistic initial goals obsolete. Accordingly, most interventions have experienced mission creep, the incremental expansion of an intervention's goals and exit strategies. Mission creep raises the cost and strains public support for military intervention. Experience with military interventions in the 1990s indicates that exit strategies based on limited goals will usually fail unless goals are expanded and exit strategies are correspondingly adjusted to address the underlying causes of internal conflict. These factors are largely nonmilitary in nature and include elements of nation building.

A final observation about defining a "successful" military intervention is in order. Despite the problems experienced by most military interventions, one must not lose sight of the fact that all of the cases in this volume are believed to have reduced potential death and human suffering, in some cases by considerable amounts. Accordingly, the "usual" practice of intervening after violent conflict has erupted with the limited goal of stopping the death and destruction has its positive aspects. It has saved lives while keeping casualties to intervention forces low and costs to intervening states fairly low.

Military Intervention and Nation Building

Perhaps the very use of the term "exit strategy" sends a misleading signal to policymakers. As I. William Zartman observed, intervening powers should look upon military intervention as part of an *engagement strategy* rather than an exit strategy, particularly in cases where no government exists or opposing groups have no political program to implement if the government falls. In such cases, only constructive engagement to reestablish basic institutions will lead to a sustainable peace. Essentially, there is no *military solution* to the problem, only a *military dimension.*[22]

Interventions in the 1990s and the recent interventions in Afghanistan and Iraq have underscored the fact that military intervention is a tactic rather than a strategy. A case has been made that intervening forces should not be withdrawn until the country involved has made significant progress toward a sustainable peace. Otherwise the country will fall back into internal conflict. It might also become a base for terrorists. The processes and initiatives that lead to a sustainable peace fall into the category of "nation-building" or "reconstruction" efforts. While these efforts have a military dimension, they also possess political, economic, legal, and civil aspects.

How does military intervention fit within an exit or engagement strategy that includes nation building as a goal? Military intervention should ideally be located within a four-stage process:

1. A coalition of willing states should conduct military intervention.
2. Overwhelming force must be used to impose an effective cease-fire.
3. The military should hand over authority to appropriate civilian leaders and organizations as soon as the situation is stable and remain as the "junior partner" to help reestablish law and order.
4. Military forces should be removed once law and order is reestablished.

A coalition of willing states should conduct intervention. States should not wait for a UN resolution authorizing military intervention if this results in delays that cause more death and destruction, but UN endorsement for intervention is preferred for reasons of legitimacy. Considerable latitude exists regarding the exact role the United Nations should play in interventions. For example, in chapter 3, David Laitin describes the command-and-control problems that arose in Somalia when the UN was given command of troops of various nationalities and it became necessary to engage in combat. Similar problems occurred in Bosnia, Rwanda, and Sierra Leone. Events in East Timor and Haiti support this view as well, but from the opposite side. They demonstrate how smoothly intervention can proceed when a single state with a capable military runs the intervention under a UN mandate. Cambodia is one case in which UN control has worked reasonably well, but it is also a case in which forces under UN command have not needed to engage in combat operations.

Another way of handling military command-and-control is being tested in Afghanistan. While the intervention has UN authorization, the United Nations is only in direct charge of certain military-related duties such as peacekeeping operations (primarily the provision of a police presence in Kabul) that do not involve large-scale combat operations. The U.S. military is responsible for combat operations to eliminate the threat posed by Taliban and al Qaeda forces remaining in the country. This arrangement allows the United States to capitalize on its effective command-and-control capabilities as well as its intelligence, surveillance, and reconnaissance assets. Detachments of troops from other countries sometimes support this effort but are under the control of the U.S. military command when doing so.[23]

In Iraq, the United States, in close consultation with the United Kingdom, has thus far reserved the right to direct all elements of intervention unless it agrees to relinquish control to the United Nations. In the military dimension, the United States and the United Kingdom (which also possesses excellent command-and-control capabilities) have divided Iraq into sectors that each administers. Other countries have provided some military assistance, but the United States retains overall control of any military forces in its sector of Iraq.

Overwhelming force must be used to impose an effective cease-fire. The outcome of military intervention should never be in doubt. Experiences in the 1990s have shown that any military intervention force must be configured to engage in combat operations regardless of whether the need for combat is considered highly likely or only remotely possible. For example, in Sierra Leone, Bosnia, Rwanda, and Somalia, the initial UN peacekeeping force was improperly structured for operations in a combat environment. As a result, intervening forces presented one or more of the warring factions with an irresistible target once they no longer perceived the intervention to be impartial.

The military should hand over authority to appropriate civilian leaders and organizations as soon as the situation is stable and remain as the "junior partner" to help reestablish law and order. Military forces are not trained to engage successfully in the many other missions associated with the nation-building process. As noted below, the handoff of control is rarely a smooth exercise because identifying the "appropriate civilian authorities" is difficult at best. Military forces often retain responsibility for several of the nonmilitary aspects of nation building.

The military's role as "junior partner" is an extremely important one. If intervening forces are unable to reestablish law and order, it is virtually certain that the process of nation building will fail. Events in Afghanistan and Iraq appear to demonstrate this lesson. In Afghanistan, most experts continue to criticize the failure to establish contingents of peacekeeping troops outside of Kabul because this omission has hurt the reestablishment of law and order by preserving arbitrary rule by warlords in most parts of the country. In Iraq, the initial numbers of troops on the ground have been inadequate to prevent wide-scale looting, rioting, and other forms of lawlessness, including attacks on U.S. and British occupation troops.[24]

Military forces should be removed once law and order is reestablished. The military should not organize civil society. Rather, international organizations such as the UN, various nongovernmental organizations, such as the major food donor agencies, and members of the civil services of national governments should perform this role. Since it is difficult to determine when a sufficient degree of law and order has been reestablished, the bias should be toward having military forces remain in place slightly too long rather than pulling them out too soon.

The need to view military intervention as one of the elements of a larger intervention strategy was the subject of debate throughout the 1990s. For example, in early 2001, a study by the Army War College compared developments in the intervention doctrines of several major powers. It indicated that, while most doctrines were converging toward a common approach to intervention in internal conflict, U.S. doctrine diverged from the others in several significant ways. First, U.S. doctrine primarily focused on the military aspects of intervention, while the doctrines of other wealthy nations focused on civil *and* military aspects. As a result, all doctrines except that of the United States emphasized nation building as an important element of intervention. Second, U.S. doctrine did not list humanitarian assistance as a reason for intervention, while most others did. Third, U.S. doctrine stressed that it was possible for U.S. forces to provide the military aspects of intervention without otherwise becoming involved in the intervention process. The other doctrines contended that this was not the case. Fourth, U.S doctrine considered peacekeeping (considered a noncombat activity) and peace enforcement (considered a combat activity) to be separate missions. The other doctrines listed both as part of the same continuum of military operations. [25]

Since that time, U.S. doctrine has converged with those of the other powers. Today there is virtual consensus about the need to define successful military intervention in broad terms. The current U.S. administration's switch from a policy that originally rejected the need for nation building to one that now embraces it is the most evident example of this convergence. Its rhetoric about the need to rebuild both Afghanistan and Iraq is further evidence. [26]

In summary, military intervention is a means to an end, where the end is a lasting end to internal conflict and a lasting peace. Military intervention is thus a tactic rather than a strategy. This strategy inevitably contains some elements of nation building or reconstruction because they are necessary to produce a lasting peace. Most nation-building tasks are nonmilitary in nature. Intervening forces are primarily concerned with restoring and then maintaining law and order so that civilian administrators can conduct the nonmilitary aspects of intervention. In practice, the absence of civil organizations to conduct the nonmilitary dimensions of intervention means that intervening forces become responsible for carrying out both military and nonmilitary aspects of nation building.

Nation-Building Challenges

Even when policymakers fully commit to nation building as part of an intervention strategy, achieving this goal remains difficult for a number of reasons:

1.   Nation building takes time.
2.   No single group or organization is structured to take over responsibility

from the military.

3. Little proven knowledge exists about how best to perform the process of nation building.
4. Scholarly research and expert opinion about nation building send conflicting signals to policymakers.
5. Countries that require military intervention are usually those in which the likelihood of successful reconstruction is the lowest.

Nation building takes time. Societies ravaged by war, whose populations have been subjected to severe human rights abuses, cannot be restored to functioning civil societies overnight. Self-sustaining economies take years to grow and legitimate institutions decades to develop under the best of conditions. This requires long-term involvement by the intervening powers, which strains public support for nation building as the causes for intervention become dim memories and other issues affecting the intervening countries compete for attention and funding. The military phase of intervention might end long before nation building is complete, or intervening troops might stay for years, depending on the situation and how skillfully nation building is conducted.

No single group or organization is structured to take over responsibility from the military after violent conflict has ended and basic law and order have been established. As a result, the military is forced to remain in control of both the military and nonmilitary aspects of reconstruction. A standing international police force and civil service would be the ideal tool for conducting nation building, but such an organization does not exist. The military is ill equipped to perform the nonmilitary aspects of nation building.

Little proven knowledge exists about how best to perform the process of nation building. Nation building requires making fundamental changes to a country's political culture, especially when lawlessness and privation have become the norm. The general requirements for nation building are fairly well understood. For example, law and order must be established, basic institutions of governance must be restored, a working economy must be developed, a democratic form of government must be created, and a civil society that respects human rights must be developed. However, the specific steps for achieving these goals are not well established and will emerge only with experience. In any event, since each candidate for nation building possesses cultural, political, and economic traditions that are to some extent unique, there probably is no single best way to accomplish nation building for all cases.

Consider just two of the many ingredients of a successful reconstruction effort: the development of a working democracy and a sustainable economy in the occupied state. Both of these tasks require the regeneration of civil society, including a respect for civil rights and the rule of law. Democratic governance assumes that citizens are reasonably well educated in the political process, which presumes some form of universal education that emphasizes the benefits of tolerance and pluralism rather than ethnic or racial superiority. These attitudes arguably cannot become ingrained in a society without some reasonable assurance that individual and collective human rights will be respected. Economic development requires a reasonably fair mechanism for allocating and respecting private property and the achievement of minimum standards of workers' rights and consumer protection, as well as a workforce that possesses skills to enable the country's products to be competitive in the world economy. A legal structure that can impartially adjudicate disputes also is necessary to support trade as well as to encourage foreign investment.

But exactly how does one accomplish these processes? For nation building to be successful, the intervening powers must oversee the accomplishment of many complex, interdependent processes, the exact elements of which are far from well understood. Thus, the emphasis on coalition building before intervention takes place becomes clearer, as does the preference to have the UN's endorsement and involvement in such operations. Many hands lighten the load, many minds produce more constructive ideas than only a few, and many partners reduce the burden of an intervention's expense.

Scholarly research and expert opinion about nation building send conflicting signals to policymakers. The "impartiality" issue is one such case. Many experts stress that intervening forces must remain impartial in order to be viewed as legitimate by the population of the occupied country.[27] However, several chapters in this volume have detailed how attempts by intervening forces to remain impartial failed. These cases showed that such a posture was all but impossible to maintain because, sooner or later, local groups perceived that actions by the intervening forces favored their opponents. Their perceptions led these factions to impede efforts by intervening forces to reestablish law and order in the occupied country.

Given these considerations, some experts recommend that intervening forces abandon attempts at impartiality and actively support one of the warring factions in an internal conflict.[28] Apart from avoiding the difficulties of trying to remain impartial, allying with one of the warring factions might resolve hostilities more quickly by decisively defeating the opposing factions. However, the governments of wealthy states are usually unwilling to support a dictatorial regime or a faction (e.g., a warlord) that possesses a private army. In addition, finding a faction with an acceptable human rights policy can prove impossible in practice.[29] The remaining option is to ally oneself with a faction that has a history of human rights violations, the logic being that it is more important to halt violent conflict as quickly as possible and then deal with lesser types of human rights abuses. This is the approach that was used in Afghanistan. The U.S.-led coalition allied itself with the Northern Alliance, which consisted of the combined forces of a group of warlords opposed to the Taliban. This alliance hastened the downfall of the Taliban but also enhanced the power of the various warlords. Following the Taliban's defeat, several of these leaders returned to their respective regions of Afghanistan and have worked to solidify their local power at the expense of the central government,[30] thus impeding nation-building efforts.

Past interventions also send competing signals about disarmament. Many experts assert that it is preferable to disarm to some degree the population of a country in which intervention has occurred because this improves prospects for restoring law and order. However, attempts to disarm virtually guarantee that one or more of the previously warring parties will perceive that the intervening force favors an opposing faction. So disarmament attempts appear to belie efforts to remain impartial, unless factions disarm voluntarily.

Thus, conventional wisdom on impartiality and disarmament creates a conundrum. If disarmament is achieved by creating the conditions in which people voluntarily turn in their weapons, then first people must feel secure enough to do so. To achieve this condition, basic law and order must be restored. But most agree that it is necessary to disarm the population before law and order can be restored.

One way to resolve this apparent tautology is to focus on the ultimate objective, which is the need to restore law and order as soon as possible so that the nonmilitary aspects of nation building may succeed. Maintaining impartiality and disarming the population are means to achieve this end. If the ready availability of weapons manifests itself in attacks on intervention forces, then disarmament—by force if necessary—should be a priority, while attempts to remain impartial should be secondary. On the other hand, if the availability of arms has not led to resumption of conflict or to frequent attacks on intervening forces, it might be appropriate to emphasize attempts to remain impartial and deemphasize disarmament plans.

For example, in Iraq, frequent attacks on U.S. and British forces point toward the need to attach a high priority to disarming the population or at least certain factions (how to distinguish among groups is another problem). In Afghanistan, where the population is also heavily armed, attacks have been less frequent. In this case, it might be more appropriate to deemphasize disarmament and stress the role of the U.S. and its coalition partners as honest brokers interested in improving the condition of all Afghanis.

Some things about disarmament are clear. First, if disarmament is to be performed by forceful methods, experience shows that lightly armed intervention forces are not effective to carry out this mission and might in fact cause factions to use force to resist disarmament efforts. Second, when disarming members of former militias or armies, it is critical to remember that disarmed soldiers need to find civilian employment. Simply disarming them will not work.

Countries that require military intervention are usually those in which the likelihood of successful reconstruction is the lowest. Internal conflicts have tended to occur in a so-called "arc of instability"[31] comprised of Africa, the Middle East, Central Asia, and Southeast Asia. Most of the states in these regions have nondemocratic governments, and many can be classified as "weak," "failing," or "failed" states. These characteristics detract from successful interventions, regardless of how narrowly or broadly one defines success. In addition, if these kinds of states border an occupied state, it is likely that the intervening powers must become involved in solving regional problems to reconstruct the state in which intervention has occurred.

A "weak" state is not necessarily weak militarily, but institutionally. Its leaders possess low levels of legitimacy. Its population lacks social cohesion. Its government possesses frail public institutions, has limited resources, and exhibits poor economic management. As a result, activities often occur in weak states that undermine civil society and the rule of law, encourage violations of human rights, and pose security threats to their neighbors. These activities include arms proliferation, smuggling, currency manipulation, conflicting water rights issues, cross-border attacks on neighboring states, the export of terrorism, and environmental degradation.

"Failing" and "failed" states are subcategories of weak states. A failing state is one in which government services are inadequate to prevent civil unrest from developing and possibly erupting into internal conflict, while a failed state is one in which governance has ceased to exist at a national level. Governance, such as it exists, is performed by local or regional actors such as warlords or other self-proclaimed leaders, and violent internal conflict of some kind is very likely.

Weak, failing, or failed states can destabilize entire regions. Refugees from internal conflict in a weak state can destabilize a neighboring state if they commit crimes and carry their conflicts across the border. In fact, the presence of such activities in a weak state could incline neighboring states to consider military intervention to prevent internal conflict from spreading. Intervention by neighboring states might worsen rather than stabilize the situation, since predatory motives might also drive the intervention in addition to a desire to stop the violence (Nigeria's desire to corner the diamond trade in Sierra Leone is used as a prime example of such activity). Alternatively, neighboring states could refrain from intervening because they might benefit from an internal conflict in a neighbor and want to see hostilities prolonged.[32] An intervening power must deal with these structural factors. It cannot modify them in the short-term through its policies but must take them into account and ideally incorporate them into its goals and exit strategy.

All of the states examined in this volume fit into the categories of weak, failing, or failed states. Afghanistan under the Taliban and Iraq under Saddam Hussein were weak states. Even though both of these countries had effective repressive governments, neither regime controlled all of its country's territory. In Afghanistan, the Northern Alliance controlled portions of the country prior to the U.S. invasion and internal conflict had been raging for several years. In Iraq, Saddam Hussein's regime had lost full control of both the northern and southern areas of the country through U.S.-imposed no-fly zones, and Kurdish people in northern Iraq were conducting an ongoing rebellion against the central government.

In summary, several significant challenges to nation building exist. However, the main purpose in examining major challenges is not to argue that reconstruction efforts are doomed to failure. In fact, nation-building efforts are gaining ground in most of the countries examined in this volume, but progress has been slow. In particular, the military aspects of intervention have continued longer than anticipated in almost all cases, but some degree of troop withdrawal has occurred in almost all of the cases studied. Instead, the purpose for examining the challenges that will confront any nation-building campaign is to help inform policymakers and the public of the difficulties and uncertainties inherent in any nation-building effort. In particular, one should be wary when the argument is made that a particular military intervention will be a short, tidy affair with few or no linkages to political, social, and economic conditions within the country that is a candidate for intervention. Experience has shown that this is rarely, if ever, the case.

Summary and Conclusions

This chapter has offered broad observations about military intervention in internal conflict in an effort to place this complex phenomenon in context. Most military interventions during this period used the United Nations as the coordinating organization. This imparted legitimacy, which eased the way for many states to participate and share the costs and risks.

Policymakers in wealthy states perceived that most interventions in the 1990s were driven primarily by humanitarian concerns rather than threats to national interests. This tended to produce interventions that occurred too late to avert widespread death and destruction due to internal conflict (although significant additional violence and abuses of human rights were prevented following intervention in many cases). Additionally, several factors inclined policymakers to set limited initial goals that were unrealistic. In particular, it was common for policymakers to underestimate the level of military force required to halt internal conflict. This led to intervention by forces inadequate to accomplish their mission. This resulted in "mission creep," the incremental expansion of an intervention's goals and exit strategies. Mission creep raised the cost and strained public support for military intervention.

Realistic planning prior to military intervention is essential to avoid mission creep. Planning should address the underlying causes of internal conflict as well as military factors. These underlying factors are largely nonmilitary in nature and include elements of nation building. Some degree of nation building is required to produce a lasting peace. This, in turn, is a necessary condition for declaring the military phase of intervention a success because it allows troops to be withdrawn without a resumption of civil violence. In practice, however, the absence of civil organizations to conduct the nonmilitary dimensions of intervention means that intervening forces become responsible for carrying out both military and nonmilitary aspects. Even under the best of conditions, several significant challenges to nation building still exist.

In addition to providing contextual information, the case studies in chapters 3 through 8 contain important specific lessons about how to conduct military intervention. These are listed below. Although listed in bullet format, they should not be construed as a "laundry list" of items that, if successfully performed, guarantee a successful military intervention. All cases of military intervention are highly situational. While potentially valuable, specific lessons must be considered within the tapestry of the history, culture, politics, and economic backdrop that make each case of military intervention unique.

Somalia

- The Somalia interventions indicate that one's allies in the military phase of a mission are not necessarily allies for the transitional administration. Fulfilling goals of the military phase (for example, using local alliance partners to help intervening powers defeat or weaken rival factions) might undermine the program of the transitional administration (when local alliance partners emerge in strengthened military and political positions after rival factions have been defeated). These newly empowered local allies might then pursue independent agendas that make the transitional authority's task more difficult.

- Somalia also offers the idea that an intervening force should ally itself with a strong local faction (whose conduct meets minimal human rights standards) in order to hasten the end of conflict. U.S. and UN attempts to remain impartial didn't work in Somalia.

- Somalia strongly shows the danger in emphasizing manhunts, for example, going after Aideed. It is better to focus on shaping governing structures rather than eliminating individuals.

- Consider using the United Nations as the principal, rather than the agent of intervention. As principal, UN monitoring of the intervention process provides legitimacy to the operation. Using others as agent—the United States and its allies, who possess capable militaries and effective command-and-control structures—matches the unit to the task. For example, UN forces in Somalia had a divided command structure that seriously impaired its military effectiveness.

Bosnia

- In contrast to Somalia, Bosnia offers a case where none of the local factions could have made acceptable alliance partners because of their uniform disregard for human rights. Allying oneself with such actors corrupts the legitimacy of the intervening force.

- Bosnia is a case where attempts by the intervening force to remain impartial failed. It appears that this failure resulted when intervention forces began to disarm the population. In short order, each faction perceived that the disarmament program favored the other side.

- Under the best of reconstruction programs, it was argued that it would take about thirty years to produce a functioning, stable state out of Bosnia's current conditions. This observation should serve as a sobering reminder that the scars of systematic human rights violations run deep and that reconstruction is a complex, long-term, and probably expensive undertaking.

Rwanda

- Rwanda highlighted the difficulty of intervening on the basis of a weak peace agreement, in this case the 1993 Arusha Accords. The initial intervention force was configured to monitor implementation of this agreement and was accordingly a small, lightly armed mission only authorized to use force in self-defense. It was soon apparent that neither side intended to abide by the terms of the agreement, and, in such an environment, UNAMIR was impotent against the armed Rwandan factions.

- Rwanda seems to demonstrate that early intervention with a sizeable force (sufficiently large and heavily armed to overcome any possible resistance) with robust rules of engagement can prevent the escalation of internal conflict and save large numbers of lives at relatively small cost.

- In the case of Rwanda, no outside country was willing to take responsibility for the implementation of the Arusha Accords. This contrasts with the East Timor intervention, in which the leadership role played by Australia was considered to be a decisive cause of that intervention's success.

Cambodia

- Cambodia is a case in which domestic political factions traditionally used foreign allies to strengthen their positions. As long as these foreign powers provided support, Cambodia continued to experience internal conflict. When these powers finally grew tired of providing support, the warring factions soon lost the wherewithal to continue fighting, and the peace process and state reconstruction began to make real progress. Events in Cambodia indicate that every effort should be made to shut down external sources of support for factions engaged in internal conflict.

- The Cambodia case study provides a model for devising excellent voter education and registration programs and establishing secure conditions for holding national elections.

- The Cambodian intervention provides a model for conducting an excellent refugee repatriation program.

- The Cambodia case demonstrates how reconstruction efforts can include a strong human rights component.

Haiti

- Political factions should not be the only focus of attempts to build lasting peace; such attempts should be embedded in broader processes of dialogue involving different social sectors, so that consensus on policy is not easily shaken by the short-term calculations of the factions.

- Societies in transition cannot deliver immediately on the high expectations of their members. Crises of "social patience" may disrupt the fragile peace. Hence, local and international authorities should ensure maximum participation by civic representatives in the development and implementation of initiatives designed for their benefit. Such participation will help to reduce alienation.

- The availability of security and justice for the common person is critical for the stabilization of peace. If factions continue to dominate political processes through fear and impunity, then politics will be deadlocked along the lines of their contradictory interests. The emergence of other voices, however, will open new spaces for compromise. Hence, the establishment of the rule of law, including through interim means such as community policing and alternate dispute resolution, should be a top priority.
- An economic strategy that supports the emergence of a viable polity may not often coincide with conventional economic wisdom. For example, fiscal discipline in order to attract significant foreign investment might stress immature political systems to the point of collapse. On the other hand, non-capital intensive schemes focused on providing the simple means (title, credit, etc.) for entrepreneurial activity may generate greater longer-term wherewithal for political stability. Common persons engaged in sound productive activity might not succumb to blandishments toward violence.
- International efforts should take into account the possibility of significant variation between local and international approaches to building peace. If local understandings emerge through open and participatory processes (as happened in 1987 in Haiti) or reflect agreement between key sectors, then they should be honored, even if they differ from preferred international courses of action. A genuine local process of interaction and learning will lead to lasting democratic participation.
- The ideological polarization generated by extended periods of conflict can significantly erode the ability of key actors in a society to bargain concretely around specific policy issues. Great emphasis should be placed on reviving or strengthening this ability.

Sierra Leone
- Military intervention is not sufficient to end a conflict whose source is state collapse, but intervention is a necessary ingredient in engaging the road to conflict's end. In a collapsed state, the conflict needs to be brought under control and the anarchic rebels defeated in order for state rebuilding to proceed.
- An internal conflict should be separated from its external sources of support, optimally by an agreement among these external sources. Then the internal conflict can be resolved.
- To isolate (quarantine) a conflict area, it is necessary to strengthen the states around it, not just by reinforcing the apparatus of each state but by enabling its services so that it can perform its functions.
- Anarchic rebels need to be brought into the political system but separated from their military leaders.
- The preferred agent for action in a regional conflict is a regional organization or coalition, if it exists, but it needs support and resources from the in-

ternational community (outside powers and the United Nations).

East Timor

- In the context of intervention, the size of a military deployment is probably less important than the capability of the troops, the nature of the Rules of Engagement (ROE), and the clear willingness of the interveners to use force to protect the mandate.
- In agreement with the Rwanda case, East Timor demonstrated that, in an insecure environment that includes large numbers of combatants under arms, officials should be skeptical that a symbolic or monitoring military presence can play an effective role in limiting violence.
- East Timor seems to illustrate the major advantage of having a capable nation play a leadership role throughout the transition period. There are also advantages if the international military and civilian presence is reduced gradually as the transition proceeds.
- There may be significant benefits to having a capable yet relatively disinterested regional actor take the lead in international intervention.

Looking Ahead

What has experience with military intervention in internal conflict taught us? How is this knowledge likely to affect future behavior? It seems safe to say that the need for military intervention will continue to arise, since military intervention is often an essential ingredient for halting internal conflict. The considerable qualitative and quantitative military superiority of the United States will continue to make it the only state for which military intervention is more or less always an option. Accordingly, the United States will be asked to participate in most future military interventions, either as the principal agent or in a number of lesser roles.

The metadoctrine will continue to develop, making military intervention in internal conflict a standard feature of international law. Concerns about the legitimacy of military intervention will become increasingly important. Events surrounding the war with Iraq have strengthened the importance of UN authorization as a sign of legitimacy. An awareness of this fact will place increasing value on obtaining UN authorization prior to future interventions both to validate the motives of the intervening powers and to ensure that some measure of burden sharing will occur. While this holds the promise of strengthening international law, it also will continue to delay most humanitarian interventions until concerns about possible aggressive motives by the intervening powers are laid to rest.

However, states might use the new importance associated with UN authorization for self-serving reasons. For example, states might attempt to prevent UN authorization for a particular intervention to diminish U.S. influence in a region or enhance their own role as leaders of the international system. If such activities were to become commonplace, they would deal a blow to the potentially enhanced role of the United Nations as a positive influence on international stability and human rights.

It is difficult to forecast trends in the timing and magnitude of future military interventions, but it seems safe to say that events with regard to Afghanistan and Iraq will have a greater effect on these factors than anything learned from interventions in the 1990s. On one hand, the terrorist attacks of September 11 gave increased credence to the globalist argument that, in a globalizing and increasingly interdependent world, weak, failing, and failed states can provide safe havens for radical movements capable of inflicting death and destruction on the U.S. homeland. In addition, systematic violations of human rights within a state could constitute a potential threat to U.S. national interests because, under certain circumstances, human rights abuses spawn the kind of hopelessness and desperation that lead individuals to join the ranks of radical movements. This awareness gives new importance to the need to intervene for "purely humanitarian reasons." On the other hand, poverty and human rights violations are pervasive throughout the world and the United States and others can't intervene everywhere these conditions exist.

How should the United States and other countries incorporate this new awareness into their foreign policies? Will September 11 and experience with interventions in Iraq and Afghanistan result in new doctrines for guiding when to intervene in the future? The September 11 terrorist attacks appear to have added a new category to cases of military intervention, one that will take precedence over the types of interventions generally seen during the 1990s. U.S. policymakers will give priority to military intervention in countries where regimes, terrorist groups, or systematic abuses of human rights present clear and present dangers to the American people and the U.S. homeland. As U.S. actions toward Afghanistan and Iraq have demonstrated, U.S. intervention would be swift and decisive if a particular country appeared to be harboring terrorists or developing weapons of mass destruction. However, U.S. resolve might not be any greater than before September 11 if a state is in the grip of a humanitarian emergency. In fact, the United States might be even more reluctant to intervene in humanitarian emergencies than before September 11 because of the demands and expenses incurred by the war on terrorism.

The increasing recognition that cases of military intervention must include a strategy for nation building can help avoid past mistakes. However, it also has the potential to decrease the frequency with which the United States and other wealthy states engage in new military interventions. Policymakers should now have few illusions that military intervention can be performed "on the cheap" or terminated quickly. While each potential new case of military intervention will be unique and thus be evaluated on its own set of issues, it is likely that U.S. policymakers might decide against a potential future intervention because they would anticipate the full scale of the actions required, the time involved for a successful intervention, and the expense that will be incurred.

Developments in Afghanistan and Iraq will influence the nature and the conduct of future interventions. Failure in either of these large-scale operations has the potential to prejudice policymakers against military intervention in future cases of internal conflict, independent of any other considerations.

Interestingly, the current military interventions in the Democratic Republic of the Congo and Liberia[33] appear to follow the pattern of the limited interventions of the 1990s (Somalia, early Bosnia, Rwanda, early Sierra Leone). While these latest interventions have the potential to reduce the violence in those countries, experience indicates it is unlikely that these current small-scale, short-term, exclusively military events will prove successful by themselves, since both countries have experienced massive shocks to their institutions, societies, economies, and governance structures over periods of many years. As a result, both countries will require significant nation-building efforts before a lasting peace will become possible.

Perhaps the most important question is not how to improve current practices associated with military intervention. A better question might be whether the lessons learned from past and current military interventions will lead the wealthy nations to experiment with new approaches. How can wealthy states commit the necessary resources to enable troops and civilian administrators from a wide variety of states and organizations to exert a consistent, long-term effort that avoids the pitfalls of the past?

Notes

I wish to thank Robin Bisland for commenting on an earlier draft of this chapter.

1. As described in the introduction, the case studies were part of the *Project on Internal Conflict*, which was conducted by the *National Intelligence Council Project* at the University of Maryland with funding from the National Intelligence Council. The *Project on Internal Conflict* conducted several workshops and conferences in addition to the seven case studies contained in this volume to explore the phenomenon of military intervention in internal conflict. The names and affiliations of the scholars and other nongovernment experts who participated in the project are listed in the acknowledgments at the beginning of the volume. For more information about the NIC Project, see www.cissm.umd.edu/NIC.html. For information about the National Intelligence Council, see www.cia.gov/nic.

2. Remarks by I. William Zartman, National Intelligence Council Project *Workshop on the Future of Internal Conflict*, College Park, Md., 11 August 2000.

3. Chapter 1, pages 11–12.

4. Remarks by Barbara Harff, National Intelligence Council Project *Workshop on the Future of Internal Conflict*, College Park, Md., 11 August 2000.

5. For a description of the roles of power and principle in U.S. foreign policy, see Charles W. Kegley, Jr., and Eugene R. Wittkopf, *American Foreign Policy: Pattern and Process*, 5th ed. (New York: St. Martin's Press, 1996), 31–86. See also Michael H. Hunt, *Ideology and U.S. Foreign Policy* (New Haven, Conn.: Yale University Press, 1987).

6. Remarks by Deborah Avant et al., National Intelligence Council Project *Workshop on Strategies for Military Intervention in Internal Conflict*, College Park, Md., 27 October 2000.

7. Remarks by Charles Stevenson et al., National Intelligence Council Project *Workshop on Intervention in Internal Conflict*, College Park, Md., 12 July 2001.

8. Avant et al., *Workshop on Strategies for Military Intervention.*

9. Chapter 2, pages 40–41.

10. Glenn Kessler, "Powell Making Key Trip to Turkey; U.S. Aims to Mend Relationship, Forestall Invasion of Iraq," *Washington Post*, 1 April 2003, A24.

11. For a concise summary of events, see John Tagliabue, "Threats and Responses: Discord; France and Russia Ready to Use Veto against Iraq War," *New York Times*, 6 March 2003, A1; Robert D. McFadden, "Threats and Responses: An Overview—March 8, 2003; Squabbling Diplomats, a Mixed Report Card from Iraq and a Ticking Clock," *New York Times*, 8 March 2003, A7; Robert D. McFadden, "Threats and Responses: An Overview: March 16, 2003; An Ultimatum, Frayed French Relations and Stockpiling in Iraq," *New York Times*, 17 March 2003, A11; Steven R. Weisman, "Threats and Responses: Foreign Policy; A Long, Winding Road to a Diplomatic Dead End," *New York Times*, 17 March 2003, A1.

12. For an explanation of UN Security Council voting procedures, see A. LeRoy Bennett, *International Organizations: Principles and Issues*, 5th ed. (Englewood Cliffs, N.J.: Prentice Hall, 1991), 45–46, 62–65, 441–442. See also the UN Charter, Articles 23–27 and 43.

13. Article 2 of the UN Charter states, "The Organization is based on the principle of the sovereign equality of all its members."

14. Chantal de Jonge Oudraat, *Intervention in Internal Conflicts: Legal and Political Conundrums*, working paper, Global Policy Program of the Carnegie Endowment for International Peace, Washington, D.C., 15 August 2000, 4.

15. Remarks by Ted Robert Gurr, National Intelligence Council Project *Workshop on the Future of Internal Conflict*, College Park, Md., 11 August 2000.

16. For a concise treatment of these concepts, see D. Robert Worley, "Waging Ancient War: Limits on Preemptive Force," Strategic Studies Institute, U.S. Army War College, Carlisle, Pa., 19–21. See also Jack S. Levy, "Declining Power and the Preventive Motivation for War," *World Politics* 40, no. 1 (October 1987): 91.

17. Remarks by I. William Zartman, National Intelligence Council Project *Workshop on Intervention in Internal Conflict*, College Park, Md., 12 July 2001. See also chapter 7, pages 149–150.

18. Rajiv Chandrasekaran and Colum Lynch, "U.N. Officials Say Intelligence to Prove U.S. Claims Is Lacking; Best Information Still Being Withheld from Inspectors," *Washington Post*, 27 January 2003, A12.

19. For example, see Patrick E. Tyler, "Threats and Responses: Postwar Plans; Panel Faults Bush on War Costs and Risks," *New York Times*, 12 March 2003, A15; Vernon Loeb, "Postwar Window Closing in Iraq, Study Says," *New York Times*, 18 July 2003, A9.

20. Remarks by Barry Posen, National Intelligence Council Project Workshop on *Strategies for Military Intervention in Internal Conflict*, College Park, Md., 27 October 2000.

21. Chapter 3, page 48.

22. Zartman, *Workshop on Intervention in Internal Conflict.*

23. Vernon Loeb, "U.S. Hopeful on Afghan Security; Regional Bases Plan Reflects Emphasis on 'Stability' Operations," *Washington Post*, 23 December 2002, A14; Tonda McCharles, "Canada Sending Troops to Kabul," *Toronto Star*, 13 February 2003, A1; Barry Neild, "Italians Get a Pizza the Action in Afghanistan," *Agence France Presse*, 16 March 2003.

24. See Loeb, "Postwar Window Closing in Iraq."

25. Remarks by William Flavin, National Intelligence Council Project Workshop on *Strategies for Military Intervention in Internal Conflict*, College Park, Md., 27 October 2000.

26. Joint Statement by President George W. Bush and Chairman Hamid Karzai on a "New Partnership between the United States and Afghanistan," White House Press Release, 28 January 2002; "Dr. Condoleezza Rice Discusses Iraq Reconstruction," White House Press Release, 4 April 2003; and "President Discusses the Future of Iraq," White House Press Release, 28 April 2003.

27. Gurr, *Workshop on the Future of Internal Conflict*.

28. Remarks by David Laitin et al., National Intelligence Council Project *Workshop on Intervention in Internal Conflict*, College Park, Md., 12 July 2001. Also see chapter 2, page 36.

29. Remarks by Steven Burg, National Intelligence Council Project *Workshop on Intervention in Internal Conflict*, College Park, Md., 12 July 2001.

30. Carlotta Gall, "In Warlord Land, Democracy Tries Baby Steps," *New York Times*, 11 June 2003, A4.

31. Policymakers have used this term at least as far back as 1978, when Zbigniew Brzezinski, National Security Advisor in the Carter administration, used it to describe the area running from Angola to Afghanistan where the United States was losing ground to a number of Soviet-sponsored revolutionary movements. See Robert Levgold, "The Super Rivals: Conflict in the Third World," *Foreign Affairs* 57, no. 4 (Spring 1979): 755. Since this time, the term has been used in several contexts. The National Intelligence Council's use of the term expands upon Brzezinski's meaning to include all of Africa, the Middle East, Central Asia, and Southeast Asia.

32. Remarks by Donald Rothchild et al., National Intelligence Council Project *Workshop on Internal Conflict and Regional Instability*, College Park, Md., 25 September 2000. For additional information, see I. William Zartman, ed., *Collapsed States: The Disintegration and Restoration of Legitimate Authority* (Boulder, Colo.: Lynne Rienner, 1995).

33. Felicity Barringer, "U.S. and Britain, at U.N., Back French Congo Plan," *New York Times*, 16 July 2003, A6; Richard W. Stevenson and Christopher Marquis, "Bush Team Faces Widespread Pressure to Act on Liberia," *New York Times*, 23 July 2003, A3; and Tim Weiner, "Two Hundred U.S. Marines Land in Liberia to Aid African Force," *New York Times*, 15 August 2003, A1.

Bibliography

Abdullah, Ibrahim. "Bush Path to Destruction: The Origin and Character of the Revolutionary United Front/Sierra Leone." *Journal of Modern African Studies* 36, no. 2 (1998): 203–235.

Abraham, Arthur. "Dancing with the Chameleon: Sierra Leone and the Elusive Quest for Peace." *Journal of Contemporary African Studies* 19, no. 2 (July 2001): 205–228.

Adebajo, Adekeye. *Building Peace in West Africa: Liberia, Sierra-Leone, and Guinea Bissau.* Boulder, Colo.: Lynne Rienner, 2002.

Adelman, Howard. *Early Warning and Conflict Management, International Response to Conflict and Genocide: Lessons from the Rwanda Experience,* vol. 2. Copenhagen: DANIDA, 1996.

Alao, Abiodun. "Sierra Leone: Tracing the Genesis of a Controversy." Briefing paper no. 50, Royal Institute of International Affairs, London, June 1998.

Allard, Kenneth. *Somalia Operations: Lessons Learned.* Washington, D.C.: National Defense University Press, 1995.

Amnesty International. "Afghanistan—Police Reconstruction Essential for the Protection of Human Rights." ASA 11/003/2003, March 2003.

Annan, Kofi. "Agreement of 5 June 1992 on the Reopening of Sarajevo Airport for Humanitarian Purposes." *Report of the Secretary General Pursuant to Security Council Resolution 757.* UN Security Council, S/24075, June 1992.

———. *Report of the Secretary General on the Situation in Somalia.* UN Security Council, S/2002/709, 27 June 2002.

Anyindoho, Henry Kwami. *Guns over Kigali: The Rwandese Civil War–1994, A Personal Account.* Accra, Ghana: Woeli Publishing Services, 1997.

Aristide, Marx V., and Laurie Richardson. "The Popular Movement." In *The Haiti Files: Decoding the Crisis,* edited by James Ridgeway. Washington, D.C.: Essential, 1994.

Asian Development Bank, United Nations Development Program, and World Bank. *Afghanistan: Preliminary Needs Assessment for Recovery and Reconstruction,* January 2002.

Ball, Patrick, Paul Kobrak, and Herbert F. Spirer. *State Violence in Guatemala, 1960–1996: A Quantitative Reflection.* AAAS/CIIDH database of human rights violations in Guatemala (ATV20.1), 1999. hrdata.aaas.org/ciidh/data.html (July 2000).

Barnett, Michael N. "The UN Security Council, Indifference, and Genocide in Rwanda." *Cultural Anthropology* 12, no. 4 (1997): 551–578.

Barringer, Felicity. "U.S. and Britain, at U.N., Back French Congo Plan." *New York Times,* 16 July 2003, A6.

Bennett, A. LeRoy. *International Organizations: Principles and Issues.* 5th ed. Englewood Cliffs, N.J.: Prentice Hall, 1991.

Bentley, David. "Operation Uphold Democracy: Military Support for Democracy in Haiti." *Stategic Forum,* no. 78, Institute for National Strategic Studies, National Defense University, Washington, D.C., June 1996.

Berggren, G., S. Castle, L. Chen, W. Fitzgerald, C. Michaud, and M. Simunovic. "Sanctions in Haiti: Crisis in Humanitarian Action." Working paper, Program on Human Security, Harvard Center for Population and Development Studies, Harvard University, Cambridge, Mass., 1993.

Boucher, Richard, spokesman, U.S. Department of State. "U.S. Delegation in Brussels to Reaffirm Its Commitment to Afghanistan." Press statement, 17 March 2003.

Boutros-Gali, Boutros, ed. "Joint Request by the Rwandese Government and the Rwandese Patriotic Front to the Secretary General of the United Nations Concerning the Stationing of a Neutral International Force in Rwanda." *The United Nations and Rwanda, 1993–1996,* vol. 10, New York: United Nations Publications, 1996.

Brady, Christopher. *U.S. Foreign Policy towards Cambodia, 1977–1992: A Question of Realities.* New York: St. Martin's Press, 1999.

Brahimi, Lakhdar. "Open Meeting of the Security Council: Afghanistan." Briefing by the Special Representative to the Secretary General, 30 October 2002.

———. "Report of the Panel on United Nations Peace Operations." UN Security Council, A/55/305, S/2000/809, 21 August 2000.

Brown, Frederick Z, and David G. Timberman, eds. *Cambodia and the International Community: The Quest for Peace, Development, and Democracy.* Singapore: The Asia Society, 1998.

Brown, McAlister, and Joseph Zasloff. *Cambodia Confounds the Peace-Makers.* Ithaca, N.Y.: Cornell University Press, 1998.

Burg, Steven L. "Nationalism and Democratization in Yugoslavia." *Washington Quarterly* 14, no. 4 (Autumn 1991): 5–19.

———. *War or Peace? Nationalism, Democracy, and American Foreign Policy in Post-Communist Europe.* New York: New York University Press, 1996.

Burg, Steven L., and Paul S. Shoup. *The War in Bosnia-Herzegovina: Ethnic Conflict and International Intervention.* Armonk, N.Y.: M. E. Sharpe, 1999.

Bush, George W., and Hamid Karzail. "New Partnership between the United States and Afghanistan." Joint statement, White House press release, 28 January 2002.

CAREUSA. "NGO Position Paper Concerning the Provisional Reconstruction Teams." ACBAR policy brief. www.careusa.org/newsroom/specialreports/afghanistan/01152003_ngorec.pdf

Chandler, David. *Cambodia before the French: Politics in a Tributary Kingdom,*

1794–1848. Ann Arbor, Mich.: University Microfilms, 1974.
————. *A History of Cambodia*. 3rd ed. Boulder, Colo.: Westview Press, 2000.
————. *The Tragedy of Cambodian History: Politics, War, and Revolution since 1945*. New Haven, Conn.: Yale University Press, 1991.
————. "Will There Be a Trial for the Khmer Rouge?" *Ethics and International Affairs* 14 (2000): 67–82.
Chandrasekaran, Rajiv, and Colum Lynch. "U.N. Officials Say Intelligence to Prove U.S. Claims Is Lacking; Best Information Still Being Withheld from Inspectors." *Washington Post*, 27 January 2003, A12.
Collier, Paul. "Economic Causes of Civil Conflict and Their Implications for Policy." World Bank, 15 June 2000, 6.
Collier, Paul, Lani Elliott, Havard Hegre, Anke Hoeffler, Marta Reynal-Querol, and Nicholas Sambanis. *Breaking the Conflict Trap: Civil War and Development Policy*. Washington, D.C.: World Bank, 2003.
Collier, Paul, and Anke Hoeffler, "Greed and Grievance in Civil War." World Bank, 21 October 2001, 12.
Collier, Paul, and Nicholas Sambanis. "Understanding Civil War: A New Agenda." *Journal of Conflict Resolution* 46, no. 1 (February 2002): 3.
Corfield, Justin. *Khmers Stand Up!* Clayton, Australia: Monash Asia Institute, 1994.
Crocker, Chester. "Lessons of Somalia: Not Everything Went Wrong." *Foreign Affairs* 74, no. 3 (May-June 1995): 2–8.
Curtis, Grant. *Cambodia Reborn?* Washington, D.C.: Brookings Institution Press, 1998.
Dallaire, Romeo. "The Changing Role of UN Peacekeeping Forces: The Relationship between UN Peacekeepers and NGOs in Rwanda." In *The Role of Peacekeeping*, edited by Randolph Kent and Shashi Tharoor. New York: St. Martin's Press, 1996.
Dao, James. "Pentagon Official Wants to Speed Rebuilding of Afghanistan." *New York Times*, 15 January 2003.
de Jonge Oudraat, Chantal. "Intervention in Internal Conflicts: Legal and Political Conundrums." Working paper, Global Policy Program, Carnegie Endowment for International Peace, Washington, D.C., August 2000.
De Waal, Alex. *Times Literary Supplement* (December 1995): 29.
Des Forges, Alison. *Leave None to Tell the Story: Genocide in Rwanda*. New York: Human Rights Watch, 1999.
Dobbins, James. "Afghanistan's Faltering Reconstruction." *New York Times*, 12 September 2002, A27.
Doyle, Leonard. "Rwanda Warns of Congo Reinvasion If Militias Advance." *The Independent* (London), 18 October 2002, 10.
Doyle, Michael W., Ian Johnstone, and Robert C. Orr, eds. *Keeping the Peace: Multidimensional UN Operations in Cambodia and El Salvador*. New York: Cambridge University Press, 1997.
"Dr. Condoleezza Rice Discusses Iraq Reconstruction." White House press release, 4 April 2003.
Dupuy, Alex. "Free Trade and Underdevelopment in Haiti: The World Bank/USAID Agenda for Social Change in the Post-Duvalier Era." In *The Caribbean in the Global Political Economy*, edited by Hilbourne A. Watson. Boulder, Colo.: Lynne Rienner, 1994.
————. *Haiti in the New World Order: The Limits of the Democratic Revolution*. Boulder, Colo.: Westview Press, 1997.
Epstein, Joshua M., John D. Steinbruner, and Miles T. Parker. "Modeling Civil Violence: An Agent-Based Computational Approach." Working paper no. 20, Center on Social

and Economic Dynamics, Brookings Institution, Washington, D.C., 2001.

Esty, Daniel C., Jack A. Goldstone, Ted Robert Gurr, Pamela T. Surko, and Alan N. Unger. "State Failure Task Force Report." Working paper, Center for International Development and Conflict Management, University of Maryland, College Park, 1995.

Feil, Scott R. "Preventing Genocide: How the Early Use of Force Might Have Succeeded in Rwanda." Report to the Carnegie Commission on Preventing Deadly Conflict. New York: Carnegie Corporation, April 1998.

Findlay, Trevor. *Cambodia: The Legacy and Lessons of UNTAC.* Oxford: Oxford University Press, 1995.

Food and Agricultural Organization. "FAO Global Information and Early Warning System on Food and Agriculture." Special alert no. 319, 13 November 2001.

Gall, Carlotta. "In Warlord Land, Democracy Tries Baby Steps." *New York Times*, 11 June 2003, A4.

George, Alexander L. *Forceful Persuasion: Coercive Diplomacy as an Alternative to War.* Washington, D.C.: U.S. Institute of Peace Press, 1991.

Gershoni, Y. "War without End and an End to a War: The Prolonged Wars in Liberia and Sierra Leone." *African Studies Review* 40, no. 3 (1997): 55.

Gibbons, Elizabeth. *Sanctions in Haiti: Human Rights and Democracy under Assault.* Washington, D.C.: Center for Security and International Studies Press, 1999.

Gilmore, Gerry J. "Rumsfeld Praises Civil Affairs Work in Afghanistan." *Armed Forces Information Service.* 20 August 2002. www.defenselink.mil/news/Aug2002/n08202002_200208202.html.

Goering, Laurie. "Africans Pin Hope on Dawn of Peace; Congo, Rwanda Reach Agreement." *Chicago Tribune*, 31 July 2002, 1.

Gonzalez, David. "Port-au-Prince Journal: A Haitian Bank Takes to the Streets." *New York Times*, 17 April 2001, A4.

Gottesman, Evan. *Cambodia after the Khmer Rouge.* New Haven, Conn.: Yale University Press, 2002.

Gowing, Nik. "Real-Time Television Coverage of Armed Conflicts and Diplomatic Crises: Does It Pressure or Distort Foreign Policy Decisions?" Working paper 94-1, Joan Shorenstein Barone Center on the Press, Politics and Public Policy, John F. Kennedy School of Government, Harvard University, Cambridge, Mass., 1994.

Graham, Bradley. "Wolfowitz Pushes Faster Afghan Reconstruction." *Washington Post*, 16 January 2003, A20.

Gray, Clive. "Alternative Models for Haiti's Economic Reconstruction." In *Haiti Renewed: Political and Economic Prospects,* edited by Robert Rotberg. Washington, D.C.: Brookings Institution Press, 1997.

Gros, Jean-Germain. "Haiti's Flagging Transition." *Journal of Democracy* 8, no. 4 (October 1997): 104.

Gulden, Timothy. "Spatial and Temporal Patterns of Civil Violence: Guatemala, 1977–1986." Working paper no. 26, Center on Social and Economic Dynamics, Brookings Institution, Washington, D.C., 2002.

Gurr, Ted Robert, Deepa Khosla, and Monty G. Marshall. *Peace and Conflict, 2001.* Center for International Development and Conflict Management, University of Maryland, College Park, 1 January 2001.

Gurr, Ted Robert, and Monty G. Marshall. *Peace and Conflict, 2003.* Center for International Development and Conflict Management, University of Maryland, College Park, 11 February 2003.

"Haiti—Building Democracy." *Comment.* London, Catholic Institute for International

Relations, 1995.

Hansch, Steven, S. R. Lillibridge, G. Egeland, C. Teller, and M. J. Toole. *Lives Lost, Lives Saved: Excess Mortality and the Impact of Health Interventions in the Somalia Humanitarian Emergency.* Washington, D.C.: Refugee Policy Group, 1994.

Hayward, Fred. "State Consolidation, Fragmentation and Decay." In *West African States,* edited by Donald Cruise O'Brien, John Dunn, and Richard Rathbone. New York: Cambridge University Press, 1989.

Hirsh, John. *Sierra Leone: Diamonds and the Struggle for Democracy.* Boulder, Colo.: Lynne Rienner, 2001.

————. "War in Sierra Leone." *Survival* 43, no. 3 (2001): 145–162.

Hirsh, John L., and Robert B. Oakley. *Somalia and Operation Restore Hope: Reflections on Peacemaking and Peacekeeping.* Washington, D.C.: United States Institute of Peace Press, 1995.

Honig, Jan Willem, and Norbert Both. *Srebrenica: Record of a War Crime.* New York: Penguin Books, 1997.

Hunt, Michael H. *Ideology and U.S. Foreign Policy.* New Haven, Conn.: Yale University Press, 1987.

International Crisis Group. "Salvaging Somalia's Chance for Peace." Africa briefing, 9 December 2002.

————. "Sierra Leone: Managing Uncertainty." *Africa Report* 35 (24 October 2001): 14.

————. "Somalia: Countering Terrorism in a Failed State." *Africa Report* 45 (23 May 2002).

Jakobsen, Peter Viggo. *Western Use of Coercive Diplomacy after the Cold War: A Challenge for Theory and Practice.* New York: St. Martin's Press, 1998.

Jones, Bruce D. "The Arusha Peace Process." In *The Path of a Genocide: The Rwanda Crisis from Uganda to Zaire,* edited by Howard Adelman and Astri Suhrke. New Brunswick, N.J.: Transaction Publishers, 1999.

————. "'Intervention without Borders': Humanitarian Intervention in Rwanda, 1990–1994." *Millennium: Journal of International Studies* 24, no. 2 (1995): 225–249.

Kayigamba, John Baptiste. "Rwandan Human Rights Groups Plea to International Community." Inter Press Service Feature, 26 March 1994.

Kegley, Charles W., Jr., and Eugene R. Wittkopf. *American Foreign Policy: Pattern and Process,* 5th ed. New York: St. Martin's Press, 1996.

Kessler, Glenn. "Powell Making Key Trip to Turkey; U.S. Aims to Mend Relationship, Forestall Invasion of Iraq." *Washington Post,* 1 April 2003, A24.

Klinghoffer, Arthur Jay. *The International Dimension of Genocide in Rwanda.* New York: New York University Press, 1998.

Koroma, Abdul. *Sierra Leone: The Agony of a Nation.* Freetown: Andromeda Publications, 1996.

Kumar, Krishna. "Rebuilding Post-War Rwanda." *Hunger Notes* 22, no. 1 (1996).

Kuperman, Alan J. *The Limits of Humanitarian Intervention: Genocide in Rwanda.* Washington, D.C.: Brookings Institution Press, 2001.

————. "Rwanda in Retrospect." *Foreign Affairs* 79, no. 1 (January-February 2000): 94–118.

Laitin, David D. "Somalia—Civil War and International Intervention." In *Civil Wars, Insecurity, and Intervention,* edited by Jack Snyder. New York: Columbia University Press, 1999.

————. "Somalia: Intervention in Internal Conflict." Stanford University, Stanford, Calif., 12 October 2001.

Leitenberg, Milton. "Deaths in Wars and Conflicts between 1945 and 2000." Occasional paper 29, Peace Studies Program, Cornell University, Ithaca, N.Y., 2003.

Levgold, Robert. "The Super Rivals: Conflict in the Third World." *Foreign Affairs* 57, no. 4 (Spring 1979): 755.

Levy, Jack S. "Declining Power and the Preventive Motivation for War." *World Politics* 40, no. 1 (October 1987): 91.

Lewis, Peter M. "Economic Reform and Political Transition in Africa: The Quest for a Politics of Development." *World Politics* 49 (October 1996): 92–129.

Loeb, Vernon. "Postwar Window Closing in Iraq, Study Says." *New York Times*, 18 July 2003, A09.

———. "U.S. Hopeful on Afghan Security; Regional Bases Plan Reflects Emphasis on 'Stability' Operations." *Washington Post*, 23 December 2002, A14.

Luke, David Fashole, and Stephen Riley. "The Politics of Economic Decline in Sierra Leone." *Journal of Modern African Studies* 27, no. 1 (1989): 133–141.

Lundahl, Mats. "The Haitian Dilemma Reexamined." In *Haiti Renewed: Political and Economic Prospects,* edited by Robert Rotberg. Washington, D.C.: Brookings Institution Press, 1997.

Lyons, Terrence, and Ahmed I. Samatar. *Somalia: State Collapse, Multilateral Intervention, and Strategies for Political Reconstruction.* Brookings Occasional Papers, The Brookings Institution, Washington, D.C., 1995.

Maguire, Robert, Edwige Balutansky, Jacques Fomerand, Larry Minear, and William G. O'Neill. "Haiti Held Hostage: International Responses to the Quest for Nationhood, 1986 to 1996." Occasional paper 23, Thomas J. Watson Institute for International Studies, Brown University, Providence, R.I, 1996.

Malone, David. *Decision-Making in the UN Security Council: The Case of Haiti, 1990–1997.* Oxford: Clarendon Press, 1998.

Mamdani, Mahmood. "From Conquest to Consent: Reflections on Rwanda." *New Left Review* 26, no. 2 (March-April 1996): 15–16.

Mandelbaum, Michael. "Foreign Policy as Social Work." *Foreign Affairs* 75, no. 1 (January-February 1996): 16–32.

Maren, Michael. *The Road to Hell: The Ravaging Effects of Foreign Aid and International Charity.* New York: Free Press, 1997.

McCarthy, Rory. "The Bombing of Afghanistan." *Guardian* (London), 7 October 2002, 4.

McCharles, Tonda. "Canada Sending Troops to Kabul." *Toronto Star*, 13 February 2003, A1.

McFadden, Robert D. "Threats and Responses: An Overview—March 8, 2003; Squabbling Diplomats, a Mixed Report Card from Iraq and a Ticking Clock." *New York Times*, 8 March 2003, A7.

———. "Threats and Responses: An Overview—March 16, 2003; An Ultimatum, Frayed French Relations and Stockpiling in Iraq." *New York Times*, 16 March 2003, A11.

Melvern, Linda. *A People Betrayed: The Role of the West in Rwanda's Genocide.* London: Zed Books, 2000.

Milbank, Dana. "Bush Bids to End Impasse at UN, Outlines Iraq Plans." *Washington Post*, 12 October 2002, A1.

Mintz, Sidney. "Can Haiti Change?" *Foreign Affairs* 74, no. 1 (January-February 1995): 74–81.

Misliwiec, Eva. *Punishing the Poor: The International Isolation of Kampuchea.* Oxford: Oxford University Press, 1988.

Montague, D. "The Business of War and the Prospects for Peace in Sierra Leone."

Brown Journal of World Affairs 9, no. 1 (2002): 229–238.

Mortimer, Robert. "ECOMOG, Liberia, and Regional Security in West Africa." In *Africa in the New International Order,* edited by E. Keller and D. Rothchild (Boulder, Colo.: Lynne Rienner, 1996).

———. "From ECOMOG to ECOMOG II: Intervention in Sierra Leone." In *Africa in World Politics, The African State System in Flux,* edited by J. Harbesson and D. Rothchild (Boulder, Colo.: Westview Press, 2000).

———. "Senegal's Role in ECOMOG: The Francophone Dimension in the Liberian Crisis." *Journal of Modern African Studies* 34, no. 2 (1996): 293–306 .

Murphy, John. "Hopes High as Rwanda, Congo Sign Peace Pact." *Baltimore Sun,* 31 July 2002, 1A.

Neild, Barry. "Italians Get a Pizza the Action in Afghanistan." *Agence France Presse,* 16 March 2003.

Norton, Michael. "UN Suspends Election Aid in Haiti." Associated Press, 22 August 1997.

Nylund, Norah. "Rwanda: What Lessons Have Humanitarians Learned?" *Hunger Notes* 22, no. 1 (1996).

O'Halloran, Patrick J. *Humanitarian Intervention and the Genocide in Rwanda.* London: Research Institute for the Study of Conflict, 1995.

Owen, Col. Robert C., USAF. "The Balkans Air Campaign Study," part 2. *Airpower Journal* 11, no. 3 (Fall 1997): 8–20.

Peou, Sorpong. *Intervention and Change in Cambodia: Toward Democracy?* New York: ISEAS, 2000.

Platteau, Philippe. "Land Relations under Unbearable Stress: Rwanda Caught in the Malthusian Trap." *Journal of Economic Behavior and Organization* 34 (1998): 1–47.

"Population-Based Mortality Assessment—Baidoa and Agfoi, Somalia, 1992." *Morbidity and Mortality Weekly Report* 41, no. 49 (11 December 1992): 913–917.

"President Discusses the Future of Iraq." White House press release, 28 April 2003.

Prunier, Gerard. "Operation Turquoise: A Humanitarian Escape from a Political Dead End." In *The Path of a Genocide: The Rwanda Crisis from Uganda to Zaire,* edited by Howard Adelman and Astri Suhrke. New Brunswick, N.J.: Transaction Publishers, 1999.

———. *The Rwanda Crisis: History of a Genocide, 1959–1994.* Kampala: Fountain Publishers, 1995.

Reding, Andrew. "Exorcising Haiti's Ghosts." *World Policy Journal* 13, no. 1 (Spring 1996): 21.

Reno, William. "Privatizing War in Sierra Leone." *Current History* 96, no. 610 (1997): 227.

———. "War and the Failure of Peacekeeping in Sierra Leone." *Sipri Yearbook.* Oxford: Oxford University Press (2001): 149–161.

Reyntjens, Filip. "Constitution-Making in Situations of Extreme Crisis: The Case of Rwanda and Burundi." *Journal of African Law* 40, no. 2 (1996): 234–243.

———."War and Peace in Sierra Leone." *Fletcher Forum of World Affairs* 25, no. 2 (2001): 41–50.

Richards, P. "Militia Conscription in Sierra Leone: Recruitment of Young Fighters in an African War." *Comparative Social Research* 20 (2002): 255–276.

Ridgeway, James, ed. *The Haiti Files: Decoding the Crisis.* Washington, D.C.: Essential, 1994.

Roberts, David W. *Political Transition in Cambodia, 1991–1999: Power, Elitism, and Democracy.* London: Curzon, 2001.

Rosegrant, Susan. "A 'Seamless' Transition: United States and United Nations Operations in Somalia—1992–1993." Case Program paper CO9-96-1324.0, John F. Kennedy School of Government, Harvard University, Cambridge, Mass., 1996.

Sahnoun, Mohamed. *Somalia: The Missed Opportunities.* Washington, D.C.: United States Institute of Peace Press, 1994.

Sambanis, Nicholas. "Do Ethnic and Nonethnic Wars Have the Same Causes?" *Journal of Conflict Resolution* 45, no. 3 (June 2001): 264.

Schulz, Donald E., and Gabriel Marcella. *Reconciling the Irreconcilable: The Troubled Outlook for U.S. Policy toward Haiti.* Carlisle, Pa.: U.S. Army War College, Strategic Studies Institute, March 1994.

Shacochis, Bob. *The Immaculate Invasion.* New York: Penguin Books, 1999.

Shawcross, William. *Sideshow: Nixon, Kissinger, and the Destruction of Cambodia.* New York: Simon & Schuster, 1979.

SIPRI Yearbook, 1999. Armaments, Disarmament and International Security. Stockholm International Peace Research Institute. Oxford: Oxford University Press, 1999.

Smith, David Norman. "The Genesis of Genocide in Rwanda: The Fatal Dialectic of Class and Ethnicity." *Humanity and Society* 19, no. 4 (November 1995): 65–67, 150.

Sok, Khin. *Le Cambodge entre le Vietnam et le Thailande.* Paris: EFEO, 1991.

Sommer, John G. *Hope Restored? Humanitarian Aid in Somalia, 1990–1994.* Washington, D.C.: Refugee Policy Group, Center for Policy Analysis and Research on Refugee Issues, 1994.

Steering Committee of the Joint Evaluation of Emergency Assistance to Rwanda. "Recommendations and Lessons Learned—Chapter 12." *The International Response to Conflict and Genocide: Lessons from the Rwanda Experience*, vol. 4, *Rebuilding Post-War Rwanda.* Copenhagen: Steering Committee of the Join Evaluation of Emergency Assistance to Rwanda, March 1996.

Steinbruner, John D. *Principles of Global Security.* Washington, D.C.: Brookings Institution Press, 2000.

Stevenson, Richard W., and Christopher Marquis. "Bush Team Faces Widespread Pressure to Act on Liberia." *New York Times*, 23 July 2003, A3.

Sutter, Robert. *The Cambodian Crisis and U.S. Policy Dilemmas.* Boulder, Colo.: Westview Press, 1990.

Tagliabue, John. "Threats and Responses: Discord; France and Russia Ready to Use Veto against Iraq War." *New York Times*, 6 March 2003, A1.

Thakur, Ramesh. "From Peacekeeping to Peace Enforcement: The UN Operation in Somalia." *Journal of Modern African Studies* 32, no. 3 (1994): 393.

Traub, James. "Inventing East Timor." *Foreign Affairs* 79, no. 4 (July-August 2000): 74–89.

Trouillot, Michel-Rolph. *Haiti—State against Nation: The Origins and Legacy of Duvalierism.* New York: Monthly Review Press, 1990.

Tyler, Patrick E. "Threats and Responses: Postwar Plans; Panel Faults Bush on War Costs and Risks." *New York Times*, 12 March 2003, A15.

UN Charter. 26 June 1945.

UN Security Council. "Report of the Panel on United Nations Peace Operations." A/55/305, S/2000/809, 21 August 2000.

UN Security Council. Resolution 758, on UN involvement in Bosnia and Herzegovina, S/RES758, 8 June 1992.

UN Security Council. Resolution 872, on establishing UNAMIR for a six-month period and approving the integration of UNOMUR and UNAMIR, S/RES/872, 5 October

1993.

UN Security Council. Resolution 1410, on the establishment of the UN Mission of Support in East Timor (UNMISET), S/RES/1410, 17 May 2002.

The United Nations and Somalia, 1992–1996. New York: United Nations Press, 1996.

U.S. Department of State Dispatch 2, no. 22 (3 June 1991): 395–396.

U.S. Foreign Broadcast Information Service, *Daily Reports*, 7 October 1977.

Vickery, Michael. *Cambodia 1975–1982.* Boston: South End Press, 1983.

———. *Kampuchea.* London: Lynn Rienner, 1984.

Wagner, Jim. "Civil Affairs Soldiers Adapt to a New Mission." www.defendamerica.mil/articles/feb2003/a010303a.html.

Walsh, Declan. "Congolese Hope a Ragged Army of Thousands Will Go Home to Rwanda." *Irish Times*, 16 December 2002, 10.

Weiner, Tim. "Two Hundred U.S. Marines Land in Liberia to Aid African Force." *New York Times*, 15 August 2003, A1.

Weisman, Steven R. "Threats and Responses: Foreign Policy; A Long, Winding Road to a Diplomatic Dead End." *New York Times*, 17 March 2003, A1.

White House Office of Global Communication. "Rebuilding Afghanistan." Fact sheet, 27 February 2003.

Whitfield, Mimi. "Clean water, Garbage Pickup Slated for Cite Soleil Slum." *Miami Herald*, 3 November 1997.

Winner, Andrew. "You and What Army? Coalitions and Coercive Diplomacy." Ph.D. diss., University of Maryland, College Park, 2002.

Wongibe, E. "A Miracle of Peace and Reconciliation Post-War Recovery in Sierra Leone." *Development and Cooperation* no. 5 (2002): 18–20.

Woodward, Bob. *The Choice.* New York: Simon & Schuster, 1996.

Worley, D. Robert. "Waging Ancient War: Limits on Preemptive Force." Strategic Studies Institute, U.S. Army War College, Carlisle, Pa., 2003.

Zartman, I. William, ed. *Collapsed States: The Disintegration and Restoration of Legitimate Authority.* Boulder, Colo.: Lynne Rienner, 1995.

———. *Preventive Negotiation: Avoiding Conflict Escalation.* Lanham, Md.: Rowman & Littlefield, 2001.

———. *Ripe for Resolution: Conflict and Intervention in Africa.* New York: Oxford University Press, 1989.

———. "The Unfinished Agenda: Negotiating Internal Conflicts." In *Stopping the Killing: How Civil Wars End*, edited by Roy Licklider. New York: New York University Press, 1993.

Index

About the Contributors

Steven L. Burg is Adlai E. Stevenson Professor of International Politics and chair of the Department of Politics, Brandeis University. His most recent book, coauthored with Paul S. Shoup (University of Virginia), *The War in Bosnia-Herzegovina: Ethnic Conflict and International Intervention*, was awarded the year 2000 Ralph J. Bunche Prize of the American Political Science Association for "the best scholarly work in political science which explores the phenomenon of ethnic and cultural pluralism."

David Chandler is an adjunct professor of Asian studies at Georgetown University and an emeritus professor of history at Monash University in Melbourne, Australia, where he taught for twenty-five years. He has held visiting appointments at the University of Wisconsin, Cornell University, the University of Paris, and the University of Michigan. From 1958 to 1966, Professor Chandler was a U.S. Foreign Service officer and was posted for two years to Phnom Penh. His major publications include *A History of Cambodia, The Tragedy of Cambodian History, Voices from S-21: Terror and History in Pol Pot's Secret Prison,* and *Facing the Cambodian Past: Selected Essays, 1973–1994.*

Jason Forrester is research director of the Nuclear Threat Reduction Campaign (NTRC). Before NTRC, he was a senior researcher in the Foreign Policy Studies Program at the Brookings Institution. He has also worked for the Gore/Lieberman 2000 foreign policy team, the CNN nuclear weapons documentary, *Rehearsing for Doomsday*, the Carnegie Commission on Preventing Deadly Conflict, and the Carter Center. He is a term member of the Council on Foreign Relations and was a member of the 2001 Carter Center election observation mission to Guyana, led by former president Carter. He was also awarded a Thomas J. Watson Foundation Fellowship, a Fulbright Scholarship, and an NCAA postgraduate scholarship. He received a master's from the Fletcher School of Law and Diplomacy, Tufts University, and graduated Phi Beta Kappa with a B.A. in political science from the University of the South, Sewanee, Tennessee.

Gilbert M. Khadiagala is an associate professor of comparative politics and African studies and acting director of the African Studies Program at the Paul H. Nitze School of Advanced International Studies (SAIS), Washington, D.C. He is also the project director of the Africa Program at the Woodrow Wilson Center, Washington, D.C. He studied in Kenya, Canada, and the United States, obtaining his doctorate at SAIS in 1990. He is the author of *Allies in Adversity: The Frontline States in Southern Africa Security,* coeditor with Terrence Lyons of *African Foreign Policies: Power and Process,* and has recently completed a manuscript, *Meddlers or Mediators? African Interveners in Civil Conflicts.* He is currently working on a project on refugees, citizenship, and statelessness in eastern Africa.

Chetan Kumar is the political liaison for the Bureau for Crisis Prevention and Recovery of the United Nations Development Programme (UNDP). He has previously coedited *Peacebuilding as Politics: Cultivating Peace in Fragile Societies* and authored *Peacebuilding in Haiti.* The views expressed in his chapter are strictly his own and not those of UNDP.

William J. Lahneman is program coordinator at the Center for International and Security Studies at Maryland (CISSM) at the University of Maryland, College Park. His research interests include American foreign policy, the future of intelligence analysis, counterterrorism, and international relations theory. A former career naval officer, Commander Lahneman, U.S. Navy (ret.) was a surface warfare officer with specializations in international negotiations, strategic planning, and nuclear propulsion. Lahneman holds a Ph.D. in international relations from the Johns Hopkins School of Advanced International Studies and is a graduate of the U.S. Naval Academy. Recent publications include "Restructuring U.S. Intelligence: Outsourcing the Stovepipes?" in the *International Journal of Intelligence and Counterintelligence* and "Changing Power Cycles and Foreign Policy Role-Power Realignments: Asia, Europe, and North America" in the *International Political Science Review.*

David D. Laitin is professor of political science at Stanford University. He has conducted field research on issues of language, religion, and nationalism in Somalia, Yorubaland (Nigeria), Catalonia (Spain), and Estonia. His books include

Politics, Language, and Thought: The Somali Experience, Hegemony and Culture: Politics and Religious Change among the Yoruba, Somalia: Nation in Search of a State (with Said Samatar), *Language Repertoires and State Construction in Africa,* and *Identity in Formation: The Russian-Speaking Populations in the Near Abroad.* He has also published, in collaboration with James Fearon, "Ethnicity, Insurgency, and Civil War" in the *American Political Science Review.*

Kwaku Nuamah is completing a doctoral dissertation on the sources and nature of leverage in third-party mediation at the Johns Hopkins University's School of Advanced International Studies (SAIS). He has extensive field experience in conflict management research and has published on conflicts in Liberia, Peru, Ecuador, Sierra Leone, Ghana, Uganda, Northern Ireland, Eritrea, and Ethiopia. He has taught in the Conflict Management Department of SAIS and has served as consultant on various governance and security-related issues to several institutions, including the International Foundation for Election Systems (IFES), Management Systems International (MSI), and the Ghana Center for Democratic Development.

Eric Schwartz serves as chief of office for the United Nations High Commissioner for Human Rights in Geneva. Between 1993 and 2001, he worked at the National Security Council, finishing his tenure there as special assistant to the president and senior director for multilateral and humanitarian affairs. After leaving the White House in 2001, he served as a fellow at the Woodrow Wilson International Center for Scholars (2001), the U.S. Institute of Peace (2001–2002), and the Council on Foreign Relations (2002–2003). In his writings at these institutions, he focused on postconflict peace stabilization, humanitarian issues, and accountability for grave abuses of human rights. He has also been a visiting lecturer of public and international affairs at the Woodrow Wilson School at Princeton University.

John Steinbruner is the director of the Center for International and Security Studies at Maryland (CISSM) at the University of Maryland, College Park. He previously served for eighteen years as director of foreign policy studies at the Brookings Institution and prior to that appointment held academic positions at Harvard University and the Yale University School of Organization. He has authored or coauthored five books, including *The Cybernetic Theory of Decision* and *Principles of Global Security.* Steinbruner has served on major commissions and advisory committees, including the Defense Policy Board, the Carnegie Commission on Preventing Deadly Conflict, and the National Academy of Sciences Committee on International Security and Arms Control. He is also a member of the American Academy of Arts and Sciences.

I. William Zartman is the Jacob Blaustein Distinguished Professor of International Organization and Conflict Resolution at the Paul H. Nitze School of Advanced International Studies (SAIS) at Johns Hopkins University, and former director of African studies at SAIS. He is the author of *Ripe for Resolution: Conflict and Intervention in Africa* and *Cowardly Lions: Missed Opportunities to Prevent State Collapse and Deadly Conflict*, and editor of *Elusive Peace: Negotiating to End Civil Wars*, *Preventive Negotiations: Avoiding Conflict Escalation*, and *Escalation and Negotiation*.